NURTURING SPIRIT
THROUGH SONG

NURTURING SPIRIT THROUGH SONG
The Life of Mary K. Oyer

Rebecca Slough and Shirley Sprunger King, Editors

Cascadia

Publishing House
Telford, Pennsylvania

copublished with
Institute of Mennonite Studies
Elkhart, Indiana and
Herald Press
Scottdale, Pennsylvania

Cascadia Publishing House orders, information, reprint permissions
contact@CascadiaPublishingHouse.com
1-215-723-9125
126 Klingerman Road, Telford PA 18969
www.CascadiaPublishingHouse.com

Nurturing Spirit through Song
Copyright © 2007 by Cascadia Publishing House
Telford PA 18969
All rights reserved

Copublished with Institute of Mennonite Studies, Elkhart IN 46517
and Herald Press, Scottdale PA 15683

Library of Congress Catalog Number: 2006025897
ISBN: 1-931038-42-2
Printed in the United States of America
Book and cover design by Alison King

The paper used in this publication is recycled and meets the
minimum requirements of American National Standard for Information
Sciences—Permanence of Paper for Printed Library Materials, ANSI
Z39.48-1984.

Library of Congress Cataloging-in-Publication Data

Nurturing spirit through song : the life of Mary K. Oyer / Rebecca Slough and
Shirley Sprunger King, editors.
   p. cm.
   Includes bibliographical references (p.   ).
   ISBN-13: 978-1-931038-42-3 (6 x 9" trade pbk. : alk. paper)
   ISBN-10: 1-931038-42-2 (6 x 9" trade pbk. : alk. paper)
   1. Oyer, Mary K. 2. Music teachers—Biography. 3. Church music—Menno-
nite Church. I. Slough, Rebecca. II. King, Shirley Sprunger. III. Title.

   ML423.O89N87 2007
   781.71'970092—dc22
   [B]

                              2006025897

      15 14 13 12 11 10 09 08 07 06   10 9 8 7 6 5 4 3 2 1

CONTENTS

Contents

AH! BRIGHT WINGS
Part 3: Selected Writings from the Life of Mary K. Oyer

A JOYFUL SONG I'LL RAISE
Bibliography of Works by and about Mary K. Oyer

CONTRIBUTORS

E. Douglas Bomberger is Professor of Musicology and Chair of Fine and Performing Arts, Elizabethtown College, Elizabethtown, Pennsylvania.

Lu Chen-Tiong is a pastor of The Methodist Church in Malaysia, and Lecturer in Worship and Church Music, Methodist Theological School, Sibu, Sarawak, Malaysia.

Philip K. Clemens is Pastor of Pike Street Mennonite Church, Elida, Ohio.

John Enz is an orchestra director at West Windsor–Plainsboro High School North, Conductor of the Youth Orchestra of Central Jersey, and a private cello teacher. He performs with the Princeton Symphony in New Jersey.

Rachel Waltner Goossen is Associate Professor of History, Washburn University, Topeka, Kansas.

Jean Ngoya Kidula is Associate Professor of Ethnomusicology, University of Georgia, Athens, Georgia.

Shirley S. King is Director of Academic Advising and Adjunct Professor of Organ and Harpsichord, Dickinson College, and Organist at First Presbyterian Church in Carlisle, Pennsylvania.

James Miller is Emeritus Professor of Voice, University of Oregon, Eugene, Oregon.

Julia Moss, Nairobi, Kenya, teaches piano and woodwinds.

J. Harold Moyer is Professor Emeritus of Music, Bethel College, North Newton, Kansas.

Contributors

Luzili R. Mulindi-King is a music educator, choral director, freelance lecturer in ethnomusicology, and workshop presenter in African music. She is currently teaching in the United Kingdom.

Justus M. Ogembo is Associate Professor of Anthropology and Education, University of New Hampshire, Durham.

Rebecca Slough is Associate Professor of Worship and the Arts, Associated Mennonite Biblical Seminary, Elkhart, Indiana.

Mary Swartley, Elkhart, Indiana, is a retired business educator/administrator and is Moderator, Indiana–Michigan Mennonite Conference.

Robert L. Weaver, Lititz, Pennsylvania, is Professor Emeritus of Music and Humanities, Centre College, Danville, Kentucky.

Photographs

SOMETIMES A LIGHT SURPRISES

Introduction

Sometimes a Light Surprises

Sometimes a light surprises The Christian while he sings;
It is the Lord who rises With healing in His wings;
When comforts are declining, He grants the soul again
A season of clear shining, To cheer it after rain.

In holy contemplation We sweetly then pursue
The theme of God's salvation, And find it ever new;
Set free from present sorrow, We cheerfully can say,
Let the unknown tomorrow Bring with it what it may.

It can bring with it nothing But He will bear us through;
Who gives the lilies clothing Will clothe His people, too:
Beneath the spreading heavens No creature but is fed,
And He who feeds the ravens Will give His children bread.

Though vine nor fig tree neither Their wonted fruit should bear,
Though all the fields should wither, Nor flocks nor herds be there;
Yet God, the same abiding, His praise shall tune my voice;
For while in Him confiding I cannot but rejoice.

William Cowper, 1779

PREFACE

At the dawn of the new millennium, the editorial staff of *The Mennonite*,[1] with help from their readers, named twentieth-century Mennonite individuals or organizations whose impact on the life and belief of the church had been most significant. Among the twenty notables selected were five women: Edna Ruth Byler, Katie Funk Wiebe, Elfrieda Dyck (with her husband, Peter Dyck), Doris Janzen Longacre,[2] and Mary K. Oyer, beloved teacher and well-known song leader, who "blazed trails for the arts and for women."

Mary—through her extensive knowledge of the fine arts, exacting standards, infectious leadership, and generous sharing of herself—has influenced, even profoundly shaped, the lives of many people. Her creative energies have taught us to use our aesthetic senses to understand the world and our place in it. She has helped us value the experience of others in faraway places, and through her insight and excitement we have come to grasp the depth of our shared humanity. *Nurturing Spirit through Song: The Life of Mary K. Oyer* surveys this woman's life (to date!) and celebrates her contributions to the many students around the world who encountered her as a teacher, and to professional colleagues within the Mennonite Church and beyond.

In her more than eighty years, Mary has been daughter, middle child, sister, aunt, Mennonite, resident of Goshen (Indiana), pianist, cellist, student, music teacher, fine arts professor, musi-

---

[1] *The Mennonite*, 22 February 2000, 4–7. *The Mennonite* is a biweekly publication of Mennonite Church USA.

[2] Doris Janzen Longacre edited the widely acclaimed *More-with-Less Cookbook*. Edna Ruth Byler's idea of marketing the needlework of poor Puerto Rican woman blossomed into the global craft enterprise now known as Ten Thousand Villages. Elfrieda Dyck, with her husband Peter, shaped Mennonite imagination with their stories of World War II Mennonite refugees. Katie Funk Wiebe's writing opened the way for women's experiences and gifts to be taken seriously by the church.

cologist, hymnologist, public speaker, lecturer, song leader, editor, author, cross-cultural observer and interpreter, African music specialist, Mennonite Central Committee liaison, seminary professor, enlivener, mentor, sage, colleague, and friend. Each of these identities opens a world of exploration. Taken together they offer perspective on Mary's personality and character. They entail abiding commitments to people who link her to the world of sight, sound, and spirit.

We began the Life and Legacy of Mary K. Oyer project in the spring of 2003. Both of us—Rebecca Slough and Shirley Sprunger King—had known Mary in various situations.

The origins of this project

I (Rebecca Slough) met the awesome Mary Oyer at the joint Mennonite Assembly at Bethlehem, Pennsylvania, in 1983. I was coordinator of morning worship, and Mary was song leader one of those mornings. Though I am a Goshen College graduate, I did not have Mary as a teacher because of my unorthodox approach to undergraduate education. I was a transfer student to Goshen who needed to work more than half time to avoid overwhelming college debts. By the time I was completing my general education requirements, the "Aesthetic Experience" course had replaced Mary's classic "Introduction to Fine Arts." I met the introductory arts requirement with an independent study that further removed me from Mary's sphere.

I got to know Mary during her years of work (1984–89) on the project that eventually resulted in publication of *Hymnal: A Worship Book*. Although we served on different working committees, we both were members of the committee that met regularly to coordinate the work of the project. With fear and trepidation, I became the hymnal's managing editor in 1989 after Mary left the project. Her support and cooperation were a great help to me in the months and years that followed.

In 1997 I was selected as "Mary's replacement" at Associated Mennonite Biblical Seminary (Elkhart, Indiana), when she decided to finish her work as a professor of church music there. The prospect of following Mary in a second position has given me moments of terror—after all, who could possibly replace Mary Oyer?—as

well as deep blessing. I have learned much from her understanding of the power of a well-chosen song for congregational singing
at critical moments in worship. Our conversations frequently turn
to how certain hymns or songs might sound at a particular place
in a worship service. I always find this kind of playful imagining
stimulating, instructive, and enjoyable.

Several times before 2003 I suggested to Mary that when she
was ready to sort through the vast accumulation of papers and
books from almost six decades of teaching, I would be willing to
help her. I knew we would find there the makings of a book on her
life and legacy. Shirley Sprunger King also expressed to Mary her
desire to do something that would honor her life and teaching.
Thus, Mary, Shirley, and I met in the spring of 2003 and began our
collaboration for the Life and Legacy of Mary K. Oyer project.

As Mary prepared to move from her home on Eighth Street in
Goshen to Greencroft's Juniper Place, she sifted through a teaching career's worth of files. One afternoon she gave me four grocery
bags full of old class notes, duplicated material she used in teaching fine arts, and copies of papers she had written for lectures.
Sorting these disparate artifacts of a teaching life, some of them
mere scraps of paper, was interesting, instructive, and at times
maddening. In the midst of much redundancy were sparks of new
insight and traces of new directions that Mary would eventually
pursue. I borrowed folders of neatly organized teaching material
that Mary wanted to keep and looked through everything she sent
to the Mennonite Church USA Archives–Goshen.

Thumbing through the *Gospel Herald* from 1940 until 1970
with an eye for music-related articles provided me with a sense
of what was happening with music in the life of the Mennonite
Church as Mary was coming of age and beginning to find her way
as a scholar. Thumbing through Goshen College catalogs published in her early years of teaching also proved to be useful. I
knew that some sadness and frustration surrounding the committee work on the 1927 *Church Hymnal* still reverberated for some
committee members of the 1969 *Mennonite Hymnal*, and I gleaned
insights through reading music committee reports to the Mennonite Church General Conferences related to both revisions. This

research gave me a greater sense of the contexts in which Mary developed as a scholar and teacher.

I (Shirley Sprunger King) first remember hearing about Goshen College music professor Mary Oyer in the early 1960s, when I was a high school student in Elkhart County. Although I have never had the privilege of formally studying with Mary, my interactions with her over the years have been important learning opportunities, and I continue to value how much I have learned from Mary.

In June 1969, when I married into the King family (Mary's mother was my husband's great aunt), Mary agreed to play cello for the Bach wedding cantata we used. She recently reminded me that our wedding was just a few days before she made her first trip to Africa. Five years later, energized by her study of African music, Mary came to visit us in Haiti, only weeks after we began a three-year term with Mennonite Central Committee there. I remember sitting under our mango tree, fielding Mary's barrage of questions on Haitian music, about which I had no knowledge and no sources of information.

Mary soon sensed my frustration; although I had grown up in Africa, I had no real understanding of non-Western music. Picking up on my culture shock, Mary tried to empathize with me, by saying that every time she had taken a sabbatical (and had not continued to perform regularly), she had lost some technique, "but I've always returned to teaching a better musician." I started to feel better—until she added, "But for *three* years?" Her honesty still makes me laugh. Although I never studied Haitian music in much depth, remembering Mary's genuine interest in and enthusiasm for African (and Haitian) music provided a constructive alternative to my brooding during those years.

Four years later, in 1978, I was honored to be invited to play the organ for the opening service of Mennonite World Conference in Wichita. Mary was the song leader, and I remember discussing much more than hymn tempos with her. (It would be the first of many more discussions and collaborations.) What I recall most clearly almost thirty years later is the ease with which Mary led more than 5,000 voices in singing at her brisk and energetic tempos.

The early 1990s brought new encounters with Mary. I have accompanied her when she introduced the new hymnal in a variety of settings, and I sat in on several of her classes at Associated Mennonite Biblical Seminary. I have particularly appreciated her thoroughness and her insight as a scholar, her delightful ways of communicating, and her endless enthusiasm.

But although I will always respect Mary as one of the finest musicians I've had the privilege of knowing, she has modeled far more than music making or scholarship. The impetus for this project arose in 2002, from our more general conversations about life and transitions. From Mary I heard about what she has gained through taking advantage of new opportunities, and I became convinced that her story needs to be shared. Mary's generous sharing of wisdom gained through her varied life experiences and her infectious desire to keep learning continue to inspire us and make us grateful for her life and legacy. Mary's influence reaches far beyond this continent—as expressions of appreciation from many quarters attest.

This book is a chorus of voices from around the world. Mary Oyer's students, friends, and colleagues—and Mary herself—offer a wide range of perspectives on her life. No one voice can adequately reflect the breadth of Mary's approaches to topics or her ways of engaging people as her interest and curiosity develop. A conventional Festschrift seemed out of keeping with her approach to scholarly work. Since the 1960s her lectures and presentations have become more narrative, and she has had less patience with academic papers, which are often poorly presented—in writing or speech. A book of many voices seemed to us to be the best way of honoring her influence.

Sometimes a Light Surprises

"Sometimes a Light Surprises," by William Cowper (with which this introduction opens), is one of Mary's favorite hymn texts. It appeared in *Olney Hymns* (1779), edited by John Newton, author of "Amazing Grace." Cowper, who struggled with debilitating bouts of depression, eloquently captures the healing of mind, soul, body, and spirit that can happen in a moment of singing. Mary Oyer is particularly fond of the first lines of Cowper's text, because she too believes that singing holds potential for our transformation.

Arguably, the five poems with which the parts of this book begin offer the clearest window on Mary's spirituality, on the joy she continues to find in life. The presence of these poems in this book provides a large space of wonder, in which the voices of the various contributors can be heard.

Part 1: Love Him in the World of the Flesh

Historian Rachel Waltner Goossen's opening essay, "Let the Sound Run through You," traces Mary's childhood and young adulthood. Waltner Goossen situates Mary's early years against the backdrop of North American Mennonite experience, particularly in relationship to women in the church and the role of women faculty at Goshen College after it reopened in 1924. She tells about Mary's early music education and the aptitudes evident already in her childhood. Goshen, Indiana—as home that encompassed the overlapping worlds of family, college, and congregation—is firmly established as the geography of Mary's early life. Rachel Waltner Goossen's scholarly interests in women's history and Mennonite history in the U.S. equip her to deal with this subject in a particularly illuminating way.

The second essay, "Following the Way," by Rebecca Slough, picks up the biographical thread to narrate some of the most significant turning points in Mary's evolving adult life. Most of these changes in direction are well known to many people, because Mary herself has often told these stories. In recent years interviews with her have appeared in church papers and scholarly publications. She described these turning points during an Afternoon Sabbatical presentation at Goshen College in the spring of 2004. What Slough's essay attempts to provide are additional reflections and continuities that undergird the various changes in Mary's life.

Lines from W. H. Auden's poem "He is the Way" (which opens part one of this book) provide headings for various sections of the essay. Mary is fond of this poem, written in 1941–42, as a chorus to conclude the final section ("The Flight into Egypt") of the libretto of a Christmas oratorio, *For the Time Being*.[3] The theme of incarnation ("Love him in the World of the Flesh") is central to this poem and also to Mary's claiming of the validity of the arts in the life of the believer and the church.

After discovering a setting of this poem in the Episcopal *Hymnal 1982*, with a tune by Richard Wetzel, Mary introduced it to many Mennonite congregations. With provocative imagery, Auden's words capture the richness of Mary's life experience as a disciple of the Way, the Truth, and the Life.

Part 2: Ways of Looking

One of Mary's favorite poems, Wallace Stevens's "Thirteen Ways of Looking at a Blackbird," reflects her delight in seeing something from a variety of angles. In the spirit of Stevens's contemplation of the blackbird, eleven contributors—Mary's former students and colleagues—offer their perspectives on Mary's life. All the essayists have pursued music professionally, most of them as teachers. They were invited to address these questions: (1) What have you learned from Mary? (2) How has Mary influenced your work? Their relationships with Mary span her entire teaching career, from her early days at Goshen College to her time at Tainan Theological College and Seminary. The editors have made no attempt to find a consistent voice or style for these essays, because each reflects something deeply personal about the contributor's relationship with Mary. The honorific essay of an African student stands alongside the jotted note style of a former student and friend. What unifies this collection is the personal warmth the contributors have received from Mary and gratefully offer her in return.

Since 1969, when Mary first introduced "Praise God from Whom All Blessings Flow," 606 in the *Mennonite Hymnal*, to the Mennonite Church General Assembly in Turner, Oregon, she has led people from many cultures in singing this enduring song of praise. This section, in which we hear voices from various decades and places speaking of Mary's influence, begins with the text of this doxology in the languages of several parts of the globe in which Mary has invested significant parts of her life.

---

[3] British composer Benjamin Britten never completed his score for Auden's libretto.

Part 3: Ah! Bright Wings

The book's third section contains a selection of Mary Oyer's own writings, some of them unpublished, and others that have been printed in sources not readily available now. References to "God's Grandeur," written by Gerard Manley Hopkins (included at the beginning of this part of the book), begin appearing in Mary's lectures and notes for other presentations in the 1950s. The lines "There lives the dearest freshness deep down things" and "Because the Holy Ghost over the bent / World broods with warm breast and with ah! bright wings" provide insight into Mary's understanding of meaning in the arts and—perhaps more importantly—into her spirituality.

Mary Oyer's influence as a scholar has been felt primarily through her lectures and other oral presentations, interviews, and song leading. The trail of her written work is neither long nor wide. The majority of pieces in this section are end products of multiple presentations on a central topic in which she rehearsed her arguments or polished her illustrations. These essays span more than fifty years and represent her interrelated yet divergent intellectual interests. The earliest piece dates from 1955, and the most recent is a presentation to the June 2006 meeting of American Theological Library Association. The essays illustrate her varied forms of address and display the development of her concerns, interests, thought, and voice.

This collection demonstrates that Mary's mind has changed over the years. When she reviewed the selections to be included in this book, she confessed to feeling some embarrassment about what she had written, especially early in her life. Yet she had spoken with honesty about the truth she knew at the time. What remains constant throughout these examples of her thinking is a desire that the arts strengthen people's connections to one another, broaden their experience of and delight in their world, and deepen their faith in their Creator.

A Joyful Song I'll Raise

The joyful song Mary's life raises is evident in her written works (many of them derived from oral presentations), which are itemized by date, with some annotations of her longer and more recent works, in the final section of this book. A second section lists works about Mary Oyer. Reading the bibliography makes obvious the purpose of Mary's written work: to serve the church. To a great extent, her scholarly pursuits were intended to strengthen Mennonite understanding of the arts and to expand the expressive horizons of people of faith as they respond to the astonishing wonder of God.

"There is not a more pleasing exercise of the mind than gratitude. It is accompanied with such an inward satisfaction, that the duty is sufficiently rewarded by performance."[4] So writes Joseph Addison in an essay on gratitude, followed by the hymn "When All Thy Mercies, O My God."[5] Mary's contributions elicit gratitude for her teaching vocation; for the many lives she has touched; for her pioneering ethnomusicological work that has contributed to cross-cultural respect and church unity; and for her hymn interpretation and inspired song leading, through which many worshipers have been "lost in wonder, love and praise."

Visual Motifs

The book's Pennsylvania Dutch images were created for the 1943 Goshen College *Maple Leaf,* for which Mary Oyer (as a sophomore) was the art editor. In her recent move from Eighth Street, Mary found a large stack of pages with these patterns, which would have been reprinted on heavier paper, with color, then carefully cut apart and glued into each yearbook. The yearbook was likely the most labor-intensive that Goshen College has ever seen.

A Companion DVD

We have no illusions that a book can adequately reflect Mary Oyer's influence on generations of students and colleagues in the several institutions she has served. No "dumb book" can bring to life the energy and passion with which Mary teaches, leads congregational singing, or engages people. From the beginning of our imaginings of this project, we recognized that a book might best record aspects of her life, but the legacy of her teaching needed something

---

[4] Quoted in *Exploring the Mennonite Hymnal: Essays* (Newton, KS: Faith and Life Press; Scottdale, PA: Mennonite Publishing House, 1980), 122.
[5] Joseph Addison, "Gratitude," in *The Spectator,* 19 August 1712.

visually alive and active. The companion piece to this book is a DVD created and produced by Mennonite Media, *Nurturing Spirit through Song: The Legacy of Mary K. Oyer* (for order information, see the back page of this book). It contains interviews with Mary, interviews with former students who have become professional teachers and performers, and conversations with colleagues. It focuses on Mary the teacher and the ways her approaches to the fine arts (especially music), hymns, and worship have shaped the understandings of music leaders of the Christian church.

Acknowledgements

We offer our gratitude to the Institute of Mennonite Studies at Associated Mennonite Biblical Seminary (Elkhart, Indiana), and to Mary Schertz, its director, for IMS's early endorsement of this project, which helped get it off the ground. The generous financial support of J. Evan Kreider and the Anabaptist Foundation (Vancouver, British Columbia) ensured that we would be able to bring this aspect of the project to completion. Contributions from other donors specifically for the book were gratefully received.

Publisher Michael A. King of Cascadia Publishing House has earned our gratitude for taking on this project when we presented it in its initial sketchy form. He worked with us even when we missed every imaginable deadline. His generosity also allowed for co-publication of this book with Herald Press and Institute of Mennonite Studies.

Thanks to Rachel Waltner Goossen for bringing her understanding of women's history in the U.S. and among Mennonites to bear in her fine essay, and to Mary Swartley for updating the bibliography she created ten years ago in an earlier attempt to see Mary Oyer's life in larger perspective. We are grateful to Mary's former students and colleagues, who sent their essays in a timely way and must have feared that their work had disappeared into a black hole of forgetfulness. Thanks to Douglas Bomberger, Philip Clemens, John Enz, Jean Kidula, Luzili Mulindi-King, James Miller, Harold Moyer, Julia Moss, Justus Ogembo, Lu Chen-Tiong, and Robert Weaver, for lending their voices to the testimonial chorus. And we are grateful to Mary herself for generously giving her time and for her open spirit. She has accepted with grace and courage the attention—even scrutiny—that receiving such an honor entails.

Our gratitude also extends to those involved in the book's design and production: to Alison King, for her graceful and pleasing design work on the book; to Mary E. Klassen, who stepped in with her customary grace and skill to help with the inevitable refinements in design when Alison's youth sponsor obligations took her to Honduras just as formatting got underway. Thanks, too, to James Nelson Gingerich, for his careful and expeditious efforts in typesetting the book and preparing the musical examples during late evening and early morning hours, around the demands of his day job as a physician. Lastly, thanks to Barbara Nelson Gingerich, whose calm spirit, steady patience, perfect pitch for tone and voice, and impeccable editorial sense brought the various voices of this book into a melodious concert.

Rebecca Slough
Shirley Sprunger King

A CHRONOLOGY OF THE LIFE OF MARY K. OYER

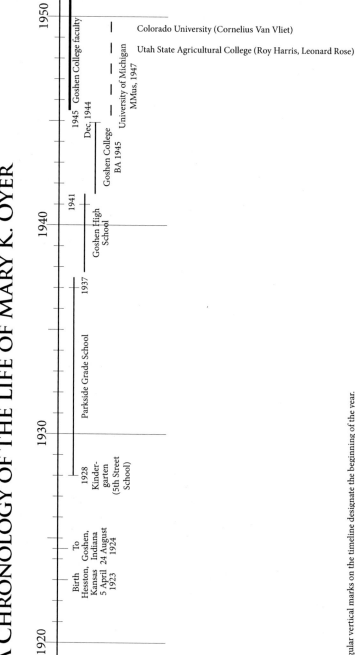

Colorado University (Cornelius Van Vliet)

Utah State Agricultural College (Roy Harris, Leonard Rose)

1945 Goshen College faculty

Dec, 1944

University of Michigan
MMus, 1947

Goshen College
BA 1945

1941

Goshen High
School

1937

Parkside Grade School

1928
Kinder-
garten
(5th Street
School)

Birth   To
Hesston, Goshen,
Kansas   Indiana
5 April   24 August
1923   1924

1920   1930   1940   1950

Regular vertical marks on the timeline designate the beginning of the year.
Interrupted horizontal lines below the timeline generally designate summer activity.

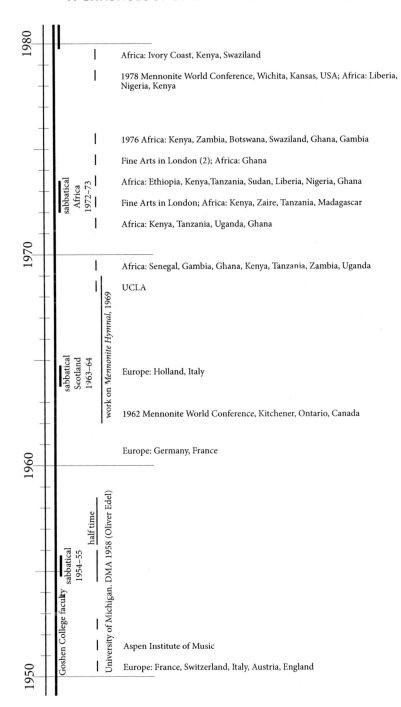

Africa: Ivory Coast, Kenya, Swaziland

1978 Mennonite World Conference, Wichita, Kansas, USA; Africa: Liberia, Nigeria, Kenya

1976 Africa: Kenya, Zambia, Botswana, Swaziland, Ghana, Gambia

Fine Arts in London (2); Africa: Ghana

Africa: Ethiopia, Kenya, Tanzania, Sudan, Liberia, Nigeria, Ghana

Fine Arts in London; Africa: Kenya, Zaire, Tanzania, Madagascar

Africa: Kenya, Tanzania, Uganda, Ghana

Africa: Senegal, Gambia, Ghana, Kenya, Tanzania, Zambia, Uganda

UCLA

Europe: Holland, Italy

1962 Mennonite World Conference, Kitchener, Ontario, Canada

Europe: Germany, France

Aspen Institute of Music

Europe: France, Switzerland, Italy, Austria, England

1980

1970

1960

1950

sabbatical
Africa
1972–73

work on *Mennonite Hymnal*, 1969

sabbatical
Scotland
1963–64

half time

University of Michigan. DMA 1958 (Oliver Edel)

sabbatical
1954–55

Goshen College faculty

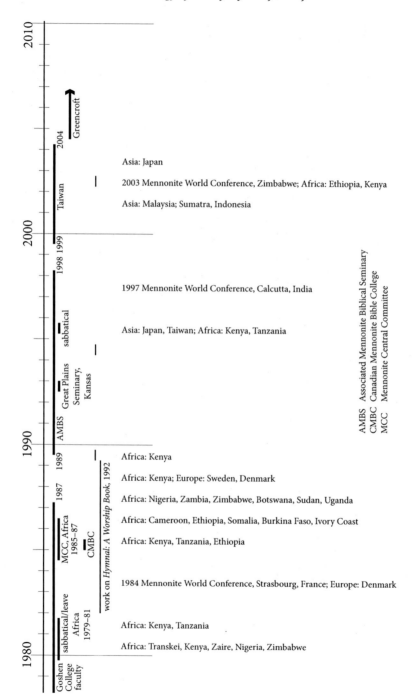

Part 1

Love Him in the World of the Flesh

Essays on the Life of Mary K. Oyer

He Is the Way

He is the Way.
Follow him through the Land of Unlikeness;
You will see rare beasts, and have unique adventures.

He is the Truth.
Seek him in the Kingdom of Anxiety;
You will come to a great city
that has expected your return for years.

He is the Life. Love him in the World of the Flesh;
And at your marriage all its occasions shall dance for joy.

W. H. Auden, 1941–42

Chapter 1

LET THE SOUND RUN THROUGH YOU

Rachel Waltner Goossen

At the opening of the new millennium, Mary Oyer received recognition as one of the twenty most influential Mennonites of the twentieth century. Editors of the *The Mennonite* cited her contributions to church music and her consummate leadership, noting that "she has blazed trails for the arts and for women. She has pushed Mennonite music beyond the traditional with new influences."[1]

Mary Oyer is a champion of vocal music, well known especially for her insistence on the value of congregational singing. She points out that "music is very important in the church—it's basically the only place in America where ordinary people still sing. Keep singing!"[2] Drawing on knowledge acquired through a lifetime of performing, studying, and teaching, she advocates singing as the most accessible and egalitarian gateway to the world of music. "You let the sound run through you," she says. "It's as fundamental as breath and life."[3]

Trained in the 1940s and 1950s as a classical musician, Mary cultivated an anthropologist's sensibilities about teaching and learning. In recent decades she fused cross-cultural insights with her career as a music scholar and educator. Immersing herself in her own community's choral traditions and the music making of others, Mary has explored the wide-ranging terrains of sacred hymnody, Mennonite folk and popular music, and African and

---

[1] "20 for the 20th Century," *The Mennonite*, 22 February 2000, 6.
[2] Quoted by Linea Reimer Geiser, "Worship," in *College Mennonite Church, 1903–2003*, ed. Ervin Beck (Goshen, IN: College Mennonite Church, 2003), 161.
[3] Denise Thornton, "For Mennonite Teacher, Music Opened Doors around the World," *South Bend Tribune,* 31 March 1991. For a comparable perspective, see Cynthia Neufeld Smith, "Singing Our Way to Heaven" (sermon, Topeka, KS, 26 June 2005), in the author's possession.

Asian traditions. As someone who began her career convention-
ally, focused on her own instrumental interpretations of notes on
the page, her teaching and traveling eventually led her into ethnomusicology—the study of people who create and perform music,
the places and ways they sing and play, and the meaning of music
in their lives.[4]

Mary's lifework of performing, teaching, conducting, editing,
collecting, and promoting music has spanned three continents.
Underlying her world outlook is a remarkable taproot of Mennonite history and culture. Throughout her international travel
and work assignments, Mary's home remained for eighty years
the house on Eighth Street in Goshen, Indiana, where she grew
up. Across the street are the two institutions that have been most
formative in her life: Goshen College and College Mennonite
Church. In these distinctive and intertwined places, Mary's musical talents and interests have led her into creative collaborations
across professional, ecumenical, and international boundaries. In
a century and a society characterized by geographic mobility, Mary
remained grounded in one place—her Mennonite community of
Goshen—while going out from there, repeatedly, over a lifetime of
exploring music.

Speaking in 2004 to a hometown audience of Goshen friends
and acquaintances about her varied career as a music educator,
Mary mused that she might just as well have focused her remarks
on "My Life in Teaching" or "My Life as a Woman" or "My Life
in the Church" or "The Single Life" or "My Cross-Cultural Life."[5]
Each of these strands of her identity is woven deeply into her musical experience, which began in childhood with congregational
singing and in learning to play the piano and cello.

Like the noted American anthropologist Margaret Mead, who
in the 1920s and 1930s traveled to Samoa in the South Pacific and
New Guinea in the Malay archipelago to investigate gender role
differences in indigenous societies, Mary found herself gradually

---

[4] I am indebted to Rebecca Slough for her perspective on Mary Oyer's orientation to ethnomusicology.

[5] Mary Oyer, "My Life with Music" (Afternoon Sabbatical presentation, Goshen, IN,
16 March 2004); typescript in the author's possession. Goshen College publicized this
event under the title "Music in My Life—A Retrospect."

drawn to cultural traditions and practices far from home. A generation after Margaret Mead published her findings on the societies she had studied, Mary, supported by a Fulbright grant, began her own forays into non-Western music, language, and culture.

In the summer of 1969, her reasons for going to Kenya and other African nations were complex. She wanted to enrich course offerings at Goshen College, where she had already taught for more than two decades. She saw the opportunity to travel to Africa as a way to learn more about African-American studies, in response to the national and international civil rights movements. And as an art historian, Mary was intrigued that Picasso and Matisse had changed their styles after their exposure to African art.[6]

Her initial visit to Africa in the late 1960s led her to return again and again to study African music and visit Mennonite Central Committee units, with eventual teaching appointments there, and later in Taiwan. In these diverse settings, Mary taught students from more than twenty different countries, adding formative cross-cultural and ecumenical experiences to her long career. After returning to her Goshen home at the age of eighty, she told friends that her years of living and working abroad had been "richer than I could have imagined."[7]

As an ethnomusicologist and Mennonite leader, Mary Oyer knew as well as anyone the distances she had traveled to make this claim. She regarded her forays into non-Western cultures as revolutionary in terms of her own intellect and experience: "The African studies changed my outlook in so many kinds of ways, in [terms of] how people think in another culture."[8] Her earlier life experiences and deep roots in Goshen had readied her for a life-work with music and people in places just a stone's throw from her family home and in locations around the globe.

Noah and Siddie (King) Oyer

Mary had spent her childhood in the Goshen community among church and college people and was herself a product of the Men-

---

[6] Duane Stoltzfus, "Still Turning to 606," *The Mennonite*, 18 November 2003, 10.
[7] Oyer, "My Life with Music," 11.
[8] Mary Oyer, interview by Rebecca Slough, Goshen, IN, 10 August 2002, 20; typescript in the author's possession.

nonite school where she taught for forty-two years. Born in 1923 in Hesston, Kansas, to Noah and Siddie (King) Oyer, Mary was the second daughter in an education-minded Mennonite family. Her father, originally from Metamora, Illinois, was ordained to the ministry in 1923. At the time of Mary's birth, he was the newly appointed academic dean at Hesston College, then a four-year institution, which like Goshen operated under the direction of the Mennonite Board of Education. His theological training had been at Princeton, and before serving as dean at Hesston, he had completed graduate coursework at Franklin and Marshall College in Pennsylvania.

Siddie King had been raised in West Liberty, Ohio, and came to Kansas to attend Hesston College. She enjoyed singing and occasionally sang solos at Hesston. There she met Noah Oyer, whom she married in 1916. The couple's first child, Verna, was already three when Mary was born. A year and a half later, in January 1925, a son, John, joined the family. In the summer of 1924, the Oyers had moved from central Kansas to Goshen, Indiana, where Noah had accepted a position as academic dean at Goshen College and also began serving as the pastor of the Goshen College Mennonite Church.

The Oyers moved to Goshen at a troubled time in the northern Indiana college's history. During the academic year 1923–24, Goshen College was closed as a result of a complicated set of struggles over theology, biblical interpretation, cultural accommodation, and power. At the center of the struggle lay competing visions of the future of the Mennonite Church. Insiders to this conflict, including a number of progressive Goshen College faculty members, had left the college, some involuntarily. Conservatives in the Indiana-Michigan regional church conference with oversight for the college and its congregation were gaining ground in this ideological battle.

In the fall of 1924, Goshen College reopened with new leadership and a reconstituted faculty. Sanford C. Yoder, a minister and Mennonite Board of Education leader, had arrived from Iowa to take on Goshen's presidency. Before coming, Yoder had recruited Mary's father, Noah Oyer, from Hesston College, to serve as the new academic dean. Preventing Goshen College from closing again in the midst of perpetual cultural wars would be Noah Oyer's raison d'être for the remainder of the decade.

The Oyers were outsiders to the wrangling that had led to Goshen College's yearlong closure. Both Sanford Yoder, the new president, and Noah Oyer, the dean, were regarded as theological moderates in the broader Mennonite fundamentalist/modernist standoffs of the 1920s. As these new leaders refashioned Goshen College and strengthened its ties with a polarized constituency, they and their supporters faced pressures to adhere to biblical and dress-code orthodoxy.

As dean, Noah Oyer divided his time between the college and the congregation. A large part of his responsibility was serving as pastor for the College Mennonite Church, which met in the second-floor chapel of Goshen College's administration building. The crisis leading to the closing of the college had also divided the congregation. Scores of members had left in the preceding months, many of them joining Eighth Street Mennonite Church, a congregation situated a mile north of the campus and affiliated with another denomination, the Central Conference Mennonite Church.

Historian Robert Kreider—son of Amos E. Kreider, who served as pastor of the Goshen College church during the turbulent 1923–24 period—has described how in 1923 his father had been "called to pastor a congregation of 213 members, who were feeling increasingly indignant and helpless. Members continued to leave and yet more than 100 remained."[9] In August 1924, although A. E. Kreider was appreciated and supported by the college church congregation, he was summarily dismissed by an Indiana-Michigan conference bishop. Noah Oyer was then installed as the congregation's new pastor. Robert Kreider, remembering his parents' loyalty to the congregation, adds that "the unfortunate fallouts of the college and congregational troubles" included "petty rumors and unkind comments among congregation members and estranged members."[10]

Eventually, however, the church's membership numbers rose again and then stabilized. Shepherding efforts by both pastors,

---

[9] Robert S. Kreider, *My Early Years: An Autobiography* (Kitchener, ON: Herald Press, 2002), 130.
[10] Ibid., 132.

A. E. Kreider and then Noah Oyer, had helped guarantee that the congregation would remain connected to Goshen College and to the Indiana-Michigan conference. In the years ahead, the congregation continued to meet on campus and draw members from among Mennonites employed there.[11]

Mary, a toddler at the time and too young to know anything about the strains and stresses of the college's closing and reopening, learned to sing in Assembly Hall, where her father preached. "I remember how much we sang [Isaac] Watts' hymns, and I realize how they shaped my piety," she later wrote.[12] During the 1920s and early 1930s she was too young to grasp how her theology was being formed by the music sung at the college church. But the linkages between hymnody and spiritual understanding would later occupy much of her professional life. From childhood, Mary knew that the hymn writer Isaac Watts was especially popular with Mennonites for his texts such as "We're Marching to Zion," "I Sing the Mighty Power of God," and "When I Survey the Wondrous Cross." Through her later work as a congregational song leader and scholar of Christian hymnody, Mary encountered the writings of this eighteenth-century figure again and again.[13]

In spite of the turmoil involving the adults around her, Mary's earliest years in Goshen were secure. Her parents were well liked, and her father developed a reputation as a gifted Bible teacher and a calm, fair-minded administrator whose dealings with men and women on the college faculty won respect. Noah Oyer had a close working relationship with several colleagues in the newly reconstituted Goshen College, including Harold S. Bender, who had also joined the Goshen faculty after the 1923–24 closing. Bender was a son-in-law of John Horsch, a Mennonite historian based in Scottdale, Pennsylvania, who published prolifically on anti-modernist

---

[11] For perspectives on the Goshen College closing and related developments, see Kreider, *My Early Years*, 123–34; John Umble, *Goshen College, 1894-1954* (Goshen, IN: Goshen College, 1955), 104–30; Susan Fisher Miller, *Culture for Service: A History of Goshen College* (Goshen, IN: Goshen College, 1994), 87–155; and Theron F. Schlabach, "History," in *College Mennonite Church, 1903-2003*, 23–30.

[12] Mary Oyer, "The Sound in the Land," 28 May 2004, 3; unpublished typescript in the author's possession. Published in *Sound in the Land: Essays on Mennonites and Music* (Kitchener, ON: Pandora Press, 2005).

[13] Ibid.

themes and had long been critical of Goshen College, because of the institution's failures to conform to fundamentalist ideologies.

But Bender, like Oyer, represented a new generation of leadership and a comparatively progressive outlook. The two men had both studied at Princeton and taught at Hesston College before coming to Goshen. Oyer, Bender, and others at the "new Goshen" wanted to develop the college's reputation among its polarized Mennonite constituencies. Oyer's gifts were in teaching, theology, and pastoral leadership. Bender's gifts were complementary, as a teacher, writer, manager, and entrepreneur within the Mennonite world of higher education and scholarship. With president Sanford C. Yoder, they hoped to lay the foundation for a biblical seminary to train future leaders for the denomination.[14]

At Home in Goshen

At the Oyer household on Eighth Street, Mary, the middle child in her family, enjoyed playing with friends from the neighborhood. The Oyers had moved into a newly renovated house just across College Avenue from Goshen College, which had been owned by Mennonite Board of Missions and Charities. Known as the missionary house, the home at 1424 South Eighth had for years been used by church workers on furlough.[15] Now, with Noah, Siddie, and their three young children in residence, the house retained its church, college, and Goshen community connections.

Mary attended kindergarten at the Fifth Street School and for the rest of her elementary years walked to the newly opened neighborhood Parkside School. Here, as a second-grader, Mary learned to read music with her classmates. Much later in life, she realized that she was dyslexic, though no one had ever noticed that she had difficulty learning. There was little outward indication of a disability, except that she read fewer books than other family members, who good-naturedly teased her for not being much of a reader.

---

[14] See Albert Keim, *Harold S. Bender, 1897–1962* (Scottdale, PA: Herald Press, 1998).
[15] When Mary moved out of the Oyer family home in 2005, she discovered a collection of twenty-eight quilts in the attic, perhaps relics of the early twentieth century when they would have been used by missionary guests (Rebecca Slough e-mail message to the author, 26 October 2005).

Remarkably, Mary never had difficulty comprehending a music score.[16]

The Oyers owned a piano, and she began taking lessons from Mary Royer, a family friend who would later be a faculty colleague at Goshen College. By the time she was seven, Mary's musical abilities—especially her perfect pitch—were apparent to the adults around her. But these childhood developments were overshadowed by a devastating turn of events at the Oyer home.

Decades later, Mary acknowledged that she had no memory of her father, attributing this gap to trauma associated with his death in 1931 when she was seven years old. She was able to recall details from school life, and she remembered the mealtime arrangements that her mother had made for her and her siblings to eat at friends' homes while Noah Oyer, at thirty-nine, lay ill with typhoid fever. For two months he struggled to regain his health. Although Mary cannot remember life with him, she recalls that after his death, friends came to the house to mourn with Siddie and the family. The entire community grieved the loss of the beloved dean, who had devoted himself to leadership of both Goshen College and the campus congregation.

In spite of Mary's struggle to remember details, she experienced the aftermath of her father's death in February 1931 as emotionally significant:

> I remember when we would sit in church in Assembly Hall.... My father had been minister of the church as well as dean of the college. So I had them confused, church and college. My mother would cry whenever we sang and so I had this strange feeling about the power of hymns. I remember that "Dear Lord and Father of Mankind" was one of my father's favorites and "The Sands of Time Are Sinking." Those were very important memories. I mean I remember those songs because people would say, "Now that was your father's favorite song." Those were etched into my memory.[17]

---

[16] Stoltzfus, "Still Turning to 606," 11.

[17] Mary Oyer, interview by Kathy Kauffman, Goshen, IN, 28 June 1993, Hist. Mss. 6–295, Box 2, folder 8, Mennonite Church USA Archives–Goshen [IN].

Throughout her childhood and adolescence, Mary continued to think of the church and college as a single, undifferentiated place. Two years after her father's death, Mary, at age nine, was baptized at the college church.[18] By that time, her mother had begun working at Goshen College. Siddie never married again. Widowed just as the Great Depression was getting underway, she took in renters and turned to service labor as a means of supporting her three young children in Goshen. She became the matron of Coffman Hall, the men's dormitory, where she sewed, cleaned, and changed the bed linens for college students for the next thirty years.

The family continued to live in their South Eighth Street home a few paces from the college. And the Oyer children grew up with an awareness of the providence of church and college friends. Siddie cooked for the family and tended a big garden in the summertime, and she sometimes sent her daughters across the street to the college kitchen to pick up tins of macaroni and cheese and other leftovers. In the leanest of times, every little bit helped. Salaries at the college were low, and Mary's mother and others had to go to the college business office to collect their money, because the institution lacked sufficient funds to pay all its employees on schedule. Although Siddie and the children did not get government relief during the Depression, they occasionally received grocery showers from the congregation. Mary recalled years later that she had never minded these gestures, "but it was embarrassing to my sister."[19]

Mary's sister, Verna, three years older, loved to draw and paint, and at home she led her younger siblings in creative play. Mary remembers that during their elementary school years, she and Verna "called the neighbors in for an art exhibit. My sister [who would become an art teacher] was in charge of this and she stood up on the table and lectured about these things that we had done."

Mary occasionally listened to classical music after a neighbor gave the family her Victrola and opera records. Without a radio at home, Mary's exposure to non-church music was limited. By the time she was in fifth grade, Mary told Verna that she wanted to be a music teacher.

---

[18] Slough interview, 20.
[19] Kauffman interview, 4, 6.

As the sisters grew older, neither liked the dress expectations imposed on them by Mennonite Church guidelines about appearance. Mary thought that she and Verna looked awful: "We had to have long hair and we dressed in an unattractive way.... [Church teachings were] very strict and because we were the children of the dean and the minister, we had to follow in line. My mother, who had come from an Amish Mennonite home, a very plain one, never saw ways to break away from that. So I felt quite inferior as a child [although] I found great pleasure in studying and in music."[20] Several of Mary's uncles, brothers of her mother, were Mennonite ministers who years earlier had been skeptical of her father's training at Princeton. Mary remembered that they disapproved of his seminary education because it was not Mennonite, and she, as a child, felt awkward and ill-at-ease with her relatives' religious conservatism.[21]

As a sixth grader, Mary began playing a school-owned cello with the guidance of a qualified teacher who traveled and gave lessons along an east-west route from Kendallville to La Porte, Indiana. Siddie paid nothing; she could not have afforded it. But Mary excelled, and her teacher gave her free cello instruction. One summer she broke a string on her cello and lacked the thirty-five cents for a new one, so a neighbor replaced it. As she reached high school, the cello was becoming a significant part of her life, and she won first division honors in a contest for young string players.[22] Through these experiences, Mary absorbed the idea that "learning music was a privilege—never, as I recall, drudgery. It always connected me with people who were giving something they valued."[23]

College Years

Like her friends growing up near the Goshen campus, Mary assumed that she was headed for college. Oberlin in Ohio was her first choice. But because the family's resources were so limited, she had few options but to follow Verna to Goshen. Verna, in the

---

[20] Kauffman interview. See also Oyer, "My Life with Music," 1.
[21] Slough interview, 26.
[22] Kauffman interview; Mary Oyer, interview by Rachel Waltner Goossen, Goshen, IN, 29 May 2004; in the author's possession.
[23] Oyer, "My Life with Music," 2.

meantime, had cut her hair and wore it in a pageboy. She was beginning to rebel against what she regarded as narrow religious and cultural restrictions in the church and at the school.[24]

Mary's passage into adulthood was more conventional for the times. She wore her long hair in braids, and then pinned up in the acceptable style for young Mennonite women her age, although her appearance remained a source of embarrassment for her.[25] By the time she was seventeen, she won a scholarship that covered most of her Goshen tuition, and she earned money by cleaning houses. During the three and a half years it took her to earn a bachelor's degree, she lived with her mother to save money. The family did not have a car. Mary learned to drive much later, at age thirty-five. But as she entered college, her world was expanding. She spent a summer as a volunteer at Ypsilanti, Michigan, working as an aide at a mental hospital alongside conscientious objectors assigned to Civilian Public Service.

Mary's years as a Goshen College student, from 1941 to 1944, were productive. She was at home in the campus community she had always known:

> I almost stopped cello but the first year there was a fine teacher around from Indiana University for string quartet. We had a very good string quartet. Then I started in the South Bend Symphony and that was helpful. I went over by bus, stayed overnight and came back. That was important for getting acquainted with the literature.... [Choir director] Walter Yoder was a fine teacher. Instrumentally I studied piano with Mrs. [Susi] Friedmann.... I loved college and did all kinds of extracurricular things. I was the first woman *Maple Leaf* [yearbook] editor. The year before that, I had been the art editor of the *Maple Leaf,* the year, 1943, that it was Pennsylvania Dutch design. It was really quite a beautiful book.[26]

While in college, Mary led a choir of younger students, including other faculty children connected to the Goshen College congregation. This was her first opportunity to practice choral

---

[24] Goossen interview.
[25] Kauffman interview, 5.
[26] Ibid.

conducting. Directing a children's choir was the only acceptable venue, at that time, in which women musicians in the Mennonite Church could exercise leadership. Conducting was a skill she was learning from Walter Yoder, a choral teacher who also taught her to lead hymn singing. Yoder was a respected mentor for her, through the 1940s and 1950s, in music scholarship and conducting, and eventually, by the 1960s, in hymnal preparation. Several decades her senior, Yoder was a skilled musician who made hymns come alive, and Mary enjoyed playing in a string quartet with his musically talented daughters.[27] "His song leading was so wonderful," she recalled. "He had a profound influence on my concept of leading a congregation. He did the big things, not the little details, like you do with a choir. It's not a choir. It's the big things that you want. So it was very enriching to live in a place like this."[28]

Her experiences of conducting hymns and other choral literature with Yoder drew Mary more deeply into the world of vocal music. While a member of the college choir, she concluded that her own voice was not her strongest attribute—it had a "thin" sound, she thought, although she tried to develop it through voice lessons. But she enjoyed being part of the sacred choral concerts that Walter Yoder led, and she watched carefully how he communicated with both choir members and audiences. A decade later, as she developed exacting standards as conductor for the Motet Singers ensemble at Goshen College, she drew on this earlier choral training. Yet during the next several decades, Mary gradually rejected this emphasis on choral performance and began experimenting with leading congregational members in church choirs. By the 1960s and 1970s, she had become deeply engaged in singing as a direct worship experience within congregations. A quarter-century after her college studies, Mary had come full circle in her preference for group singing, asserting that "I have now moved to valuing congregational singing—total participation—far beyond choirs and passive listening."[29]

---

[27] Slough interview, 6; Kauffman interview, 3, 9.
[28] Slough interview, 9.
[29] Mary K. Oyer, "Reflections of a Church Musician," *Mennonite Reporter*, 22 March 1976, 5. See also Kauffman interview, 8; and Schlabach, "History," in *College Mennonite Church, 1903–2003*, 52.

Role Models and Mentors

In the mid-1940s, as Mary finished her studies at Goshen College, she was poised to make significant contributions as a Mennonite song leader. She had come of age in a world in which women, traditionally marginalized in roles outside the home, were contributing in new ways to the public and social lives of their communities.[30] Mennonite women in Goshen and beyond had long been engaged in sewing circles, missions organizations, and Christian education. Although they had been active professionally as teachers and nurses, other career paths were emerging by midcentury. Campuses of Mennonite higher education—such as Goshen College—offered occupational mobility for young women, especially in activities that reinforced church relations and service.

The Indiana-Michigan Mennonite Conference, of which Mary's local congregation was a part, had a heritage of "singing schools" dating back to the nineteenth century. So did other Mennonite communities, especially in eastern regions of the United States, where a 150-year tradition drew on the literature of the *Harmonia Sacra* and other songbooks. Mennonite singing schools brought people together for evening sessions to lift their voices in favorite church songs—some in parts, others in unison. Unlike preaching, which was traditionally reserved for men, the public leadership of singing schools had long been available to both men and women.

Generations earlier, gifted leaders such as Mary Ann Amstutz Sommer of Ohio had established popular singing schools in Amish-Mennonite communities.[31] Several decades after the death of this pioneering Mennonite woman, Mary's leadership with music in Goshen and other communities represented a tradition different from that of the nineteenth- and early twentieth-century singing schools. As Mary pursued opportunities as a musician, educator,

---

[30] See Julia Kasdorf, "'We Weren't Always Plain': Poetry by Women of Mennonite Backgrounds," in *Strangers at Home: Amish and Mennonite Women in History*, ed. Kimberly Schmidt, Diane Zimmerman Umble, and Steven D. Reschly (Baltimore: Johns Hopkins University Press, 2002), 318.
[31] Elaine Sommers Rich, *Mennonite Women: A Story of God's Faithfulness, 1683–1983* (Scottdale, PA: Herald Press, 1983), 112.

and churchwoman, she was also bringing a broader repertoire of music into Mennonite congregations and communities.[32]

Mary planned to make her living as a music teacher. It was a conventional choice for someone of her training and ability. Although barriers remained for women hoping to enter careers in higher education, women of earlier generations had already joined campus faculties. By the 1920s, women made up approximately 25 percent of all American college faculties, and the status of women in Mennonite higher education reflected this trend. Despite these earlier gains, women's presence in academe did not yet signify integration into the campus culture or equity in salary and rank.[33] At Goshen College in the 1920s and 1930s, for example, faculty women typically earned smaller salaries than their male counterparts, because of assumptions that men had to support families, while their female colleagues—mostly unmarried—did not.

As a young woman contemplating teaching, Mary could look to role models among Goshen faculty women—Olive Wyse in home economics, Mary Royer in education, Viola Good as dean of women, and others—full-time employees of the college who had never married. These women were pioneers in Mennonite higher education in their respective fields. Olive Wyse, for example, in 1946 received an EdD degree, one of the first American Mennonite women to earn a doctorate.

Although Mary had no way of knowing it during her years as a student, these women would be her teaching colleagues within a year of her graduation. They represented a distinctive career choice in embracing the college's mission of Christian liberal arts education, and they felt valued within the campus culture. As Olive Wyse told an interviewer half a century later, she and other women (who by the 1940s had successfully lobbied for more parity in pay) felt respected by male administrators and faculty members. Wyse attributed the faculty women's collegiality to a common Amish-Mennonite congregational heritage, in which individuals were en-

---

[32] See Walter E. Yoder, "Singing Schools," *The Mennonite Encyclopedia*, vol. 4 (Scottdale, PA: Mennonite Publishing House, 1959), 533–34; and Mary K. Oyer, "A 'Singing School' for the '90s," *Festival Quarterly* 17, no. 2 (Fall 1990), 18–19.

[33] Rosalind Rosenberg, *Divided Lives: American Women in the Twentieth Century* (New York: Hill and Wang, 1992), 96; Nancy Cott, *The Grounding of Modern Feminism* (New Haven: Yale University Press, 1987), 277.

couraged to speak forthrightly with one another. In spite of their lack of representation in the college administrative hierarchy, the faculty women's voices were heard, according to Wyse, who added: "I felt you could argue from a reasonable standpoint."[34]

There were other women, too, whom Mary observed and regarded as influential. Her own mother, Siddie Oyer, did washing and cleaning work at the college. Under other circumstances, Mary thought, her mother might have been an uncommonly good teacher. Four decades earlier, around 1905, Siddie had left her Ohio family home for Nampa, Idaho, where Mennonites were engaged in mission work. From Idaho she headed for more schooling at Hesston, Kansas, where administrators liked her so much that they wanted her to join the teaching staff. According to Mary: "She loved it [at Hesston] ... but then she married my father. I think that all her life she longed to do this kind of thing.... She was so glad that we [became] academics."[35]

Siddie also approved of her daughters' inclinations toward professional careers, and she did not emphasize the need for marriage. Mary dated during her college years, but her goal was to have a career in music. Six years after her Goshen graduation, Mary fell in love with a fellow musician, Alvin King, a Mennonite violist and composer. They planned to marry in Europe, because King was pursuing music studies in Paris. In 1950 Mary traveled by boat to Europe to join him. But King's indecision, as Mary perceived it, created serious strains in the relationship, and the marriage was called off.

Returning from Europe after this unhappy experience, Mary had unwavering support from her mother, who had always been skeptical of Mary's suitors. As Mary later described it, "Mother ... never pressured Verna and me to marry. We were never put down. When I saw some of my friends and how their mothers were embarrassed when they weren't married, mine wasn't."[36] Whatever feelings Siddie Oyer may have had about her daughter's romances,

---

[34] Kathy Kauffman, "Eight Women of the Academy," 11, Oral History Project 1993–94, Hist. Mss. 6-295, Box 2, Folder 1, Mennonite Church USA Archives–Goshen. See Olive Wyse, interview by Kauffman, Box 2, folder 4.
[35] Kauffman interview, 9.
[36] Ibid., 13.

she recognized that single women were given more latitude than married women in pursuing professional goals and in offering their gifts within the church. When she measured Mary's prospects against the limitations of her own life and early widowhood, Siddie must have envisioned a wide-open future for Mary as long as she remained unmarried.[37]

Besides Siddie, there were other influential women on the Goshen campus whom Mary admired and whose work ethic provided a model for her own career. Elizabeth Horsch Bender, wife of Harold S. Bender, taught German at the college and worked as an editor on historical projects, often in collaboration with her husband. In 1945, while Mary was completing her Goshen coursework, Elizabeth Bender was embarking on a massive project. This undertaking was translation of the *Mennonitisches Lexikon* materials detailing European Anabaptist and Mennonite historical and biographical topics, which formed the nucleus of the multivolume reference work later published as *The Mennonite Encyclopedia*.[38] Known for her rigor and her knowledge of languages, Elizabeth Bender modeled scholarship in a way that was less public than that of her high-profile husband. Mary viewed Elizabeth Bender as "a very sensitive person, very open to the arts," and one whom Mary admired as she worked toward completion of her major in music performance and her minor in studio art.[39]

The Benders had known Mary and her family for a long time and were friendly to her. They had watched the Oyer children grow up in the household headed by Siddie after Noah's death, and they took an interest in Mary and in her siblings' talents. Harold Bender had become academic dean at the college after Noah Oyer's death, and he developed a reputation for launching promising Goshen students into graduate studies and careers for which he believed they were suited. Those whom Bender took under his wing often came back to Goshen to teach. Over time, he built up a cadre of loyal faculty members, including nearly a dozen women who

---

[37] See, for example, Beth Graybill, "Decades Tell the Story of Women's Activities—From Sewing Circles to Ministry," *Gospel Herald* 90, no. 54 (27 January 1998), 10.

[38] Harold S. Bender and Cornelius Krahn, "Preface," *The Mennonite Encyclopedia*, vol. 1, (Scottdale, PA: Mennonite Publishing House, 1955), vii–ix.

[39] Slough interview, 1.

would spend their entire careers at the college. Kathy Kauffman, who joined the college faculty in 1982 as a librarian, described the campus culture for women faculty in that earlier era:

> From 1920 [to] 1950 when these women were hired, none of them applied in the formal sense. All were asked to come and work at Goshen College by one of the administrators.... All the women exhibited a special loyalty to Goshen College.... The college's connection to the Mennonite Church aided in this loyalty because many of the women saw their careers as a mission.... In an era when women were not getting advanced degrees or following a career path, they ... pursued their careers with intensity and devotion.[40]

Mary's sister, Verna, who had completed her studies in German, music, and art years earlier and had begun teaching secondary school, had never quite fit in with college peers who were religious traditionalists. After graduation Verna began attending other churches and was eventually drawn to the Episcopal tradition. She and Mary remained close, and Mary noted that their mother was very accepting of Verna's decisions.[41] The immediate Oyer family was a remarkably progressive base from which both Verna and Mary were encouraged to follow their talents wherever they led—without constraints about going into traditional "women's fields" such as teaching children, nursing, or social work.[42] Mary's younger brother, John, meanwhile, had been assigned to Civilian Public Service for alternative wartime work. John had to defer his studies—college at Goshen and then graduate school—until after the war. Like Mary, John would pursue his career, as a teacher and historian of Anabaptist and European history, at Goshen College.

Mary later reflected that she always felt that the Mennonite church was where she belonged. To be sure, she had never been attracted to the more rigid elements of the denomination. And soon after completing her college degree, she began encountering criti-

---

[40] Kauffman, "Eight Women of the Academy," 8, 11. See also Albert N. Keim, *Harold S. Bender* (Scottdale, PA: Herald Press, 1998).
[41] Slough interview, 28.
[42] On prescriptions for Mennonite women in the mid-twentieth century, see Graybill, "Decades Tell the Story," 10.

cism from some Mennonites opposed to the use of instruments in the church. As a piano student and a cellist who had played in school and community orchestras throughout her teens, she had received accolades for her abilities. The Mennonite churches with which she was familiar did not use instruments for music in worship, and vehemently opposed their use—on what they believed were scriptural bases. Mary knew that many Mennonites regarded musical instruments as frivolous and therefore incompatible with practical Christian living. Later, in her doctoral studies, Mary researched historical contexts for these tensions. She studied how medieval and modern Christians had often struggled with—and even maligned—music, painting, poetry, and other art forms as expressions of faith.[43]

Despite her awareness that her own artistic talents and inclinations collided with Mennonite cultural norms, Mary's sense of identity remained firm in young adulthood: "I got along fine," she later remembered. "I stayed with the Mennonites because it was home. It felt right to do so. I felt for Verna [who had moved away from the Mennonite church] ... but I didn't have any great longing to do this."[44] She recognized that her music making would not always be considered acceptable in the prescriptive ethos of Mennonite life. Even so, she had received enough encouragement from her circle of teachers and mentors that she was determined to develop and offer her gifts of music.[45] The Mennonite world she inhabited was expansive enough for her to remain in it.

If Mennonites had collaborated more readily across narrow denominational and geographical lines at that time, Mary might have learned to know other Mennonite women in the arts. Those with similar interests and commitments to Mennonite church institutions would undoubtedly have encouraged her. In Kansas, for example, Lena Waltner and Elvera Voth, both of whom pursued careers in arts education, made significant contributions at Bethel College, a four-year liberal arts institution affiliated with

---

[43] See Mary K. Oyer, "The Holy Ghost over the Bent World Broods," in *She Has Done a Good Thing: Mennonite Women Leaders Tell Their Stories*, ed. Mary Swartley and Rhoda Keener (Scottdale, PA: Herald Press, 1999), 140–41.
[44] Slough interview, 28.
[45] Mary K. Oyer, "Reflections of a Church Musician," 5.

the General Conference Mennonite Church but not associated with the Mennonite constituencies that supported Hesston and Goshen Colleges. Lena, raised in the Mennonite community of Freeman, South Dakota, was a painter and teacher who was gradually building up the fine arts program at Bethel College, where she "believed in the importance of art in ordinary life, even that of practical Mennonites."[46] With her music faculty colleague Walter Hohmann, Lena Waltner developed an integrative humanities course at Bethel, "Appreciation of the Fine Arts," that paralleled Mary Oyer's signature fine arts class at Goshen.

Also at Bethel, in the early 1950s a native Kansan, Elvera Voth, joined the music faculty and brought new standards of professionalism to conducting in General Conference Mennonite settings and beyond. But her successes in Kansas led her to move to Alaska for a conducting position. Although she and Mary might have enjoyed fruitful collaborations, they had little contact with each other despite being aware of each other's conducting work and broadly influential careers in music. The Mennonite Church context in which Mary lived, studied, and worked rarely overlapped with the General Conference Mennonite milieu, but Mary and women with similar interests might well have benefited from contacts with one another in the 1940s and 1950s.

The theological, social, and professional constraints imposed on Mary as a Mennonite musician and arts educator were comparatively limiting. One can only speculate how Mary might have responded to the avenues that would have been available to her had she been born into the General Conference Mennonite world.

Among the Indiana-based Mennonite teachers and mentors who knew and worked with Mary, perhaps the most influential at a critical juncture in her life—during her senior year at Goshen College—was academic dean Harold S. Bender. A colleague and confidante of her father years earlier, Bender now took a direct interest in her future. As Mary fondly remembered the scene many years later, Bender told her: "You will come back and teach the related arts [on the Goshen campus]." Mary added: "It didn't occur to me to say, 'Well, who are you to tell me what I am supposed

---

[46] Ruth Unrau, *Encircled: Stories of Mennonite Women* (Newton, KS: Faith and Life Press, 1986), 210.

to do?' Times were different, and for me it released me. I was the first [Mennonite] woman to get a doctor's degree in music.... I was the first person to get a strings degree of the kind I have from the University of Michigan, a Doctor of Musical Arts degree. In the Mennonite Church, I was encouraged just to go on."[47]

Becoming a Teacher

The conversation that Harold Bender initiated with Mary was in the fall of 1944, when she was poised to finish her coursework by December. The dean was following his well-established pattern of tapping talented young people to pursue further education and then join the Goshen faculty. Mary realized that Bender envisioned a new program on campus that would integrate study of the fine arts. Few universities and colleges in the nation were offering coursework in which art history, architecture, literature, and music were conceived as an arts world for students to explore simultaneously.

Who could refuse? When Harold Bender told Mary, "Well, you're going to do this, you're going to teach here and we want you to teach music and art together," she replied, without hesitation: "Yes, I'll do that." She finished her classes at Goshen in the last full year of the war, by Christmas 1944, and then entered the University of Michigan for eight months. Mary recalls that when she returned to Goshen the following fall to begin her teaching position, "I was much too young. And I didn't know how little I knew. But ... teaching at the college was wonderful at first. I just had a great time."[48]

In the fall of 1945 she was back home again, living in the Oyer house on South Eighth Street. She was still a student, working from a distance on her master's degree at Michigan, a commitment that would stretch into a doctoral program that she completed in 1958, after summers of commuting to Ann Arbor. Later an admirer, acknowledging a pattern that began early and continued for

---

[47] Kauffman interview, 4–5.
[48] Ibid, 8.

six decades, would describe Mary as "a teacher who never stopped learning."[49]

With the opportunities offered her by the Goshen College administration, in 1945 Mary became a teacher in her own right, working on a campus that would soon change as it moved from the austere wartime climate into a more expansive postwar era. Young Mennonite men, newly released from Civilian Public Service assignments across the country, began arriving and enrolling in general education classes, including Mary Oyer's arts class. She had negotiated an arrangement with her advisor at Michigan: her new course design, integrating arts and music, would fulfill the requirements for her master's thesis. She viewed the assignment to create a new, cross-disciplinary curriculum as a valuable application of her academic preparation. Later she recalled that in this transitional moment, "I ... felt at home with my own people."[50]

In the coming years, Mary developed rapport with students and respect among her faculty colleagues. She exercised a visible and public role in the church at a time when women's roles were expanding. She cultivated her musical abilities as a performing artist on the cello, despite church-wide critique of instrumental music and in the face of stinging questions about whether a professional woman musician was acceptable in the Mennonite Church. And she interpreted church history, music, and literature for increasingly diverse Mennonite Church people, running headlong into conflicts over leadership and the maintenance of cultural traditions.

Beginning in 1945, with her return to Goshen College as a twenty-two-year-old faculty member—an age younger than that of some of her students—a series of turning points in Mary's life would serve as markers for her journey toward influential ecumenical leadership. Through all that lay ahead, Mary Oyer's investments in music, art, and education, together with her belief in their transformational power, would sustain and invigorate her for new discoveries.

---

[49] Quotation from "Goshen College Professor Received Honorary Doctorate," *Goshen News*, 25 June 1994.
[50] Kauffman interview, 8.

Chapter 2

Following the Way, Seeking the Truth, Loving the Life

Rebecca Slough

W. H. Auden's poem "He is the Way" resonates in Mary Oyer's spirit, describing in startling images the wonder of her life.[1] Some sixty years ago, in saying yes to dean Harold S. Bender's commission to teach fine arts at Goshen College (Goshen, Indiana), she chose a life that would take her through lands of unlikeness and offer unique adventures.[2] As a novice twenty-two-year-old college instructor, she could hardly have dreamed of the distant places she would go, the fascinating people she would meet, the sympathetic interpreter of cultures she would become.

This essay explores adventures that became turning points in Mary Oyer's intellectual and spiritual development. Some of these experiences enlarged on what she already knew as a teacher. Others, such as working on *The Mennonite Hymnal* (1969) and teaching in Africa, also propelled her in new directions.[3]

Through her encounters with the people she has met and taught and learned from at each new turn, Mary's life has become a song of vibrant tonal color, fascinating rhythm, and rich harmony. In each section of our review of her life's stages, we will listen

---

[1] Mary loves this poem and had hoped that it would be included in *Hymnal: A Worship Book* (Elgin, IL: Brethren Press; Newton, KS: Faith and Life Press; Scottdale, PA: Mennonite Publishing House, 1992). She has introduced it, set to a 1972 tune by Richard D. Wetzel, in a number of congregations. It appears in *The Hymnal 1982: According to the Use of the Episcopal Church* (New York: Church Hymnal Corp., 1985).

[2] H. S. Bender was dean of Goshen College, 1931–44, and dean of Goshen College Biblical Seminary, 1944–62.

[3] At a Goshen College Afternoon Sabbatical in 2004, Mary had opportunity to talk about these various turning points during a presentation entitled "Music in My Life—A Retrospect." Even the experiences that appear to be ruptures with her past in fact build on it.

for how her self-understanding changed through new discoveries, and we will notice the themes that persisted. Considering Mary's pursuit of the Way, the Truth, and Life will lead us into the wisdom of her well-lived life.

Follow Him through the Land of Unlikeness

Mary began her forty-year teaching career at Goshen College in the fall of 1945. After completing her BA degree in music (with a minor in art) in December 1944, she worked on a master's degree from January to August 1945 at the University of Michigan. There she began her study of music, aesthetics, and art history. She delved into the poetry of John Keats. Perhaps most important, as an MMus project she developed the introductory fine arts class that would become her signature course at Goshen for more than two decades. Her enlightened and inspiring professors helped her define an approach that took seriously social and cultural influences in the work of the artists she studied. Mary's teaching explored how the music and visual art of particular eras and locations reflect and interact with the events and values of those times and places. And she has shown how visual art, architecture, and music inform one another.

Mary's fine arts teaching expanded Goshen's previously functional and pragmatic approach, by raising cultural and aesthetic questions. During the 1930s and most of the 1940s, Goshen's fine arts requirement had been fulfilled by a two-hour introductory course in art that focused on basic art skills. A two-hour music course centered on basic music skills. In 1945 Mary started teaching the music section of this two-semester course. Arthur Sprunger, who had been Mary's college art instructor, taught the visual art section.[4] Mary admired Sprunger's imagination and creativity. He had inspired her selection of Pennsylvania Dutch motifs for the *Maple Leaf* in 1943, when she was sophomore art editor of the college yearbook. Sprunger's students learned a variety of graphic

---

[4] As an entering instructor in the music department, Mary taught sight singing and dictation, elementary harmony, and history and appreciation of music. She also participated as a director in campus vocal music groups as needed.

design skills, which they practiced by producing posters to adver-
tise campus events.[5]

Combining music and visual art in one course was a controver-
sial choice in 1946, when Mary began her solo teaching of the "Introduction to Fine Arts" class. For many years Goshen was among
a small number of liberals arts colleges that dealt with visual art
and music in the same course, a requirement for all students. In
the late 1950s a representative of North Central Association, Goshen's accrediting agency, expressed doubts about including both
art forms in a single fine arts course. Some Goshen professors also
complained that the visual arts would not get the kind of interpretation that a visual artist would offer. Through most of the years
she taught the course, Mary felt the skepticism of critics of this
approach.

Former students talk about their initial fear in taking the fine
arts course, because of Mary's demanding standards. Yet years later they recognize that that course, perhaps more than others they
took, opened new worlds of perception. John Blosser, professor of
art at Goshen College, says that it was Mary's fine arts course that
changed his professional direction. He had planned to major in
music, but the world her course opened lured him from music to
visual art.[6] A physician who took the course in the 1950s described
himself as an ignorant, unsophisticated Mennonite farm boy who
had not been exposed to much music or visual art. Predictably, he
found Mary's course challenging. But he remembers how generous
she was with her time, helping him see and hear things in works of
art in exchange for his service in mowing her yard.[7] Some students
did not find Mary's approach to music or visual art interesting or
useful, and she lacked understanding of what they most valued—
often sports. Others who developed an interest in the arts found
Mary to be warm and supportive even as she challenged them to
learn new vocabulary, identify musical works after hearing short

---

[5] When she moved out of her house on South Eighth Street in Goshen in 2004, Mary
found many of the design exercises that Sprunger assigned his students. Her examples
were studies in seeing, reproducing, and using the basic elements of visual design.
[6] John Blosser, in a conversation with the author, Cincinnati Mennonite Arts Weekend,
February 2004.
[7] Reported by Donald Nofsinger, Cincinnati, Ohio, on at least two occasions, the latest in
February 2006.

fragments, memorize all the visual artworks of their postcard collection, and engage aesthetic ideas.

The fine arts course, more than any other class she taught in those early years, presented Mary with perplexing questions. From 1945 until the late 1950s, as a young adult, a Christian, and a Mennonite teaching in a church-related school, she grappled with basic philosophical and theological issues that had shaped her identity and approach to teaching. These questions arose through her interactions with students, professional colleagues, and church leaders—people who challenged her commitment to the arts. Her search for answers adequate to her questions required resources beyond her family, church, and school.

In her early years of teaching, several intense and articulate students confronted Mary with questions about how she could live a disciplined Christian life as a musician. Among the most challenging were John Howard Yoder, A. Orley Swartzendruber, and John W. Miller—young men who would become influential thinkers and church leaders. Their arguments did not focus on whether it is right or wrong to play instruments, to draw or paint, or to appreciate visual art. A year before Mary began teaching, at the March 1944 meeting of the American Society of Church History, H. S. Bender had delivered his presidential address on "The Anabaptist Vision." His interpretation of the sixteenth-century Anabaptists centered on their commitment to follow Jesus, living a life of discipleship and service. Mary's critics, including these students, believed the individualistic values and pursuits of artists—including musicians—were at odds with Bender's vision of Anabaptist Christian discipleship.[8]

---

[8] In the years since Bender gave the address (see Harold S. Bender, "The Anabaptist Vision," in *The Recovery of the Anabaptist Vision*, ed. Guy F. Hershberger [Scottdale, PA: Herald Press, 1957], 29–54), scholars have explored problems with his interpretation of sixteenth-century Anabaptism—while acknowledging that the interpretation has been inspiring, creative, and useful. Bender's exclusive focus on the sixteenth-century movement means that he did not address the role the arts played among seventeenth-century Dutch Mennonites. Mostly, Mennonite scholars of Swiss German descent have not looked favorably on the ways Dutch Mennonites participated in their culture after the period of persecution was over. As they became more prosperous, the Dutch accepted the practice of acquiring visual art for the home. Swiss–South German Mennonites have not been generous in their appraisal of the artistic dimensions of Dutch Mennonite experience, believing that the Dutch became acculturated in ways that compromised high standards of Anabaptist belief and practice.

In most respects, Mary's dilemma in the early years of teaching was not unique. After graduating from college and entering the world of work, many Christian young people struggle to integrate their beliefs and values with their vocational identities. But teaching in a college supported by a denomination skeptical about the validity of visual art and instrumental music intensified Mary's professional struggle. She had been called by a respected leader to teach in subject areas that many Mennonites regarded with suspicion. Those who did recognize the validity of the arts wanted to restrict acceptable artistic pursuits to a narrow range. While Mary had the support of H. S. and Elizabeth Bender at the college, she needed to do her own work to reconcile her vocation as a musician, a teacher of visual art, and a Mennonite.

Mary tells about being in a public meeting where an influential church leader and fellow musician asked, "How can Mary Oyer be a Christian and play the cello?" She found this comment, and others like it, profoundly unsettling. For years she remained anxious and worked hard to get things "right," sometimes voicing strong opinions that belied her uncertainties. For a long time she struggled to define the essence of "good music." Articulating a justification for being a cellist, a woman in a Mennonite culture, and a person of Christian faith energized her future doctoral studies.

During this time of developing professional identity, Mary studied under the direction of composer Roy Harris[9] at Utah State Agricultural College in the summer of 1948. She took composition lessons from Harris and worked on cello with Leonard Rose of the New York Philharmonic Orchestra. Her former student, John Howard Yoder, introduced her to Alvin King. Her friendship with King deepened while they both studied at the University of Colorado, Boulder, in the summer of 1949. Later that year King went to France to study viola. Mary was to travel to Europe in 1950, and they made plans to marry in France, with a few friends as witnesses. H. S. Bender arranged her travel by boat.

The date of the wedding changed several times after Mary's departure, and she could have seen this as evidence of her fiancé's

---

[9] According to *The New Grove Dictionary of American Music*, vol. 2, ed. H. Wiley Hitchcock and Stanley Sadie (London: Macmillan, 1986), Harris helped establish an American style of symphonic music. He had been a student of Arthur Farwell.

uncertainty about the marriage. During the summer they traveled by motorcycle in France, Switzerland, and Italy. Two days before the appointed wedding date, King announced that he could not go through with the marriage. Mary returned to Goshen and began the task of refocusing her life.[10] The failed engagement added one more uncertainty in her developing identity as a woman, a Mennonite, and a musician.

In 1953 Mary enrolled in the new Doctor of Musical Arts degree program at the University of Michigan. Her study focused on performance practice. Over the course of several summers and one sabbatical year she completed the degree, the first string player to do so. She studied original manuscripts and historical resources on cello music—especially Beethoven—and performed in three recitals during the academic year 1957–58. These were her first public recitals as a solo and chamber music performer, and she found them nerve-racking.

From one side, Mary felt the doubts of her faith community about the validity of her vocation as a female Mennonite cellist teaching the arts. From the other side, she felt pressure from serious musician friends to abandon a faith that seemed to set constraints on her potential as a professional musician. In a presentation in 1955 she acknowledged that her religious tradition limited her vision of possibilities for making music with the cello.

> My teacher told me early in my study that he could tell from my playing that I was a Christian. In a kindly way, he suggested that if I wanted to be a musician I should probably give up Christianity because it was too limited and unimaginative. Unfortunately, he had encountered only unimaginative and repressed Christians. But I, too, was unimaginative and limited. I had grown up not knowing that music aside from words communicates a great deal. I had never imagined that playing had anything to do with faith.[11]

---

[10] In the mid-1980s, Mary and Alvin King renewed their friendship, in order to test whether they might now be ready to try marriage. This time Mary decided that they were better off apart.

[11] "A Philosophy of the Use of Music in Mennonite Meetings" (address, First Mennonite Musicians' Meeting, Chicago, 4–5 March 1955). Printed as chapter 14 of the present volume (quotation appears on page 155).

Mary gives no indication that she considered abandoning Christian faith, but the confusion and isolation she felt made her miserable. Perhaps it was because solo cello performance gave her little pleasure that she did not heed the voices that counseled her to abandon her faith. During these years she was captivated by the aesthetic perspective of Clive Bell, a philosopher of art who contrasted the "cold hard peaks of art" that were "far away from warm humanity." Mary commented years later,

> I shall never forget the day [my professor] read a passage from Clive Bell's *Art*.[12] After disclaiming any knowledge of music, Bell described those rare occasions when he heard music purely and rose to the lofty heights of aesthetic experience. He was unable to stay there long. Rather, he would sink into his normal state of inattention and haphazard listening: ... "Let no one imagine, because he has made merry in the warm tilth and quaint nooks of romance, that he can ever guess at the austere and thrilling raptures of those who have climbed the cold, white peaks of art."[13]

Mary's standards for performance were high, and she may have believed she could not consistently perform as the music demanded. Playing in public for its own sake did not motivate her. Participating in orchestras and especially in chamber groups gave her energy and proved enjoyable in ways that solo work never was. Mary came to see that making music with others elicits her best. Later she also recognized that she would rather talk to people about music than play alone.[14]

If solo cello performance did not offer fulfillment, Mary's studies of musicology, philosophy of art, and aesthetics thoroughly engaged her. Delving deep into the inner melodic and harmonic movements of a work to analyze its structure yielded profound satisfaction. These pursuits challenged and rewarded her capacities for seeing, organizing, and remembering details.

---

[12] Clive Bell, *Art* (New York: Frederick A. Stokes, 1913).
[13] Quoted in "The Cold, White Peaks of Art, the Foothills of Warm Humanity," *Goshen College Bulletin*, November 1983, 3.
[14] Mary Oyer, in interview with the author, August 2002.

In Palmer Throup at University of Michigan, Mary had a sympathetic advisor with whom to talk about her questions about Christianity and art. A practicing Episcopalian and a historian of medieval and Renaissance European culture, Throup guided her to early sources on aesthetics that synthesized faith, art, and the artist. During her first sabbatical in 1954–55, Mary read in these fields and compiled many annotated bibliographies. She discovered that the tension between Christianity and the arts had a long history. Michelangelo, in particular, struggled with the purpose of his work and his life as a Christian. Finding his writings and those of Petrarch and Boccaccio was liberating. She was not the first to wrestle with these questions, and she need not do so alone.

The intellectual explorations in her doctoral work gave Mary courage and perspective; through her study at Michigan she laid a foundation for her future teaching. Between 1955 and 1960 she made presentations at Mennonite church gatherings in which she attempted to synthesize her musical, aesthetic, philosophical, and theological thinking on art and faith. She sought to encourage public conversation among Mennonites on the interface between art and faith.[15]

In broad strokes, her arguments begin with the goodness of created world. Beauty is a fact of creation; it is an expression of God's character and love. God's blessing of this material world is evident in Jesus' incarnation (God's supreme revelation in human form), and his entry into the world raises questions about

---

[15] Mary rehearsed her ideas over the course of several years in a variety of settings. The following papers, some of them unpublished, attest most clearly to her efforts to draw her ideas together:

"A Philosophy of the Use of Music in Mennonite Meetings" (address, First Mennonite Musicians' Meeting, Chicago, 4–5 March 1955).

"A Philosophy of Mennonite Church Music: As Related to Beauty" (address, Second Mennonite Musicians' Meeting, Iowa City, IA, 22–23 March 1957).

"A Christian View of the Fine Arts," in *Proceedings of the Eleventh Conference on Mennonite Educational and Cultural Problems*, Bethel College, North Newton, KS, 6–7 June 1957 (N.P.: Council of Mennonite and Affiliated Colleges, 1957).

"Christianity and the Fine Arts: Basic Problems Which Confront Mennonites Participating in the Fine Arts" (paper, Goshen College Faculty Discussion Meeting, 21 November 1957).

"The Church's Responsibility in Artistic Discrimination" (paper, Mennonite Graduate Fellowship, Columbus, OH, 2 January 1959).

"The Cold, White Peaks of Art, the Foothills of Warm Humanity," *Goshen College Bulletin*, November 1983, 3–5.

the relationship between faith and culture. Mary used the typology developed by theologian and ethicist H. Richard Niebuhr, which identifies several possible postures of the church toward culture.[16] She believed that if they are to value the arts, Christians must accept culture as a social fact. Borrowing from Suzanne Langer's *Philosophy in a New Key*,[17] Mary advocated the view that the arts are expressive media that communicate in ways beyond logic. They speak on emotional and intuitive levels, in ways that words and propositions cannot fully explain. In the church, the basis for the artist's work is love—love for Christ, love for people inside and outside the church, and love for the work itself. Love is also the church's reason for accepting the gifts of artists.

These presentations include many questions, which reflect Mary's desire for discussion that could build a consensus among Mennonite scholars and educators. Her attempts to articulate new perspectives formed her as a teacher sensitive to the conflicts of mind and spirit that can trouble the soul. Her synthesis was not revolutionary; it offered few new insights in the field of aesthetics or for faith. But Mary demonstrated a way of thinking through the demands that a vocation in the arts creates for Mennonite Christians seeking to be faithful to Christ, not just to a tradition. Mary wanted to stay in the (Old) Mennonite Church as a musician and an interpreter of art and music at a time when many Mennonite-raised authors, musicians, poets, and visual artists (including her sister, Verna) found it necessary to leave the church in order to pursue their professional goals.

Mary's graduate work opened the way to a turning point in her adult life. Through music, visual art, and architecture, she grasped art's power to reveal the multifaceted truth of God's unending love. (Old) Mennonites had rejected the possibility that art has power to reveal truth about God's relationship with humankind. They have been reluctant to claim that physical materials (such as paint, canvas, stucco, clay, marble, or stained glass) could be arranged in

[16] Niebuhr's five types are Christ against culture; Christ of culture; Christ above culture; Christ and culture in paradox, and Christ transforming culture; see H. Richard Niebuhr, *Christ and Culture* (New York: Harper & Row, Publishers, Inc., 1951).
[17] *Philsophy in a New Key: A Study in the Symbolism of Reason, Rite, and Art* (Cambridge: Harvard University Press, 1951).

ways that make visible what is invisible. Surely, Mary's studies in Greek philosophy began her turning in a new direction, but the lived theology of her Mennonite community also contributed. She and many Christian artists took Christ's incarnation seriously. And Jesus used the materials of daily life—bread, wine, water, mud —to reveal the truth of God's love and mercy. The synthesis of aesthetic thought and Christian theology of incarnation, expressed most fully during the medieval and Renaissance periods, has shaped Mary's spirituality ever since.

Mary has not written or spoken much about the journey that confirmed her calling as a Christian teacher of the arts. She tested her ideas with other teachers and scholars, but for the most part her studies assured her that she was not doing something wrong: "I just didn't have the kind of fear that I had before.... That's the way it [had] felt in the church, that [playing cello] was wrong."[18]

Walter Yoder was an enduring presence and an important advocate during Mary's early years of teaching. A member of the Goshen College music faculty when Mary was a student, he was instrumental in creating a place for her to teach in the department. Mary benefited from his generosity of spirit and personal warmth. She respected him and especially admired the way he led congregational singing. Walter helped the congregation feel the music's phrasing through the use of his hand and voice. Rather than follow the conventional beat patterns, he often used fluid motions or even large circles to interpret the flow of a song. Congregations responded immediately. By the late 1950s he had become a model for Mary's intrepid leadership of congregational song. In her tribute on the occasion of his death in 1964, Mary wrote that Walter "had a remarkable intuition about congregational singing. How fast or slowly should a particular group sing on a particular day in order to find the hymn most helpful? Which hymns would be most appropriate for the occasion? His judgments in such matters were almost uncanny."[19]

Mary's graduate studies, completed in 1958, gave her an aesthetic language and a theological justification (perhaps more than

---

[18] Mary Oyer, in interview with the author, August 2002.
[19] Mary K. Oyer, "Walter Yoder: A Tribute," *Gospel Herald* 57, no. 47 (8 December 1964), 1040.

a philosophical one) for the place of the arts in a Christian's life. Ever since, she has drawn on these foundational understandings in her teaching. In all of her subsequent studies she has searched for the synthesis of art form, culture, and understanding of human experience. Her skills in formal musical analysis, well-honed through her work with critical editions of music, have been invaluable. Her views on many things have changed, but fifty years later she still draws on the basic skills and beliefs forged in her graduate studies to analyze music and visual art.

You Will See Rare Beasts

As a young woman, Mary had little interest in hymns as a subject for study. She enjoyed congregational singing and recounts vivid childhood memories of congregational singing in the administration building during Sunday services of College Mennonite Church. But she thought hymn tunes were too short to be of any real musical significance. What was ST. ANNE compared to a Beethoven cello sonata, or HAMBURG, to a Beethoven symphony? She saw that hymns are important for the church's worship, but they did not pique her intellectual curiosity. How she came to be a renowned interpreter of hymns and a respected congregational song leader is an unlikely story.

During the years of Paul Erb's editorship of the Mennonite Church weekly magazine (1944–62), *Gospel Herald* published monthly articles addressing issues of the church's music.[20] These brief pieces identified the values that should shape the use of music in Mennonite worship and in Mennonite homes. Many of the contributors served on the music committee of the Mennonite Church General Conference; regulars included J. Mark Stauffer, Walter Yoder, John Duerksen, Karl Massanari, and Paul Erb himself.

In the 1940s and 1950s, men dominated the music life of Mennonite congregations, meeting weekly to select hymns for Sunday worship and acting as song leaders. Men taught other men to lead hymns at church-wide music conferences at Little Eden Camp or Laurelville Mennonite Church Center. Article after article in *Gos-*

---

[20] Regular topics included congregational music leadership, a cappella singing, standards for congregational songs, short histories of popular hymns, and teaching children to sing in the home and at church.

pel Herald exhorted these men to take their leadership tasks seriously: to live a godly life, worthy of those carrying this responsibility; to get training for leading the congregation; to work with the preacher in making selections; to prepare the hymns selected for the service; and to lead with confidence and keen attention to the task at hand. These men were to cultivate the congregation's singing ability and to introduce new songs. Women taught children to sing in Sunday school and at home, and they led singing for women's meetings.

Walter Yoder's articles were terse, pragmatic, and to the point. His insights sparkle with energy; they also leave little room for dissent. With other members of the music committee, he had no use for gospel songs or choruses. He described as them as "light" and "trashy." He objected to the repetitive and rhythmic qualities of gospel songs and choruses. Their simplistic theology and individualistic piety seemed inappropriate for gathered worship. In unbecoming ways they excited the body and spirit with their unsophisticated sentiment.[21]

Walter edited a collection of hymns, *Songs of the Church* (1953), which appeared twenty-six years after the 1927 *Church Hymnal* and after *Life Songs Number Two*. This collection of 274 songs includes only twelve gospel songs or choruses. Yoder's goal was to provide more wholesome and—to his mind—more dignified songs for congregational worship. He tried to redirect the Mennonite Church's musical and theological tastes by widening the range of musical options for congregational singing in other directions, but the book met with limited success.

Mary could not understand Walter's strong objections to gospel songs. Although she felt no great love for these hymns, she was puzzled about why he found them so objectionable. She thought hymns for worship should be judged by criteria different from those applied to concert music, but she had not thought through what the standards for music in Mennonite worship should be. Publicly she promoted the view that gospel songs and choruses combined third-rate music and inferior theology, but privately she had doubts. Later in her life this split between private doubt and

---

[21] Forty years later many Mennonite college music teachers would make similar arguments against contemporary worship music.

public avowal would find a resolution, but in the 1950s she acquiesced in the view that these songs were inadequate.

Songs of the Church opened the way for the music committee of the Mennonite Church's General Conference[22] to consider revising *The Church Hymnal*. In 1957 Walter Yoder, then chair of the committee, submitted a rationale for revision to the General Conference of the Mennonite Church.[23] In November 1957 the General Conference approved the committee's proposal. Mary was co-opted to serve on the hymnal committee sometime between 1959 and 1961, and to work on a subcommittee appointed "to study the issues involved in the use of instruments in Mennonite Church worship."[24]

Questions about the use of instruments in Mennonite worship took on more importance in the late 1950s as organs became affordable for congregational purchase. Mary occasionally met with congregations to talk about whether it was appropriate for Mennonites to use instruments—organs or pianos—for congregational singing. Her presentations were replete with questions meant to stimulate thinking and discussion. As a cellist completing her doctoral studies, she had clear opinions about the possibilities and limitations associated with using instruments in worship, but she was not dogmatic in her views.

In her presentations on the use of instruments in worship, Mary worked with Niebuhr's typology. Historically (Old) Mennonites had interpreted the testimony of Christ to be against the values, structures, and practices of surrounding cultures; they attempted to create clear separations between the church and the world. But Mary observed that North American Mennonites in the 1950s were functioning as if the witness of Christ and the values of culture were compatible in some ways; Mennonites were even contemplating the possibility that the witness of Christians could

---

[22] This committee was elected to oversee music and worship standards in the church.

[23] Yoder gave the following reasons for revising the 1927 hymnal: (1) to remove difficult, unused tunes from the 1927 book; (2) to replace the light gospel songs with better hymn tunes; (3) to correct errors in textual materials; (4) to correct errors in notation; (5) to enlarge topic areas not fully represented [for worship]; and (6) to enrich the collection with available music of exceptional quality (proceedings of Mennonite General Conference, Eastern Mennonite College, Harrisonburg, VA, 25–27 August 1957).

[24] Proceedings of Mennonite General Conference, Johnstown, PA, 22–25 August 1961.

effect some transformation of culture. And Mary asked whether Mennonites could use instruments in worship to enrich the musical life of the congregation—without undermining the riches of four-part, a cappella singing.

Mennonite music patterns outside worship were changing. More and more Mennonites had instruments (especially pianos) in their homes. They listened to the radio. Some were buying record players and televisions. Mary recognized, as did others, that new Mennonite urban mission churches often lacked a core group of people who could read music to sing in four parts without accompaniment. Larger choral works (such as *The Messiah*), that are beneficial to hear and learn, require keyboard accompaniment at the least. Mary preferred congregational singing that was unaccompanied, but she realized that not all congregations had the training necessary to sing in the traditional a cappella style. On this issue she began to question the views of Walter Yoder, J. Mark Stauffer, and others writing for *Gospel Herald*.

Issues surrounding the use of instruments for congregational singing became more focused after the (Old) Mennonite Church and the General Conference Mennonite Church became partners in creating a shared hymnal. For the General Conference Mennonites, this collection had to have music appropriate for organ accompaniment. Traditional cultural differences between the two groups—including those surrounding use or nonuse of the organ—would need negotiation in the course of the joint hymnal project.

Here again Walter Yoder exerted a vital influence on Mary's life, taking a direct role in inviting her involvement with the committee charged with creating the new Mennonite hymnal, in the 1960s. The opportunity to work on the hymnal came at a timely moment in Mary's unfolding vocation—which Walter knew, of course. She had completed her doctoral work. She could deal competently with music history and analysis. By the late 1950s she had established herself as a teacher and a choral conductor, having directed Goshen's Motet Singers for nearly a decade. She had visited many congregations while on tour with the Motet Singers, and she frequently accepted invitations to talk about using musical instruments in worship. She had encountered the *Hymnal for Colleges and Schools* (1956) published by Yale University, which included brief articles with source information for each hymn. It impressed her favorably, and the field of hymnological study had gained credibility in her mind. And she did not have a next big project on which to focus her attention and her considerable gifts.[25]

During her second sabbatical (1963–64), Mary went to Scotland to work with Erik Routley, a pastor, musician, church historian, and hymnologist, in order to broaden her understanding of church music and the use of instruments in worship. After reading several of his books, she believed she could benefit from discussing worship and instruments with him. She learned about Routley from Nathan Scott, who had come to Goshen to make a presentation on literature and faith.[26] As it turned out, her conversations with Routley about instruments in worship went nowhere. But he introduced Mary to the historical study of hymns and tunes.

Routley was a respected hymnologist with an international reputation.[27] His quick wit and strong opinions on music and theology were startling. He helped Mary and many others see hymns—texts and tunes—as music for ordinary people. He frequently referred to hymns as "folk music," music and words that Christians sing to express a common faith.

Her year in Scotland became another turning point for Mary, and Routley's influence was decisive. Hymns are songs with histories that reflect the times and locations of the people who create and sing them. All the analytical skills she had applied to the

---

[25] When asked to serve on the hymnal revision, one of Mary's first thoughts was that she could fix all the musical errors found in *Songs for the Church* and the *Church Hymnal*. At the very least she thought she could contribute proofreading skills.

[26] Nathan Scott was an African-American professor at the University of Chicago, whose work on connections between faith and literature was helpful to Mary. She inquired more about his perspective, and he pointed her toward Routley.

[27] Selected examples of Routley's work prior to Mary's time in Scotland include *Music in Christian Hymnody* (London: West Microfilming, 1951); *I'll Praise My Maker: A Study of the Hymns of Certain Authors Who Stand In or Near the Tradition of English Calvinism* (London: Independent Press, 1951); *Companion to Congregational Praises: With Notes on the Music by Erik Routley* (London: Independent Press, 1953); *Hymns and the Faith* (Greenwich, CT: Seabury Press, 1956); *The Music of Christian Hymnody: A Study of the Development of the Hymn Tunes since the Reformation* (London: Independent Press, 1957); *The English Carol* (New York: Oxford University Press, 1958, 1959); *Ecumenical Hymnody* (London: Independent Press, 1959); *Church Music and Theology* (Philadelphia: Muhlenberg Press, 1960); and *Isaac Watts* (London: Independent Press, 1961). Routley continued to write prolifically through the remainder of his life.

critical editions of Beethoven's cello works she now began to use to understand the simpler structures of hymn tunes and texts that people have sung as expressions of faith.

Mary compared the original versions of Isaac Watts's hymns and psalm paraphrases with those she had learned through the Mennonite hymnals, and she noticed striking differences. These discrepancies raised questions in her mind about how hymnal editors made their choices. Why were certain verses from the hymnist's original work omitted? Why were words or phrases changed? Comparing the original form of the tunes GENEVA 42 or OLD HUNDREDTH in the 1565 Genevan Psalter[28] with the version she knew from the Mennonite hymnal sources helped her imagine new possibilities for congregational singing.

Mary dived into her work with a scholar's zeal, searching for the first appearances of tunes well known to Mennonites, getting facsimile copies of important collections such as the Genevan Psalter, Thomas Est's *Whole Booke of Psalms*, Catherine Winkworth's *Chorale Book for England*. She developed a deep appreciation for hymnals and historical books related to hymnody.[29] Although *Exploring the Mennonite Hymnal: Essays* was not published until seventeen years later, the fruits—still fresh—of her labor in Scotland are evident there.[30]

This new perspective on the study of hymns began a shift in Mary's teaching and presence in the life of the church. As a budding hymnologist, she felt the connection between the song and the people singing take on depth. On earlier tours with the Motet Singers she frequently sensed the gulf between the concert style music the choir had prepared and what local congregations of Mennonites were most eager (and prepared) to hear. In 1976 Mary wrote in *Gospel Herald*: "I had been influenced early in my studies by a philosopher of the arts who invited the reader to be transported to the 'cold, white peaks of art,' far away from 'warm humanity.'

---

[28] *Les Pseaumes mis en rime françoise, par Clément Marot et Théodore de Bèze; mis en musique à quatre parties par Claude Goudimel* (Geneva: François Jaqui, 1565).

[29] As a result of this newfound interest, Mary pursued acquisition of J. D. Hartzler's collection of eighteenth-century hymns for the Mennonite Historical Library at Goshen College in the mid-1960s.

[30] Mary Oyer, *Exploring the Mennonite Hymnal: Essays* (Newton, KS: Faith and Life Press; Scottdale, PA: Mennonite Publishing House, 1980).

I tried to communicate to my small choir the excitement of those 'cold, white peaks.' They could catch it over a period of time and in direct music making, but congregations for whom we sang did not care for the austerity."[31]

If the cold hard peaks represented the reified world of the artist and the solo performer, human warmth characterized the world of hymns shared by people singing together. Many times Mary has told eager students and congregations around the world stories about hymn texts and tunes, which she had picked up in Scotland. Learning to understand hymns sung by congregations over time would constitute a significant step toward her becoming an ethnomusicologist in Africa.

Mary returned to Goshen in 1964, having acquired a fund of historical information and resources. She was committed to the idea that the tune and text subcommittees of the joint hymnal committee should consult the original form of the texts and tunes as they were making decisions, and that they should select the original whenever possible, as other mainline denominations were doing in their hymnal revisions. The *Yale Hymnal for Schools and Colleges* and *Hymnal 1940* are examples of this scholarly approach to hymnal revision; they provided impetus for Mary's work. Beyond issues of historical fidelity, this approach provided the committee with ways to move beyond their partisan loyalties to the different versions of hymns each tradition had come to prize. Such differences are evident in the versions of "O[h,] for a Thousand Tongues to Sing" in *Church Hymnal* and *The Mennonite Hymnary*. (See the appendix to this chapter for Charles Wesley's original, and a comparison of the versions printed in these two hymnals.[32])

Mary advocated including historical information about the origins of the text and tune for each hymn in the new book. Not all of the other committee members shared her enthusiasm for introducing the church to the historical breadth of its hymns. Some wondered how these data would contribute to the congregation's singing. A hymnal handbook, which the revision committee and

---

[31] "Reflections of a Church Musician," *Gospel Herald* 69, no. 13 (30 March 1976), 256.
[32] From *Representative Verse of Charles Wesley* (New York: Abingdon Press, 1962), 24–26.

the Mennonite Church General Conference had already approved, eventually became the repository for this information.[33]

How did Mary work on the hymnal project's joint committee? She was the only woman among the nine representatives of the Mennonite Church[34] and the nine representatives of the General Conference Mennonite Church. She was also the only single person working on the project; with fewer family responsibilities, she may have had more time to devote to the enterprise.[35] After Walter Yoder's death, she was named executive secretary of the joint hymnal committee; she says she was chosen because women were always secretaries. Nonetheless, this position gave her scope to exercise her power as a scholar and a woman prepared to give attention to details.

It is hard to read how Mary worked on the subcommittee for selecting tunes and on the joint committee. Especially on returning from Scotland, she doubtless held strong opinions about hymnody, and negotiating differences and handling dissent have never been easy for her. She desires to be respected because of her intellect, knowledge, and passion. Most of the men on the committees were still learning how to work with women as professional colleagues. Did they listen to and honor her opinions, or were men's opinions the ones that mattered? Did she need to dwell on a point until she felt understood? Did she feel heard only when people agreed with her?

In the early 1960s, men and women had few critical tools for understanding gender differences in conversational and decision-making styles. With no other women present at the meetings—which lasted a week at a time—Mary had no respite from men's talk. She was sometimes painfully aware that her ways of thinking about things differed from those of the men on the committee. She remembers that she invariably needed a good cry at some point during the working sessions—often alone but not always. She needed affirmation.

---

[33] Alice Loewen, Harold Moyer, and Mary Oyer, *Exploring the Mennonite Hymnal: Handbook* (Newton, KS: Faith and Life Press; Scottdale, PA: Mennonite Publishing House, 1983).

[34] The preface to *The Mennonite Hymnal* notes that Arlene Hartzler served as a consultant for the hymns for children, but she did not serve on the committee.

[35] Her mother had died in 1963, so Mary was relieved of those caretaking responsibilities.

The decision to produce a joint hymnal expanded the singing horizons for both the General Conference Mennonite Church and the Mennonite Church, in several directions. The German chorale tradition, still strong among the General Conference Mennonites of Canada and Kansas, was restored to the Mennonite Church. The original rhythmic versions of these tunes were often recovered, or a Bach harmonization was used. The hymnal also included a rich selection of American folk hymns, especially from the *Harmonia Sacra*. From this collection the committee reluctantly included "Praise God from Whom All Blessings Flow" (606); they feared it would be too difficult for general congregational use. Hymn translations from the *Ausbund* set to music of the fifteenth or sixteenth century opened another direction. African-American spirituals and hymns from Japan, China, and India gave North American Mennonites connections with the global church.

The collection has few hymns or tunes composed in the twentieth century and even fewer written by Mennonites, living or dead. While in Scotland, Mary had had contact with a group of British pastors and theologians who were writing new hymns and tunes.[36] Their hymn texts were commentaries on contemporary social and political realities, and their tunes reflected the influence of popular folk music and jazz. Mary was intrigued by the vitality of their work, but she and other members of the revision committee feared that this emerging body of hymns would be too challenging for North American Mennonite congregations.

The new hymnal was officially introduced to the church at the Mennonite Church General Assembly at Turner, Oregon, in 1969. Mary was given time during the Saturday evening session to introduce its contents, and she emphasized the historical breadth and varied character of the hymns the committee had selected.[37] She was recognized as the person who did the most work on the hymnal. She led a number of hymns as part of her demonstration, including "Praise God from Whom All Blessings Flow" (MH 606),

---

[36] Brian Wren was among this group of hymn writers. Sydney Carter, though not part of this group, was also writing contemporary texts, such as "Lord of the Dance," and setting them to folk-like melodies.

[37] Paul Erb, "Gathered with a Purpose," *Gospel Herald* 52, no. 36 (16 September 1969), 804.

but she was never asked to lead congregational singing in any of the assembly worship periods.[38]

The Mennonite Hymnal is widely recognized as an exceptional book. It set a new scholarly standard for Mennonite hymnals as well as for those of other denominations. In the bulletin of the Hymn Society of Great Britain and Ireland, Erik Routley would write,

> The book shows a far more sophisticated approach to hymnody, and a much greater readiness to share with the praises of neighbouring traditions, than the Mennonites have shown before: and this is in large measure due to the remarkable work done by the committee's Executive Secretary, Dr. Mary Oyer, of Goshen College, Indiana. ... It is to Dr. Oyer that we owe most of the discoveries and arrangements[39] from that folk tradition which give the book its chief interest and character.[40]

Release of *The Mennonite Hymnal* presented Goshen College's music department with an opportunity to commission composers to write brief organ preludes to introduce some of the hymnal's new tunes. The college sponsored a church music conference in 1970, during which these pieces had their premier performance on the Walcher organ recently installed at College Mennonite Church. The project gives us a sense of Mary's vision for the use of organ music in congregational life. Charles Burkhart, J. Harold Moyer, and Alice Parker wrote the majority of the preludes. The preludes' length, relative simplicity, and crafting demonstrate how an instrument can support congregational singing by imagi-

---

[38] Mary introduced the following songs in this presentation: "Holy God, We Praise Thy Name" (1); "All Creatures of Our God and King" (52); "How Firm a Foundation" (260); "O Thou, in Whose Presence" (273); "Come, Come, Ye Saints" (312); "Thou Didst Leave Thy Throne" (563); "All Praise to Our Redeeming Lord" (383); "O Happy Day, That Fixed My Choice" (398); "Christ for the World We Sing" (425); "God of Grace and God of Glory" (434); "Holy Spirit, Truth Divine" (207); "Cry out with Joy" (618); and "Praise God from Whom" (606); *Thirty-Eighth Mennonite General Conference (Turner, Oregon), Mennonite General Conference Proceedings* (Scottdale, PA: Mennonite General Conference, 1969), 14.
[39] On this point Routley is wrong. Mary did not do arrangements of any of the folk hymns included in *The Mennonite Hymnal*. J. Harold Moyer did nearly all of the arrangements and new harmonizations.
[40] Erik Routley, "Three American Hymn Books of 1969," *Bulletin of the Hymn Society of Great Britain and Ireland* 119, no. 7 (Summer 1970), 96.

natively introducing new tunes. The congregation's voice remains the primary sound of worship, but a creative use of instruments can help educate that voice.

Before the release of the new hymnal, Mary was not known primarily as a song leader in the Mennonite Church. Congregations had seen her directing Goshen's Motet Singers when the group was on tour. She sometimes led singing during college chapel services. She had begun leading singing in her congregation, College Mennonite Church, sometime in the 1950s. Beyond these venues, her exposure as a song leader was limited; song leading in worship was still almost exclusively the prerogative of men.[41]

How did Mary become an icon of congregational singing in the Mennonite Church? It happened primarily because people were eager to learn about the songs they were singing: What is in them? Where did they come from?[42] Mary was uniquely placed to provide answers to these questions, and uniquely gifted to engage congregations in learning to sing from this new collection.

Generations of Mennonite church leaders had been preoccupied with the theological integrity of their hymn texts. Musical considerations were secondary.[43] Mary focused on the musical qualities of the tunes, believing them to have an importance for worship equal to that of the words. When she guided a group through a hymn, pointing out features of words and music that people had not noticed or had not known, they responded with surprise and delight. She interpreted the music for the congregation, demonstrating how melody, rhythm, and harmony work with the words to create a satisfying experience of worship in song. Hymns took on depth and richness as she drew singers into the truth, beauty, and love of singing.

The opportunity to work on *The Mennonite Hymnal* came as Mary was entering midlife at forty. Middle age opens possibilities

---

[41] See J. Mark Stauffer, "Mennonite Women and Music," *Gospel Herald* 42, no. 36 (6 September 1949), 880.

[42] Articles on hymnody and congregational singing appeared routinely in *Gospel Herald* during the years when Paul Erb was editor and nearly disappeared when he retired in 1962 and the editorship passed to John Drescher. Editorial leadership can exert powerful influence in shaping the discourse of the church.

[43] Gospel songs and choruses were deemed musically inferior by many Mennonite leaders, but a bigger issue was the "inferior" theology of these pieces.

for many women to claim their life's work or push into new areas of interest, and Mary was no exception. She used her aesthetic language, theological perspectives, and skills for analyzing music and text sources to research hymns. Years of teaching had forged her abilities to introduce visual art and music to people with limited exposure or vast knowledge. Mary drew on all her musical skills to move Mennonites to a deeper appreciation of the church's song. Through presentations of hymns in the new hymnal and leading singing at large Mennonite Church conferences, she became the most recognized song leader of her generation.

And Have Unique Adventures

In 1968, through the Department of Health, Education, and Welfare, the U.S. state department granted fellowships to selected college professors interested in African studies. The goal was to build international goodwill and strengthen awareness of the cultural heritage of Black Americans. Thirty scholars would spend eight weeks at University of California, Los Angeles, engaged in study of Swahili, African history, anthropology, and literature. In the summer of 1969, they would travel to sub-Saharan East Africa for a two-month study tour. A program requirement stipulated that when they returned to their campuses, participating scholars would create an Africa-related course in their discipline.

Mary was chair of the Goshen College music department when academic dean Carl Kreider asked her whether anyone on the music faculty might be interested in this study tour. In an uncharacteristic move, Mary nominated herself. She had not previously exhibited an interest in Africa (although her mother had), and she never went out of her way to engage the African students on campus. But two painters whose works she admired—Henri Matisse and Pablo Picasso—had changed their painting styles after visiting Africa, and their shift in perspective piqued her curiosity. With the hymnal work completed by 1968, Mary again needed something to engage her energies.

By this time, Mary had taught many of the same courses for more than twenty years. She introduced new elements, but basic course outlines were well established. Her exacting standards were a constant, and she continued to offer her time generously to serious students who needed help to do well in her courses. But there was an edginess in her manner that hinted at fatigue and perhaps discontent. The curriculum's new Study-Service Trimester promised to provide international experience for her faculty colleagues, but as a single woman she was not then eligible to lead SST groups.[44]

From the Goshen faculty, Mary Oyer and Howard Kauffman were nominated and then selected to participate in the UCLA program. During the time in California, she gathered bibliography and other resources on African music. This summer of study and the subsequent trip to Africa, funded by a Fulbright scholarship, opened a new world of cultural questions.

Events in the summer of 1969 introduced the kind of travel and work the next twenty years would bring Mary. After teaching a spring term at the college, she flew to Africa. Two months later she flew to Mennonite Church General Assembly in Turner, Oregon, to introduce the new hymnal. She moved easily between these three areas, using her intellectual and analytical skills, her love for the church and its music, her historical knowledge, and her widening study of culture.

For its Festival of the Holy Spirit in 1972, Goshen College asked Mary to provide leadership in compiling a book of contemporary songs, most requiring instrumental accompaniment. The *Festival of the Holy Spirit Song Book* is an example of the new thinking that was emerging in her.[45] Its pages include Jesus movement evangelical scripture songs accompanied by guitar, post–Vatican II Catholic folk songs (including then-popular Medical Mission Sisters compositions), African-American spirituals, Black gospel songs, Latin American songs, songs in a folk idiom by Mennonite writers, songs in a jazz idiom, songs by Sydney Carter, and international songs from Israel and the West Indies. This remarkable collection remained popular among Mennonite young adults throughout the 1970s.

---

[44] Study-Service Trimester (SST; now Study-Service Term) was a groundbreaking initiative of Goshen College, begun in 1968 under the leadership of provost Henry Weaver. This required international learning and service term takes faculty-led groups of 15–25 students to locations outside North America for six weeks of cultural, language, and historical study of the host country, followed by six weeks in service assignments.

[45] *Festival of the Holy Spirit Song Book* (Goshen, IN: Goshen College, 1972).

Appearing in print just three years after publication of the 1969 hymnal, this songbook signaled a new approach to Mennonite congregational song. Mary and the festival planners now assumed the use of instruments—guitars and pianos, if not organs—in worship. Many of the songs in the collection appear in unison or in two-part arrangements; some would be sung with improvised harmonies. The previous generation of church leaders would have considered these "lighter songs" more appropriate to the campsite than the congregation's worship. But because it was not an authorized book of the Mennonite Church, Mary could take risks. Her classical training, her experience with the 1969 hymnal, and her emerging awareness of African music expanded the musical sensibilities she applied to the task of selecting 125 songs.

Erik Routley has advocated the idea of the "throwaway" song; he recognized that these transient spiritual songs can serve important functions in the church's life. When they are no longer mean ingful, they fall from use. The festival songbook includes many ephemeral songs. Many have seen the sun set on their glory. Some are interesting as samples of a time of heightened religious sensibility. Several endure and continue to enliven singers' spirits.

Mary used knowledge gained from the UCLA-sponsored trip to plan her sabbatical in 1972. She traveled in Kenya, Tanzania, Zaire, and Madagascar,[46] focusing on traditional African music and arts. African culture presented her with intriguing patterns of communication, unfamiliar social values, and assumptions that she did not readily understand. Music was the primary cultural expression in which the differences between her Western classical training and an embedded folk style were most obvious. The Africans she observed learned music by ear, through imitation, not by sight. The skills for music analysis that Mary had practiced for forty years were not immediately useful for taking her into the music of sub-Saharan Africa. Her perfect pitch was almost an impedi-

---

[46] Between 1969 and 2004 Mary was in Kenya (11 times), Tanzania (5), Ethiopia (4), Ghana (4), Nigeria (4), Zambia (3), Zimbabwe (3), Botswana (2), Gambia (2), Ivory Coast (2), Liberia (2), Sudan (2), Swaziland (2), Uganda (2), Zaire (2), Burkina Faso (1), Cameroon (1), Lesotho (1), Madagascar (1), Senegal (1), Somalia (1), and Transkei (1). What Mary has learned in and from Africa cannot be easily assigned to discrete periods. This section synthesizes her learnings from those years and trips without attempting to assign particular insights to particular trips or locations.

ment in the African context, where musicians use various tuning systems for their instruments and in singing.

The Africans she met were puzzled by Mary's eagerness to learn their native music. In their experience, Westerners preferred the organization of European-style music to the "primitive" sounds of Africa. They had little use for African songs, which did not conform to their ideas of the beautiful or the sacred. Mary's challenge was to use her Western musical knowledge to explore the characteristics of African music. She was engaged in "real time" musical study—music improvised, extended and elaborated, dynamic, constantly changing. She created an audio library of music performed by Africans in their own settings. She went into the cities and the countryside and found people who played their instruments or sang their songs exceptionally well. She recorded their performances on street corners, in homes, at church, and in public gatherings. These tapes were valuable on one level but profoundly limiting on others. From them she could not tell how the singers' or drummers' bodies were involved in making the sound. Their dance—so intimately connected to the sound—was completely invisible. More than half of the music was missing.

In spite of the tapes' limitations, Mary spent time studying them, in order to learn African patterns of melody, rhythm, and harmony.[47] Through this tedious process, she regretfully discovered that her aural skills for remembering variations of songs and musical pieces were underdeveloped. The music she had valued and respected had been written down so it could be practiced and analyzed by sight. But throughout human history and in most places, the music of the vast majority of the world's people has not been written and has been learned by ear rather than by sight. This acknowledgement opened the way for perhaps the most radical turning point in Mary's intellectual development. She had to rely on individual musicians to help her enter African music, by imitating what she heard instead of relying on written transcriptions.

Over the course of several visits with one skilled musician, Mary recorded his playing and singing of a favorite local song. She

---

[47] In the summer of 2006 a Goshen College student converted Mary's recordings to a digital format. This project, with the notes Mary has had time to reorganize, serves to make her ethnomusicological collections more accessible to interested students and scholars.

noted that no two performances were the same. One time the tuning of the instrument differed from that of the previous performance. Another time the melody took a different form. Over the course of several days she recorded four versions of the same song. Mary asked the musician which version of the song was the right one, to which he answered, "Yes." It was hardly the answer she anticipated or sought, but she took note.

Since the sixteenth and seventeenth centuries, Western music has been shaped by tensions, climaxes, releases, and resolutions created by harmonic structure. Mary's music teaching had focused on these characteristics, as she pointed out to students the interplay of harmonic tensions and releases that heightened expectations for resolution. Where are the tensions and releases in African music? Certainly not in the harmony. Perhaps in the multiple and complex rhythms that are layered under the vocal or instrumental melody. But the melodies tended to keep repeating, circling back around with variations. Mary asked an African musician friend, "When does the song stop?" The response: "When the musician gets tired or wants to quit. Or when the musician is paid or the work accompanying the song is finished."

One day Mary asked a mbira[48] craftsman why he put extra noisemakers on the body of the instrument. She heard the rattle and jangle they created as distracting and superfluous. Puzzled, he asked, "Why not?" Africans know that such sounds and vibrations arouse the spirits of the musicians and the listeners, adding intensity and excitement and contributing complexity to the rhythm. Mary thought the rattles cluttered the important melodic patterns; for her they created too much excitement, too much rhythm. The brief encounter demonstrated a clash of culturally defined musical assumptions that brought both musicians up short.

Over the last thirty-five years, Mary has told and retold these three stories of encounters with African musicians. She uses them to demonstrate contrasting cultural conventions surrounding music. And she tells them to poke fun at herself and her naiveté. But these stories also describe moments of conversion in Mary's un-

---

[48] Mbiras (thumb pianos) are made of flattened bicycle spokes attached to a wooden box to create resonance. They vary in size and in the number of attached spokes (see photograph on page 93).

derstanding of music and its function in a culture. Her ears, mind, and spirit opened to the possibility that contradictory approaches to music and music making may be equally valid. Through Western music conventions, composers have created beautiful and inspiring works, and craftspeople have produced instruments of incredible quality. Mary did not abandon her classical Western training, but she expanded her musical horizons. She recognized that sometimes musical conventions of the West can help people interpret music from another culture, and sometimes those same conventions impede understanding.

Increasingly, Western music practices have separated music performance from the routines and ceremonial activities of ordinary community life. But African music is—or was—integrated organically into the movements and patterns of daily life. The rhythms of African music are infectious. They get into the body, and the body has to move. Rhythm enables a group of people to walk, dance, or work as one—like a single organism. Mary's experience of rhythm, of being part of a body of people moved by rhythm, opened new spaces of freedom in her spirit. Her body became a wiser instrument, and her knowledge of self and world expanded. She used her whole being to interpret songs, and her new knowledge showed up immediately in her leading of congregational singing back in North America.[49]

By enhancing her appreciation for the context in which people make music, Africa freed Mary to value a variety of musical styles. She came to see that questions about whether a certain type of music is good are relative: Good for whom? Good for what? Good for when?[50] If the music freed something lively, interesting, and significant in the singers, then the music was good. Judgments of what is good, beautiful, and true can only be made in a given moment, with particular people, and in a specific place. Now the church's

---

[49] At the 1978 Mennonite World Conference, after a period of singing that Mary led, a Conservative Mennonite woman spoke enthusiastically about her leadership, complimenting her on her way of helping people sing international songs. She went on to say that her husband was less excited about Mary's style: he thought you would have to be a clown to direct songs in such an "undignified" way.

[50] This functional approach to understanding music began to emerge for Mary as she introduced new hymns in Mennonite congregations. Because of her observation of the significant and obvious differences between Western music and African music, her African experience had sharpened these questions.

questions about gospel songs could be addressed from a new perspective. If gospel songs freed something lively, interesting, and important in new Christians or Black Christians, then they were good and fitting. But if they were deadening, dull, and meaningless for the singers, they were not good in that context.

Her many trips to Africa over thirty-five years taught Mary a deeper patience, which arises out of the hard work of trying to understand people of another culture. Cross-cultural communication is effortful. Sharing music is one of the quickest ways to make connections across cultures—assuming, of course, that musicians are willing to learn from one another. In the early part of the twenty-first century, integrating the influences of divergent musical cultures is almost commonplace. But in the 1970s Mary was a pioneer at the frontier in this kind of cross-cultural exchange.

During Mary's 1972–73 sabbatical, the college reorganized its curriculum. Her required introductory fine arts course for second year students was a casualty of the revision. Thereafter the class was available only as an elective. The new general education required arts course was "Aesthetic Experience," a class team-taught by three (and later by two) professors, including Mary. The change was a bitter pill for her to swallow. As she saw it, she had lost the opportunity to help young students, often artistically naïve ones, discover the wonder of studying visual arts and music in a single integrated classroom experience.

For her, perhaps the most distressing aspect of this curricular redesign was the changing view of liberal arts education at Goshen that shaped it. In the late 1950s, professors had wrestled with what a liberal arts education for Mennonite students should be. Mary was in the thick of the discussions, articulating her vision for the arts as integral to the curriculum. In the 1970s, she was marginal to the discussion, and her counsel did not help shape the decisions the college made.

Mary chaired the committee given responsibility for organizing the music and arts aspects of the Mennonite Church General Conference at Estes Park, Colorado, in 1977. Her committee represented various ethnic and language groups of the North American church. For this event she edited a supplemental songbook that reflected the cultural diversity of the church.

A group of African-Americans had been invited to sing as part of the Wednesday evening service at the conference. After the service the group started to sing again—in a louder and more spirited way. The style of singing bothered some conference participants, who confronted the group. Tempers flared. Harsh words were spoken, in which racial overtones and implications were obvious. Yet that very evening people also began working to resolve the conflict.

Mary had left immediately after the service and was not aware of the conflict until the next morning. By Thursday morning a path to reconciliation emerged. Mary and Hubert Brown, who were responsible for leading worship on Thursday, read a statement that summarized the small group work from earlier in the day.[51] The statement affirmed openness to various musical styles; freedom of expression, in a climate of order and sensitivity; the multicultural make-up of the planning committee; and the need for cross-cultural understanding. To the final question, "Do the benefits of the inter-generational experience outweigh the difficulties?" the resounding answer was: "Yes! As long as we can continue to squarely face and resolve the problems."

After the event several people sent Mary letters thanking her for speaking forthrightly and in a way that deepened understand-

---

[51] Notes from the Estes Park folders in Mary Oyer's personal papers in the Mennonite Church USA Archives–Goshen:

"Last night we experienced an unusually intense and emotional confrontation involving youth and adults and persons with varying cultural and racial backgrounds. In dealing with the confrontation we all became involved in attempting to understand and clarify the issues. The process began last night during the 5th Quarter and continued late into the night and resulted in a list of questions. The following viewpoints emerged from the small group process.

"There is considerable tolerance and openness on musical styles. Many are saying that the Christian message can come through a variety of musical media. Some are expressing discomfort at certain musical styles.

"Affirmation of the right and freedom of expression, the spirit of prophecy and the need to take risks in confrontation. However, an emphasis on the importance of order and sensitivity to all involved.

"Affirmation of the multi-cultural make-up of the planning committee and program.

"The need to continue working at cross-cultural understanding by open mindedness, exposure, confrontation, and widespread involvement of people both here and in congregations. We are learning from the process of last night and this morning. The intentional way in which the issue was handled serves as a model for use in other situations.

"Do the benefits of the inter-generational experience outweigh the difficulties? Yes! As long as we can continue to squarely face and resolve the problems."

ing between the cultures and across generations. One person wrote:

> I was particularly impressed with the efforts made at keeping the music as diverse as possible. It did my heart good to have the whole assembly sing songs from my culture.... I also appreciated very much the way in which you stood between the two generations and attempted to bring them together. I felt you did a very good job in relating from your past experiences as well as conveying the issues to the larger assembly. Who would have thought that Mary Oyer would be the one who was instrumental in bringing the generations together? Thanks again for your cultural sensitivity.[52]

The next year, Mary was the primary song leader at the 1978 Mennonite World Conference in Wichita, Kansas. Each day she demonstrated remarkable flexibility in teaching new songs, especially those from Africa, to the predominantly white, North American congregation.[53] Former students who had not seen her since her sojourns to Africa were astonished by changes in her approach to congregational singing. She made the rhythms and melodies of the songs come alive in ways that would revolutionize the singing and worship of many North American Mennonite churches.

Mary led music at the many worship sessions of the conference, until the closing communion service on Sunday morning. Conference organizers feared that some worshipers—Mennonite Brethren, Brethren in Christ, Conservative Mennonites, and Mennonites from other continents—would disapprove of having a woman lead music for this final service. So Mary flew home, frustrated and hurt, and someone else led the singing at the last service.

During this period, Goshen College faculty colleague Lon Sherer brought to Mary's attention Tony Buzan's *Use Both Sides of Your Brain* [54] Buzan's mind-mapping techniques, which promised

---

[52] Letter from Tony Brown, Assistant Secretary, Personnel Services, Mennonite Central Committee, 11 July 1977.

[53] See photograph on p. xiii. The collection prepared for the event was *International Songbook*, compiled by Clarence Hiebert and Rosemary Wyse (Lombard, IL: Mennonite World Conference, 1978).

[54] Tony Buzan, *Use Both Sides of Your Brain* (New York: Dutton, 1976).

to improve memory and creativity, influenced Mary profoundly, giving her a circle-and-spokes approach to organizing her ideas. Buzan suggests placing in the center of a page a keyword that represents a central idea, then extending spokes out from the center and adding keywords associated with the central one. Each spoke could then have other lines branching out to identify additional details. Subsequent speeches, papers, or projects could elaborate the keywords and narrate their interconnections. Since the late 1970s Mary has almost exclusively used the circle-and-spokes way of planning presentations and papers.

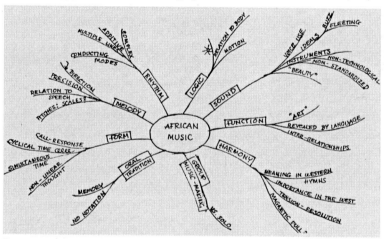

Fig. 2.1. Circle-and-spokes diagram

This mapping process creates a strong image of the topic to be explored. It is visually holistic—grasped intuitively at a glance—and allows Mary to see the vital connections within her subject matter. Her attraction to Buzan's ideas may have roots in her experiences in Africa, where she sensed the wholeness of life, but also in her years of teaching visual arts at Goshen. She claims she can improvise a talk from any spoke on one of her circles.

Exploring the Mennonite Hymnal: Essays (1980) may be the best written example of her mind-mapping technique at work. She begins each essay in the collection with a firm anchor, in a central point of reference, and then the essay branches out to related topics that span different historical eras, musical styles, or various musical sources.[55] Readers of these essays whose minds work in linear, methodical ways may find them frustrating. The branches Mary develops from the starting point are rarely sequential or predictable.

In 1979 Mary received a Lilly Faculty Fellowship to work in the Kenya National Archives. The assignment was to gather—with a team of researchers—history, literature, music, and material culture from selected ethnic groups of Kenya. Gradually she realized that nothing was happening because the director was redirecting funds for his personal use. By the time he was fired, she had little reason to remain at the archives. An invitation to teach music in Kenyatta University College opened an intriguing alternative.

The music department at the university used a British curriculum for a Bachelor of Music Education degree. The work was challenging and the students responsive. By the beginning of the new school year in September of 1980, the chairman of the music department had disappeared, and Mary was asked to head the small department. She did so, reluctantly.[56]

Every university or college department—whether in North America, Africa, or Asia—has its own character, strengths, dysfunctions, and intrigues. To Mary's eyes, the Kenyatta music department was no exception. The department included a Russian expatriate piano instructor who was reputed to have had connections with the KGB, the Soviet Union's intelligence agency. This woman apparently provided sexual favors for many people. It was the fact that she was not qualified to teach piano or the classes to which she was assigned that caused Mary distress in her role as department chair. The woman's students complained. Eventually she was transferred to another department of the university, but she took with her one of the department's four or five pianos and most of the African instruments. It was impossible to retrieve the stolen items during the remaining months of the year. The duplicity of the university officials who had refused to deal with the woman's incompetence was a source of frustration for Mary. Where she

---

[55] For an appreciative response, see Ellen Jane Porter's review in *The Hymn* 33, no. 4 (1982), 263–64.

[56] For another perspective on these events, see chapter 11 of the present volume, "An Exceptional Colleague and Friend," by Luzili R. Mulindi-King.

could not trust people to work with competence and integrity, she found it hard to function well.

Mary considers her experience as music department chair in some respects a failure. She did not understand the character of the university system and so could not work within it effectively. She also realizes that she lacked sufficient understanding of the basic thinking and reasoning patterns Kenyans use to address their circumstances.

Mary cultivated lasting friendships with a number of students and professional colleagues in the university. Some of her students have completed doctoral studies and now teach in Africa and in North American universities. In 1979 she borrowed a cello in order to play in the Nairobi orchestra when she was in Kenya. In that context she made contacts with other string players, and in 1979–81 and again in 1985–87 played string quartets with friends on Sunday afternoons for the sheer joy of making music together, with only an occasional public performance.[57] These times provided Mary with some of the greatest pleasures in playing cello that she had ever known. She says, in almost mystical terms, that the instrumentalists knew they played better in the presence of the others than they could have played alone.

From 1969 to 2003, Mary traveled to Africa about fifteen times and visited twenty-two countries. During this period her combined time in Kenya totaled more than five years. She sometimes stayed in a Nairobi club or visited at the Mennonite guesthouse, and she lived and worked with a variety of people interested in African and Western music. Mennonite missionaries were often sources of wisdom about how to live in a culture that she did not fully understand.

Africa was a transforming experience for Mary, because she felt free to define herself without regard for the approval or disapproval of professional colleagues, the church, or the college community. By leaving the contexts that had shaped her self-understanding, she could experience herself as a musician, a Mennonite, a woman, and a North American in a place that offered few constraints.

---

[57] For another perspective on this experience, see chapter 12 of the present volume, "Making Music with Mary," by Julia Moss.

Seek Him in the Kingdom of Anxiety

At the age of fifty-nine, Mary cut her hair. The traditional Mennonite prayer covering had vanished years before. Now her coiled braids disappeared, replaced by a short cut that fell into a natural part. She had kept her hair long out of convenience and uncertainty about what style would suit her. The haircut visibly signaled shifts Mary had been making throughout the 1970s. It marked a new season of intellectual and musical freedom, which set her at odds with some of her colleagues.

Early in 1982, before she cut her hair, Mary had fallen on the ice at the college and broke her ankle. The complex fracture became emblematic of the 1980s for her; it proved to be a decade of dislocations. They were perhaps the most difficult years of Mary's life.

From 1984 to 1987 Mary was away from Goshen a good deal. She and her brother John led a study tour to European Anabaptist sites after the Strasbourg Mennonite World Conference in 1984. In spring of 1985, she taught at Canadian Mennonite Bible College in Winnipeg, Manitoba, and was a featured guest for the regional Hymn Fest celebration.

From 1985 to 1987 Mary was on assignment as a visitor with Mennonite Central Committee in Africa, traveling to their program sites, leading music at retreats, helping MCC volunteers adjust to their new cultures, and doing basic pastoral care. These activities accounted for about half of her time. The other half she worked in the Kenya Conservatoire of Music. The conservatoire received $150,000 from the Ford Foundation to gather artifacts and musical examples for the archives. Officials of the conservatoire had diverted the grant money to other projects, and Mary's work never really got off the ground. She was able to find some funding for an anthropologist to gather recordings of the Rendili people of northern Kenya. Twice—in 1979 and 1985—Mary had hoped to contribute to archival projects in Kenya, and both endeavors ended in frustration. Perhaps the projects were too Western in conception.

Mary's discontent about the curricular changes of the 1970s at Goshen College continued to fester. Her Africa experiences had shifted many of her musical values and commitments. Because she was no longer chair of the department, she had less influence over the department's directions, which more and more focused on training professional performers. Music education was still strong, but the emphasis on performance had increased. Mary's personal discomfort with solo performance may have been an element in her uneasiness about this shift in direction, but she also sensed that the values and disciplines suited to success in the concert music industry did not mesh well with the qualities that fitted musicians to serve the church.

Christopher Small's *Music, Society, and Education*[58] helped clarify Mary's thinking about the role of music as a creative social activity. A classically trained musician and music educator, Small doubts the creative integrity of the concert industry of the West, in which music making is relegated to professionals who are distanced from their audiences. He observes that most late twentieth-century concert music replays past understandings of time and the organization of sound. The public hears little from professional musicians that reflects contemporary experience. Western harmonization—with its drive toward the perfect cadence[59]—has dominated the way Westerners comprehend music. Small claims that the 300-year triumph of the perfect cadence makes it difficult for Europeans and North Americans to hear, let alone understand, the organization of music made by other people of the world. His approach directly and persuasively addresses (albeit in a style somewhat prone to overstatement) significant aspects of Mary's Africa experience.

The issues of music and Mennonite values that Mary had struggled with in the 1940s and 1950s returned in a different key by the late 1970s and early 1980s. People no longer debated the religious and theological questions. No one seriously asked whether training performers was morally consistent with Christian discipleship. Mary did not argue on that level either. But in the con-

---

[58] Christopher Small, *Music, Society, and Education: An Examination of the Function of Music in Western, Eastern and African Cultures with Its Impact on Society and Its Use in Education* (New York: Schirmer Books, 1977).
[59] The perfect cadence is a chord progression (V–I) that signals the end of a section of music or the completion of an entire piece.

text of Mennonite liberal arts education, she resisted changes that moved toward greater specialization.

Already in the 1950s, when Mary took the Motet Singers on tour to Mennonite congregations, she had felt unease about singing for people rather than with them. Her Africa sojourns and her experiences of leading worshipers at large conference gatherings had reinforced a desire to make music with people. Music is a shared social activity among people with varying degrees of sophistication and competence, which takes a variety of forms in a multitude of settings. By the 1980s, the question of what constitutes good or beautiful music had acquired a new shape for her. For a variety of reasons, her faculty colleagues did not receive Mary's new views on the role of music in the life of human communities, and music department discussions did not include her perspectives in ways she found satisfying. In that setting, Mary did not feel heard or valued.[60]

Because of Mary's stature at Goshen College, her prominence in the Mennonite Church, and her achievements as a scholar, some women on campus expected her to advocate for women's causes. When Mary would not take on the political agenda of feminism at the college, these women were perplexed, disappointed, and angry. Mary does not work well in politicized situations. She does not think strategically. She has not always negotiated well. She sought people's approval, and when it was not forthcoming, she tended to become discouraged or defensive. And she does not unquestioningly lend support to causes. The climate surrounding women's issues at Goshen in the early 1980s required these dispositions, and Mary's gifts and skills lay elsewhere.

In the midst of these strained relationships, Mary chaired a committee to create *Assembly Songs*, the songbook for the first joint conference of the Mennonite Church and the General Conference Mennonite Church, in Bethlehem, Pennsylvania, in 1983.[61] The conference marked the 300th anniversary of the Mennonite settlement in Germantown, Pennsylvania.

---

[60] Later Mary would acknowledge that she probably talked too much about what she had learned in Africa about music and the arts.
[61] *Assembly Songs: A Hymnal Supplement—Hymns Both New and Old* (Scottdale, PA: Mennonite Publishing House; Newton, KS: Faith and Life Press, 1983),

The collection—subtitled *A Hymnal Supplement—Hymns Both Old and New*—displayed remarkable breadth. Mary worked with Orlando Schmidt—whose *Sing and Rejoice* had been released in 1979—Harry (later Harris) Loewen, and Leonard Gross to gather the body of hymns. They drew from sources in early Anabaptism, such as the *Ausbund,* and the writings of early Anabaptist leaders. They included contemporary hymns produced by a wide variety of English-speaking Christians since the 1970s.[62] About half of the hymns were taken directly from the 1969 *Mennonite Hymnal;* the other half were new to most Mennonites. Eleven of the 161 hymns were from Cheyenne, Indian, Japanese, African, or Portuguese cultures. As a book produced for a single event, *Assembly Songs* could take risks with songs that had a "freshness of expression and usefulness to congregations."[63]

Mary's introduction to *Assembly Songs* briefly addresses the issue of inclusive language. The committee changed masculine language where it referred to humanity; for example, "Rise Up, O Men of God" became "Rise Up, O Saints of God," an alteration other denominations had made in their hymn collections. The committee had more contentious debate about masculine language referring to or naming God. An editorial policy necessary for addressing this kind of sweeping change could not be developed in the short time the committee had been given to gather and publish the songbook.[64] This mention of inclusive language issues foreshadowed troubles to come with *Hymnal: A Worship Book.*

Mary's teaching at Goshen College was effectively over by 1985, although she did not officially retire until 1987, at sixty-five. This turning point carries painful memories for her. Both she and the college had undergone significant changes since the fall of 1945. They had seen substantial transformation in the place of liberal arts education in the vocational preparation of Mennonite students. The college was moving in one direction; Mary would

---

[62] Christians in the English-speaking church of North America and Western Europe wrote few hymns during the first sixty years of the twentieth century. The early 1970s saw a veritable explosion of new hymns and songs, partly as a result of Vatican II mandates that Roman Catholics sing in the everyday language of their communities, rising social consciousness among young Christians and church leaders, and the charismatic renewal.

[63] "Introduction," *Assembly Songs.*

[64] Ibid.

have chosen another. From a distance of several years, and with the help of a counselor, she came to see that forty-two years was too long to spend in the same academic culture. Add twenty-two years of family association and her own undergraduate education at Goshen, and Mary had accumulated sixty-four years of history with the college. After so many years, it was nearly impossible to see herself or the college clearly.

In November 1982, representatives of the Church of the Brethren, the General Conference Mennonite Church, and the Mennonite Church met to discuss whether producing a new hymnal jointly would be beneficial. Mary attended that meeting. Only fourteen years had passed since *The Mennonite Hymnal* had been published. By the early 1980s many congregations had just purchased it. Why consider another revision so soon?

The Mennonite publishers believed they were within five years of starting a revision. The period between the 1927 *Church Hymnal* and the 1969 *Mennonite Hymnal* had been too long; the average lifetime for hymnals is closer to twenty-five or thirty years. Mennonites wanted to have available in one collection many of the new hymns and tunes that had been published since 1969. Many women and men in the church were pressing for more hymns with inclusive language; they were dissatisfied with attempts to change texts piecemeal on their own. Finally, because of rising copyright fees, hymnal production was an increasingly expensive undertaking. Doing a three-way project would spread out these expenses. In 1985 the Mennonite Church General Assembly voted to support the hymnal project.

Organizationally, the structure of the project was cumbersome. Lines of communication were fuzzy, and clarity about decision-making processes was sorely lacking. The greatest fear among the partners was that the largest group—representatives of the Mennonite Church—would dominate the other two. While the committee structures included safeguards for balance, administrative responsibilities were blurry. Music, text, worship, and publishers committees did the basic work of the project. Mary served as the chair of the music committee. The publishers bore responsibility for overseeing the project, managing personnel, and communicating with their respective denominations. On average, the committees met twice a year for three to six days at a time. They scheduled conference calls and additional meetings as needed.

Mary was present for the first year of full project meetings in 1984. Though she was traveling in Africa from 1985 to 1987, she attended most of the semiannual meetings. In 1987 a cut in the Church of the Brethren denominational budget eliminated the position that Robert Bowman had filled, which included the coordinating work of the hymnal project. Before returning from Africa, Mary was invited to take the position of project manager, and she accepted. Nancy Faus became the project chair, with responsibility for running the hymnal project meetings. Mary continued as chair of the music committee and Nancy as chair of the text committee. Administrative lines of responsibility and authority remained muddled.

Not long after she began work as project manager, Mary had surgery for breast cancer. The operation and subsequent treatment were successful, but the interruption delayed her full entry into project management. Her illness also stands as an emblem of the unhappiness and dislocation Mary experienced in the 1980s. Her illness gave her greater clarity about the level of conflict she is willing to tolerate in a situation and aided her discernment about when it is time to bow out, for the sake of her health and sanity. This awareness helped her in defining her relationship with the hymnal project.

Many women and men in the supporting denominations expected the new hymnal to reduce use of or eliminate the words *men* and *man* where they referred to all human beings, male and female. These people wanted the language of the church's hymns to recognize the presence, worth, and dignity of women and their experience as people of faith. A second expectation, held by some, was that male pronouns and other male language referring to God would be reduced or even eliminated. These expectations about inclusive language presented challenges and opportunities for many North American denominations at the end of the twentieth century. Ways of working with the issue varied from making slight text revisions to making wholesale changes that eliminated specific references to gender. Those involved in the hymnal project ran the gamut from conservative to radical in their views on inclusive language. The text committee tended to favor more revision, while the music committee leaned toward a more measured, case-by-case examination, with less revision of older texts that were well known in the church. With new songs, the music committee adopted a more liberal posture.

Over a period of several months, Mary saw the need to establish a language policy that the hymnal project committees could follow. In broad strokes the policy included two points:

> Traditional hymns and prayers of the Christian church will be used essentially in their original or standard form. … Any changes will be made with great care …

> Contemporary hymns and worship resources (those written since the 1960s or whose authors are still living) will be scrutinized rigorously in order to assure us of the benefits of the current evolution of language.[65]

The full guidelines set broad editorial parameters rather than specifying the details. The entire hymnal council agreed to this policy during its fall meeting in 1987.

In the practical work of the committees, the limitations of the policy soon became evident. Some members looked to the hymnals of other denominations that included older hymns, revised—in their judgment—"with great care"; these members wanted these familiar hymns to appear in the "cleaned up" versions. Some contemporary hymns also presented problems. Some project members wanted certain contemporary hymns in the collection be-

---

[65] The full policy (from "Hymnal Council Passes First Major Language Statement," *The Mennonite*, 8 December 1987, 546) reads as follows: "Traditional hymns and prayers of the Christian church will be used essentially in their original or standard form. We want to embrace the literary value and historical context of those hymns and prayers which we find compatible with our reading of Scripture and the theology of our denominations. We also wish to respect the role of memory and deep associations that hymn singing contributes to worship. Therefore, any changes will be made with great care.

"Contemporary hymns and worship resources (those written since the 1960s or whose authors are still living) will be scrutinized rigorously in order to assure us of the benefits of the current evolution of language. We will select texts that enlarge and deepen our faith through their poetic expression in late 20th century terms.

"Because we recognize the sensitivity to language issues is in a continuous state of flux for individuals as well as for hymnal committees and congregations, we perceive our responsibility to be that of providing materials for worshipers representing a broad spectrum of needs."

cause of the songs' theological contributions, despite the fact that their texts did not use inclusive language for humans or for God. Further, some of the living authors refused to entertain requests for text revisions.

In 1987 Mary was asked to create a songbook for the joint Mennonite Church–General Conference Mennonite Church assembly in Normal, Illinois, to be held in 1989. She accepted this invitation, with the understanding that the book would serve as a sampler of the hymns, songs, and worship resources that were being selected by the hymnal council. In the end, the sampler was a great idea. It introduced the work of the hymnal project committees by providing an array of the kinds of songs that were under consideration. If the church's reaction proved to be unsupportive or even hostile, there would be time to change the direction of the final product. The Church of the Brethren eagerly supported the sampler idea and arranged to use the book at their annual conference in 1989.

From the early days of the project in 1984, the denominational partners agreed that "Move in Our Midst," an undisputed Church of the Brethren favorite, and "Praise God from Whom All Blessings Flow" (606 in *The Mennonite Hymnal*), a Mennonite favorite, would be in the book—no questions asked. What became contentious was an inclusive language version of "606" that many Church of the Brethren people had learned from the *Brethren Songbook*. Most Brethren on the project, and the majority of members on the text committee, wanted this version to appear along with the original text in the *Hymnal Sampler*. Many Mennonites—and the majority of members of the music committee—found this proposal offensive. It became the ultimate test of the inclusive language policy the hymnal council had adopted. During one turbulent meeting, in which the entire process nearly collapsed, the hymnal council voted to include only the original Thomas Ken text in the *Hymnal Sampler*. The possibility of including both texts in the future hymnal remained open.

This watershed experience sobered project participants. It shattered illusions that goodwill alone would bring the hymnal to completion. Harsh words had been said, and feelings were bruised. Trust was compromised. Creating a hymnal was going to be much harder work than anyone had anticipated, and the potential for hurt was greater than most had imagined. Peaceful negotiations ending in acceptable outcomes would require far more clarity about process than the project had yet established.

It took the project about a year to restabilize after this disastrous meeting.[66] In the process, the project manager's influence was curtailed; the person in this role was to carry out the will of the hymnal council, exercising little—if any—personal judgment or authority. As production of the *Hymnal Sampler* progressed, Mary increasingly felt tension between her role as project manager and her role as editor of the sampler. And she found it difficult—if not impossible—to act on hymnal council decisions to which she was conscientiously opposed.

Her historical work on *The Mennonite Hymnal* had energized her as a scholar and a leader of congregational song. The study of hymns had opened new possibilities for her intellectually, and she had found more freedom to move around emotionally and spiritually. She rightly felt that among the gifts she had offered that project were her best insights arising from her scholarly pursuits. But people working on the 1992 hymnal project did not care so much about the original versions of the texts or tunes, and returning to these versions no longer provided a way to move beyond disagreements surrounding preferred forms of favorite hymns. Mary found that the new approach to revising hymns seemed to diminish possibilities for musical and textual expression instead of wid-

---

[66] The 606 episode demonstrated many things, including these: (1) Commitment to the adopted inclusive language policy was adequate in the abstract, but in specific instances it left openings for a range of interpretations. (2) Inclusive language concerns could trump historical practice. (3) Inclusive language concerns crossed denominational boundaries. No single denomination championed inclusive language; rather, members from each denomination spanned the continuum from giving highest priority to language issues to weighing other considerations (for example, history, current practices) in relationship to language matters. (4) Everyone believed he or she was representing a constituency in the church, and that this constituency was of supreme importance. (5) Changing a story, song, or cultural symbol with which a group deeply identifies opens possibilities for insensitivity, misinterpretation, arrogance, and outrage. (6) Logical arguments for one position or the other were not persuasive and seemed only to confuse the issue and the process. (7) Some passions and commitments are too deep for words, and any threat to them can seem a personal threat. (8) The unclear decision-making process, along with the role confusions, created uncertainty and distrust.

ening them.[67] In other organizations a project manager could have established the policies that would guide committee decisions, but Mary did not have standing to do so in relation to this project.

Because of its structure, the hymnal project could not use Mary's greatest gifts to best advantage. With unclear lines of authority and a flawed decision-making process, in a context of distrust and fear that an individual or a denomination would exert excessive power, Mary floundered in the role of project coordinator. In the summer of 1988, she decided to resign, on completion of the *Hymnal Sampler*. She notified the publishers and the church of her decision early in 1989 and left the project in early May.

Months later, in July 1989, the Hymn Society in the United States and Canada named Mary a fellow of their society. With this honor, this group recognized Mary's outstanding contributions to the field of hymnology and the practices of congregational singing. The irony could not have been more striking: her professional colleagues validated her outstanding work in hymnology just as the hymnal project could find no effective way to use her wisdom.

In worship and in workshops at Normal '89, Mary introduced the *Hymnal Sampler*, highlighting the organization of the collection around elements of worship, and showcasing the variety of songs and other worship resources included in it. Through the sampler and her introduction of it, the church received an excellent preview of the shape of the hymnal planned for publication in 1992. Given opportunities to react, people across the two denominations immediately offered strongly positive response. The *Hymnal Sampler* had set the standard for the hymnal to follow.

The hymnal project publishers printed extra copies of the book for congregations to purchase or to rent for several weeks, to explore the contents more carefully. Frequently congregations and conferences invited Mary to teach songs and lead worship using

---

[67] In an interview with David Music of the Hymn Society in the United States and Canada, Mary alludes to her experience of growing up in a Mennonite world that was confined and confining ("An Interview with Mary Oyer," *The Hymn*, 45, no. 1 [January 1994], 16). The decisions made by members of the hymnal project felt confining in a similar way. Her graduate work, her research for the 1969 hymnal, and her experiences in Africa had given her opportunities to redefine the constraints. The values of inclusive language seemed to be applied with a legalism that Mary felt diminished the evocative qualities of language. In her mind the possibilities for living in a fully human way were diminished rather than expanded.

the sampler. While she was at first skeptical of the book's organizational concept, she came to see the value and the flexibility of that outline.[68]

Mary created distance between herself and the continued work of the hymnal project, and she promoted the sampler through her travels without endorsing the future book. But she was forthcoming with help when asked, and she remained on friendly terms with several project members. And her identification with the sampler paved the way for *Hymnal: A Worship Book* in 1992. Within a couple of months of the hymnal's release, Mary was promoting it, replacing the sampler with the new hymnal in her trips to congregations and conferences. In 1995 she was music coordinator for the Mennonite Church General Assembly in Wichita, Kansas, and used *Hymnal: A Worship Book* almost exclusively as a resource for congregational singing. When she found the new book worthy of use, Mennonites who had remained with the hymnal project breathed a sigh of relief. Without her endorsement *Hymnal: A Worship Book* would not have fared well in the North American Mennonite church.

Mary returned to Goshen in May 1989, to rest and prepare to teach at Associated Mennonite Biblical Seminary (AMBS). Orlando Schmidt had retired from AMBS that spring and had moved to Kansas, leaving no one to teach church music and fine arts courses at the seminary. At Marlin Miller's invitation Mary began teaching part-time in the fall.

You Will Come to a Great City
That Has Expected Your Return

Mary's nine years as interim professor of church music at AMBS (1989–98) provided occasion to refocus her energies, to reflect, and to heal. With no administrative responsibilities and a part-time teaching load, she was free to pick her projects and choose the ways she would be involved in the AMBS community. In the forty-five years since she had entered the classroom as a fine arts teacher, the Mennonite Church had undergone remarkable changes. In part

---

[68] See chapter 21 of the present volume, "On the Table of Contents of a Hymnal," by Mary K. Oyer.

through her influence and in part as a result of increased access to and acceptance of music and art resources, the tension between art and Christian discipleship had eased. Mary could teach fine arts in a Mennonite seminary with no cloud of distrust surrounding her or her subject matter.

At AMBS, Mary soon began teaching "Foundations of Worship and Preaching" with Marlene Kropf and June Alliman Yoder. This course introduced students to a basic theology of worship and helped them acquire skills in worship planning, leading, and preaching. The three women (students sometimes referred to them as "the trinity") formed a team rich in knowledge and experience.

Mary opened the eyes and ears of many future pastors to the power of music and visual arts in congregational worship. *Hymnal: A Worship Book* was a primary text, and Mary became more convinced of the wisdom found in the book's organization. She developed a deeper appreciation for the cycle of the Christian year and for the ecumenical lectionary that shapes each season's worship. Having taught church music and music history at Goshen College for many years, she was familiar with the structure of the Christian year, but in her teaching at AMBS, the formative character of the symbols associated with the seasons began to provide a richer way for her to think about music in worship. Analyzing lectionary texts using skills that she had honed in working with hymn texts yielded fresh insights and renewed creativity.

Mary wove her knowledge of musicology, ethnomusicology, hymnology, and fine arts into her presentations. As the speaker for the 1991 AMBS Theological Lectureship, she chose topics that demonstrate the breadth and the interweaving of her experience: "Hymnody: A Key to Culture," "Crossing Cultures—Africa and the West," "My Pilgrimage with Music and the Church," "Artistic Dimensions of a Hymn," "The Future of Hymnody among Mennonites."

Mary's conversations with Abraham Schmitt, author of *Brilliant Idiot*,[69] helped her identify her lifelong dance with dyslexia. She understood with greater grace why reading had always been a chore for her. Words wouldn't stay in the same place as her eyes

---

[69] Abraham Schmitt, *Brilliant Idiot: An Autobiography of a Dyslexic* (Intercourse, PA: Good Books, 1992).

tracked across a line of print; they sometimes jumped around. She found it helpful to use Buzan's center-and-spokes diagram approach to organize her presentations in part because she could see her talks as a whole and speak with more spontaneity; then she worried less about losing her place on a page of written text. Her unusual ways of taking in and organizing information had doubtless shaped her style of thought. A logical, linear argument is not Mary's strong suit. It is her insight and passion—not an unassailable logic—that persuades her listeners.

Mary continued to form professional relationships with church musicians and seminary instructors from a variety of denominations through the Hymn Society. Planners of the society's annual meetings regularly included her in the program. She repeatedly helped people experience the power of the unaccompanied congregational voice. For musicians in denominations in which hymns and songs are always accompanied by organ, a cappella singing under her leadership proved inspiring and invigorating.

Mary had opportunities to make presentations at other seminaries and graduate schools, such as Westminster Choir College in 1997 and 1999. She made presentations at Valparaiso University as part of the Lilly Fellows Program in Humanities and the Arts, and at the Choristers Guild Regional Meeting in Dallas, Texas, in 1994. Christian Theological Seminary in Indianapolis gave her an honorary doctorate in 1995. The Evangelical Lutheran Church of America invited her to lead singing at their conference, Jubilee 2000, at Chicago's Navy Pier. She gave the Erik Routley lectures for the Presbyterian Association of Musicians in Albuquerque in 2001.[70]

As they established mission churches in Africa, European and North American missionaries of the nineteenth and twentieth centuries had imposed Western musical values, with limited curiosity about the wisdom to be found in African cultures. Because Mary's Africa experience had taught her to think cross-culturally,

---

[70] Other ecumenical settings in which Mary has made presentations include Yale Divinity School, 1999; Regent College, University of Vancouver, Canada, 2002; Amagi Sanso Retreat Center, Japan, 2004 ("The Poetry and Music of Hymns"); Anderson (IN) University, 2004 ("Hymnody" and "African Music"); Faculty Seminar: Teaching Theology through Music, sponsored by Wabash Center for Teaching and Learning, 2004 ("Issues in Ethnic Music"); and Institute for Sacred Music, 2005 ("Crossing Cultures in Hymnody").

her ethnomusicological work proved to be of great interest for mission agencies. In her experience, listening to and participating in the music of the people is a good way to gain entry into a new culture. As a symbolic medium, music reveals cultural values and worldviews. She suggested ways people could use music to enter another culture, prepared to have their assumptions challenged as hers had been.

In an essay on hymnody and world mission given at a meeting of the European Hymn Society in Sweden, Mary outlines several approaches she has found helpful for bridging the gaps between cultures, with music.[71] She recommends that people (1) participate in music-making activities with local people; (2) talk about the character and function of hymns with leaders in local congregations; (3) read novels written by people who are natives of the country or who know it well; and (4) read the work of anthropologists, ethnomusicologists, linguists, and theologians who have studied the culture. Her insights and experiences gained from doing these things have helped prepare many missionaries and Mennonite Central Committee workers for immersion in a new culture.

Mary assisted in leading singing at the August 1997 Mennonite World Conference assembly in Calcutta, India, nineteen years after her first MWC experience. This honor and responsibility speaks volumes about her ability to interpret music cross-culturally and to draw people from around the world into the song of the gathered church.

In late spring of 1997 Mary was a guest at Salford Mennonite Church in Harleysville, Pennsylvania. As she was leading Sunday morning worship, her speech became disjointed. In her confusion, she panicked. Somehow the service ended—she does not know quite how—and people came to her aid. Soon she was able to orient herself again. She rested all afternoon, cancelled the evening hymnsing, and returned to Goshen after a couple days of rest. Her doctor confirmed what the medical people in the congregation suspected: she had had a transient ischemic attack (TIA). The experience frightened her not only because of the medical risk but because she felt she had looked foolish in public.

---

[71] "Hymnody in the Context of World Mission," *I.A.H. Bulletin* 16 (June 1988): 53–74

That summer Mary tendered her resignation at AMBS; the 1997–98 school year would be her last. Through the fall Mary began eating better, losing weight, exercising conscientiously, and slowing down a bit. By the end of the school year, she was in good health and ready for something new.

The nine years Mary taught at AMBS reconfirmed her identity as a teacher, this time in a graduate institution. The early 1990s were unsettling at AMBS, because of a difficult curricular review and extraordinary financial constraints. Mary participated in faculty discussions and helped formulate departmental proposals, but as an interim professor, she could steer clear of the thorniest decision-making processes. Teaching "Foundations of Worship and Preaching," "Hymnology," and "Christianity and the Fine Arts"; rehearsing the choir; and leading worship there pleasurably filled her time.

AMBS honored Mary's retirement from teaching there with a two-day hymnsing. Song leaders, many of them serving on faculties of Mennonite colleges, took turns leading hymns from each historical period of congregational song found in *Hymnal: A Worship Book*. Mary opened the hymnsing by leading several songs, and then her friends and colleagues led in turn throughout the event. There were no long-winded speeches, no academic papers, no elaborate introductions to educate the singers. People simply sang until mid-afternoon on Saturday. The event concluded with a banquet and testimonies by Mary's family and friends about her contributions to their lives. That evening the seminary marked the establishment of an endowed chair of church music in her honor.

The "contemporary" worship music idiom was notably absent from this event. *Hymnal: A Worship Book* has few examples of this rock-based idiom, and Mary has little interest in this musical style. She does not dismiss it; she is too culturally sensitive to deny its significance for a large segment of the church. But she has little intellectual curiosity about it. The most interesting features of many of these songs are found in their accompaniments. The melodies are often weak and uninteresting apart from the accompanying instrumentation. In the late 1980s and early 1990s, debates over appropriate styles of music for congregational singing reached a level of fierceness equal to that of arguments about gospel songs in the earlier part of the century. Mary, wisely, did not take sides. She thought introducing people to new songs that expanded their musical horizons was the better approach. With this understanding she followed the example of her mentor, Walter Yoder.

Love Him in the World of the Flesh

On Mary's last day at AMBS, she received a telephone call from executives of the Reformed Church in America, inviting her to teach in Taiwan at Tainan Theological College and Seminary. The RCA does not create and support its own mission projects but rather works in partnership with existing programs by supplying personnel. James Goldsworthy of Westminster Choir College[72] had suggested Mary for a teaching position in the school's church music program, because of her specialty in African music.

Mary felt healthy and was eager to find a new direction in her retirement. During the late spring and early summer of 1999, she met with representatives of the RCA to determine whether her theological commitments were close enough to theirs to allow them to support her work in Tainan. After several interviews and proof of her good health, they gave her clearance to go to Taiwan for a three-year term. She would teach from September until the end of the spring term, returning to North America during the summer.

During a leave from Associated Mennonite Biblical Seminary in the fall of 1995, Mary made a trip to Japan and Taiwan. Mary Beyler, a Mennonite missionary in Hokkaido, introduced her to Japanese culture. In Tokyo Mary consulted with a committee that was revising a Japanese hymnal. She also stopped in Taiwan to see Goshen College graduates Edgar and Kathleen Lin in Taichung, whom she had visited in 1973 in Tumutumu, Kenya, where they were serving as teachers with Mennonite Central Committee. She also planned to visit I-to Loh, whom she had met in 1985 at a Hymn Society meeting in Bethlehem, Pennsylvania. He was known for collecting and publishing hymns from many Asian countries in *Sound of Bamboo* (1990). Mary wanted his counsel on how American churches might understand and sing Asian hymns.

---

[72] Goldsworthy had taught piano at Goshen College for several years prior to going to Westminster Choir College (Princeton, NJ), which is now part of Rider University.

Coincidentally, he was installed as president of Tainan Theological College and Seminary during her visit, and she was able to attend the celebration. Little did she imagine that in four years she would be teaching there.

Tainan Theological College and Seminary, supported by the Presbyterian Church of Taiwan, offered a new program in church music for Asians, to be taught in English. Mary was recruited to teach core courses in this program. It was an ideal job for a retired teacher, although learning a new language is a challenging proposition for a seventy-six-year-old. The Taiwanese value elderly people (as do the Africans) and treated Mary with respect and kindness. Students were responsive and appreciative. Some have remained good friends. Teachers at the college received her with warmth and grace. The group of (mostly) women who exercised in the park each morning welcomed her participation and occasionally invited her to a meal at one of Tainan's fine restaurants. The fact that only one woman spoke English did not stand in the way of their offering gracious hospitality.

The students in the church music program were from Malaysia, Indonesia, and India, as well as Taiwan. Taiwanese students came from Chinese and from indigenous backgrounds. The students studied "Research Methods and Materials" (a library course), "Reformations in Western Hymnody," and "Arts and Symbol in Christian Worship." In the latter course they were usually joined by young pastors sent by Christian World Mission from Presbyterian churches in other parts of the world—Europe, Africa, Pacific islands, and other Asian countries. The diversity opened Mary's eyes to the meanings a single visual symbol could have in the various cultures represented by the students. Her African music course was not among the curriculum's requirements, but she taught it three times as a specialized area.

Mary was asked to direct the undergraduate choir for her first two years at Tainan, an assignment that presented much challenge and was a source of some stress for her. Although for the most part the choir sang Western music, the words were translated into Taiwanese. Because Taiwanese is a tonal language, while the music relies on syllabic accents characteristic of European languages, the experience necessitated finding new ways of making music.

Fortunately, she had a fine Malaysian translator to help make her explanations clear to the choir.

Mary taught core courses for five years, two of them for the entire year, the other three in more concentrated blocks for a shorter time. Opportunity to work with I-to Loh, a skilled ethnomusicologist and hymnologist, enriched her involvement with the Asian world. By providing translation in many of Mary's classes, his wife, So Hui-Chin, eased the language difficulties for students who came to Tainan with less proficiency in English.

Both I-to Loh and Mary were surprised to be recipients of Distinguished Service Awards on July 16, 2006, given by the Global Consultation on Music and Missions in St. Paul, Minnesota. Members of this international consultation are missionaries and ethnomusicologists.

Asia did not have the impact on Mary's intellectual development that Africa had had. Since her return to live in Goshen, she is more likely to make presentations on African music and fine arts than on Asian arts. Why?

Mary went to Tainan at seventy-six; she went to Africa for the first time at forty-six. Her African experiences opened new ways of perceiving and understanding music, which in turn reshaped her thinking about culture and the arts. Her Asian experiences fit into a larger interpretive framework that she had developed earlier. These experiences did not significantly challenge that framework. Her many stays in Africa offered opportunities to live more deeply into African cultures, to test what she was learning, and to make refinements in her understanding. Her time in Taiwan, less than five years, did not afford her the same opportunities to enter deeply into Taiwanese culture.

Because she did not learn much Mandarin or Taiwanese, Mary's travels and interactions with people outside the school were far more limited. She never hired a driver to take her out into towns or nearby villages to hear local people singing, as she had done in Africa. She did not take music lessons from local musicians. Overall, Mary came away from Taiwan with less clarity about how music fit into people's everyday lives than she had gained in Africa.

Her primary interactions in Taiwan were with church people; she had fewer professional contacts than in Africa, and far less access to intellectuals or musicians who were of other religious traditions. She did enjoy attending a small English-speaking congregation, the primary group she related to outside the school community.

Mary did not have significant Mennonite Central Committee connections in Taiwan. MCC had sponsored, promoted, or encouraged much of her travel in Africa. Neither the Presbyterians nor people from the Reformed Church in America used her gifts for visiting and teaching in local congregations or schools. Perhaps language difficulties presented obstacles.

The subjects Mary taught in Taiwan did not push her into new avenues of inquiry. The school's commitment to learning about Western-style hymnody and Protestant traditions did not require her to gain new skills. She thoroughly learned the resources in *Songs of Bamboo* (2000) because she served as proofreader for the English edition.

The grants Mary received in 1968 stipulated that on her return from Africa, Mary would create and teach a course in African arts. This obligation focused her inquiry during her first and subsequent trips to that continent. No such obligation was linked with her going to Taiwan. She was the specialist coming to the college and seminary, not the novice going to Kenya. Her expectations and responsibilities were radically different.

Teaching at Tainan provided Mary with the intellectual and social stimulation that gave this phase of her retirement meaning and purpose, without the strain that comes from having to manage a department and keep a program going. She had time to prepare for classes, make and maintain friendships, and take care of her health. Her living conditions were more than adequate, the food plentiful and good, and the warmth of Asian women welcoming. But the most enjoyable part of teaching at Tainan was the people who enrolled in her classes. Their diverse perspectives gave discussions a depth and richness that brought Mary great satisfaction. The fall semester of 2003 was her last at Tainan.

Since 1998 Mennonite Central Committee has invited Mary to lead daily music sessions during orientation for international visitors coming to North America for a year of service through the International Visitor Exchange Program, who need help with their

English. For three weeks each August, the Archbold, Ohio, Mennonite community hosts these visitors as they learn about North American culture, work on their English, and begin the process of acculturation. Singing together provides opportunities for these young adults to share something musical from their cultures and to sense themselves as a community of friends. Few people in the Mennonite Church could work with such a group with sensitivity and integrity. Mary draws on her vast experience of leading North American hymns, spirituals, African songs, Asian songs, and Spanish-language songs, when she selects music for these guests to learn together. Almost every year, the volunteers create a meal made up of their favorite dishes from home, and they invite their host families from the Archbold community to share it with them. After the meal, the IVEP participants sing the songs they have learned together. Everyone has come to love these occasions of friendship and music-making.

And at Your Marriage All Its Occasions Shall Dance for Joy

One factor in Mary's decision to make the fall 2003 semester at Tainan her last was a painful knee that made walking difficult. In June 2004, she had surgery to replace the joint. By the end of July she was walking without pain or assistance. During her recuperation she finalized plans to move from her home on Eighth Street to Juniper Place, part of the Greencroft Retirement Community in Goshen.

Moving from the house where she had lived for eighty years was a monumental task and another significant turning point in her life. She embraced the move with energy and without regret. As she and her family and friends cleaned out the attic of her home, they unearthed twenty-eight quilts and comforters, which had belonged to the Oyer family or were left behind when Mennonite Board of Missions and Charities sold the house to the Oyers.[73] Boxes of her parents' books; antique furniture; games and toys that Verna, Mary, and John had played with—memories of a rich family life—she gave to nieces or nephew, sold, or stored elsewhere for future sorting. Books on visual arts, music, and hymnology she

---

[73] Goshen College Library Gallery exhibited some of these mystery "Quilts from the Attic," 12 March–7 July 2006.

sold, sent to Taiwan, or gave to local libraries. Some of her hymnals went to Mennonite Historical Library. File folders holding a life-time of work, stretching back to the earliest days of teaching, were sorted, organized, and archived with Mennonite Church USA or thrown away.

The move dramatically reduced what Mary possesses, but enough remains for her to continue her studies. All her African instruments went with her to her condominium. Bookshelves in her new home office soon filled with art and music books, hym-nals, tapes and CDs, and books for pleasure reading. More than eighty feet of shelving built into a large walk-in closet and a den hold the overflow. Brightly colored African fabrics are safely stored in a large overhead cupboard. The dry sink, piano, modern liv-ing room furniture, wall hangings, and paintings have their places. Her living arrangement suits her, and she has been surprised at how much she enjoys being around interesting and intellectually curious people of her own age.

Mary is still in demand as a speaker, teacher, and song leader. Since leaving AMBS, she has been invited by many organizations to speak on African music or to lead hymn festivals or hymnsings. She has led music at Hymn Society meetings and at the Calvin In-stitute of Worship weekend. Local Mennonite congregations have invited her for Sunday services and weekend music retreats. Her talks to organizations for older adults focus on lifelong learning, on African music, visual arts, hymnology, and her own interesting life. She was the keynote lecturer at the 2004 Sound in the Land conference at Conrad Grebel College. She has lectured at profes-sional and academic meetings, on music in Africa and in the life of the church. During the summer of 2006 she helped supervise a Ministry Inquiry student from Eastern Mennonite University who was serving at College Mennonite Church. Many people have in-terviewed her on a variety of topics or written short articles about some aspect of her life. Mary generously shares her insights, and she warmly engages people with her interest in them and their pursuits.

He Is the Way, the Truth, and the Life

In *Composing a Life*,[74] Mary Catherine Bateson describes how women improvise their lives in and through their commitments to family, marriage, work, and community service. Bateson draws on her experience as a university professor and administrator and on the experiences of four other professional women. At various points stable patterns that had ordered their lives were upset. Rather than let go of their commitments or drop out of life, these women adapted creatively—sometimes slowly, sometimes rapidly—to their changing circumstances. From a distance of months or years, they could look back and discern continuities in their lives, which created a rich and meaningful whole.

What dominant themes have composed Mary's life? Her shifts in perspective after the first trip to Africa in 1969, which seem dramatically reorienting, in fact build on other turning points. The continuities of her life have provided stability that has freed her to embrace significant change in intellectual outlook and to garner deeper wisdom and grace.

Living a lifetime in the same town is a rarity for North Americans. To call the same residence home for eighty years is extraordinary. After her mother's death in 1963, Mary traveled and lived abroad for extended periods, but she always returned to Goshen. The town and the college grounded her identity and gave her roots. Her friendships with high school classmates, College Mennonite Church members, Goshen College faculty, and her brother John's family have provided a network of relationships that she could reenter as soon as she returned to town. She has been so strongly identified with Goshen that people always know where to find her when she is not abroad.

After all the dislocations of the 1980s, she returned to Goshen to heal. When she moved from her house on Eighth Street to Juniper Place, she moved closer to friends she had known for decades and expanded her circle with new neighbors. Her local ties did not bind her or make her afraid of traveling into the unknown. Her ability to engage other cultures deeply was grounded in a character and identity shaped by a particular place. She could dare making

---

[74] Mary Catherine Bateson, *Composing a Life* (New York: Atlantic Monthly Press, 1989).

changes in her intellectual perspective because she had a secure sense of home to which she could always return.

Mary's life has been persistently linked with Goshen College—as a child, a student, a teacher, a critic, and increasingly as a reconciled friend. Colleagues there have nurtured and supported her, angered and hurt her, and reached out to welcome her. She has given her best and been at her worst there. She has pushed new ideas and rejected new directions. Several influential people wanted the music building to be named for Mary, but she withheld her consent. Nonetheless, she gladly participated in its dedication in October 2002, leading the audience in singing "606." On the weekend of her eightieth birthday in April 2003, she collaborated with Vance George, a Goshen alumnus and director of the San Francisco Symphony Chorus; she led the audience in singing the chorale portions of J. S. Bach's *St. John's Passion*. In 2004 she spoke at an Afternoon Sabbatical in Sauder Hall of that building. She wrote a brief history of the organ at Goshen College for the dedication of the new Opus 41 organ in Rieth Recital Hall. Her ties with the college are conflicted and contradictory but deep and strong. She has never stopped caring about what happens there.

Looking back all these years later, it is difficult to imagine who Mary might have become had she married. Perhaps she would have stayed close to the Mennonite Church, but perhaps not. If she had married a string player who enjoyed performing, maybe she would have chosen cello as the focus of her teaching. Perhaps she would have lived in Africa or taught in Asia, but likely not.

Few married women of her generation, Mennonite or otherwise, have had the freedom to accept new opportunities for travel, learning, and growth that Mary has known. Even fewer married women have touched so many people's lives. Mary achieved a depth of knowledge about the arts and a breadth of friendships in part because she remained a single woman. Her primary energies could focus outward—beyond the constraints of spouse, children, and home. Mary recognizes that she has never known the intimacy that can come with being a spouse or a mother, but she has no regrets. Her mother supported her daughters' decisions not to marry; Siddie Oyer's work as a college matron and mother had constrained the development of her own gifts and skills. As a single woman raising three children, she had had few opportunities to study or travel. She had wanted to go to Africa as a missionary but never traveled outside the United States.

Adolescents and young adults are rarely presented with single-ness as a viable and legitimate life calling. The persistent message is that personal fulfillment is found only in marriage and family. In recent years, when so much public attention has focused on the intimacy and privacy of the nuclear family, Mary is a startling example of commitment that moves beyond the confines of that circle. She eagerly enters the experience of others and explores their worlds. Many people around the world feel Mary's personal interest in them. She has given them her attention, undistracted by parental or spousal cares. She has nurtured many people into a fuller sense of their dignity and potential as human beings. People she has met in Goshen and around the world have shown her who God is—a God of relationship, infinite variety, creativity, imagina-tion, warmth, and beauty.[75]

Each new phase in Mary's intellectual development opened through opportunities offered to her by an influential man. Few interests in her life came first from an internal or intrinsic call to pursue something that needed investigation. No long-held desire drove her to Scotland to study hymns, to UCLA and Africa to study indigenous music, or to Asia to teach. As a woman of keen intellect and curiosity, Mary went to new places and let those places teach her. The questions that arose from these contexts and the insights gleaned there captivated her fully. Her friends and colleagues did not always share her sometimes single-minded enthusiasm. Nor did they always like the ways these experiences changed her. At the various turning points of her life, opportunities chose Mary. She had freedom to embrace or reject them, but she did not initially plan any of them.

In later life Mary recognized her unspoken desire to be the center of attention—the "show-off," the performer.[76] As a teacher,

---

[75] *Growing in Faith: Practices That Shape the Changing Lives of Christians,* videocassette, produced and directed by Christopher Salvadore (Notre Dame, IN: Institute of Church Life, University of Notre Dame, 2000).

[76] Mary recognizes herself as a three on the Enneagram, an ancient system developed in the Middle East for classifying nine types of personality and character. In *Understanding the Enneagram: The Practical Guide to Personality Types,* Don Riso describes threes at their

she is at the center of a class's attention, guiding students to hear or see more in a work of art. As she leads singing, she holds the congregation's attention. In these situations she thrives. But as a solo cellist she was too much at the center of attention. There she faltered, sometimes feeling cut off from the people who listened. Mary attributes the ambivalence evident in her performance anxiety to the Amish-Mennonite ethos of her family and community; drawing attention to herself was considered prideful. Her greatest enjoyment with the cello was playing string quartets, especially in Africa, where the synergy of making music for the unalloyed pleasure of doing so helped everyone in the group play better than they could play alone.

In the Goshen College music department and on other church or professional committees where she served, Mary needed to be heard. She wanted to be able to talk about things, even topics that were difficult or even taboo in some way. But she struggled to find a style that would allow her coworkers to air their different viewpoints and then come to agreement. This leadership task was especially difficult for her when group discussion moved in directions that conflicted with her convictions. After leaving the hymnal project in 1989, Mary realized that committee work had frequently been difficult for her. She had reached a point in life where it was no longer obligatory. She has served on few committees since that time and has been much happier.

Mary's desire to be the center of attention changed over the years as she grew more sure of herself as a teacher, music leader, and friend. She still has definite opinions. She still finds some personalities insufferable. She still digs in her heels when one of her principles is threatened. But as she has matured, Mary has let other people's lives be the focus of her attention, and whenever possible she uses her influence for their good. A former student marveled that when he meets Mary, she always asks what is interesting in his life. And then she listens. His life matters to her.

---

best as inner-directed, genuine and authentic, accepting of themselves, and living within their own "center." When they are less than their best, threes can be competitive, continually comparing themselves with others, and too concerned with how others perceive them. Fearing failure or humiliation, they can become exploitative and caring only for themselves (Boston: Houghton Mifflin Company, 1990), 49–50.

For more than sixty years Mary has taught in school settings and informally in congregations, in small interest group settings, and at conferences. Mostly she talks and sings. Sometimes she demonstrates a key idea with an instrument. She is low on technical wizardry and high on warmth, energy, and personal engagement—characteristics typical of those at home in an oral tradition.

As a young teacher she took an analytical and formal approach to her presentations. But in time she began telling stories, conveying much of the same information but embedding it in an engaging narrative. Her stories do not always have beginnings, middles, and endings, and few of them drive to a resolution. Africa taught her to seek what makes for wholeness in a thing, and a resolution does not always make for wholeness. Often her stories show the surprising interrelationships between ideas, musical characteristics, visual symbols, and ways of perceiving time; these connections give a sense of completeness. Her circle-and-spokes diagrams (see figure 2.1) help her keep the wholeness in mind.

Her essay on "The Sands of Time Are Sinking" in *Exploring the Mennonite Hymnal: Essays*[77] is illustrative. It covers a wide territory in just a few pages. She opens the essay with a brief history of the hymn text, followed by a discussion of the power of images in hymns. This song is among her favorites, and next she writes appreciatively of the way its poetic images captured her imagination already in childhood: "In spite of my mistaking the sand of the hourglass for sinking quicksand, I loved the song, which still holds a kind of magic for me."[78] She proceeds to note that images make us (Mennonites, presumably) uneasy, as seen in the fact that the 1927 *Church Hymnal* version of the song puts the phrase "house of wine" in stanza 5 in quotation marks—"undoubtedly to control the image."

She moves on to consider the interplay of the concrete and abstract in "God Be in My Head" and expresses gratitude for the strong images of "Come O Thou Traveler Unknown" and "O Have You Not Heard of that Beautiful Stream." Then she returns to "The Sands of Time Are Sinking" and presents all the verses of the song, as published in the 1876 edition of author Annie Ross Cousin's

---

[77] Oyer, *Exploring the Mennonite Hymnal: Essays*, 43–47.
[78] Ibid., 44.

poems. She gives a brief description of the tune and comments that logical analysis suggests that it should be dreary, but in her experience it is not. She moves to an exploration of what makes something good, quotes from the writing of Chinua Achebe, and concludes by claiming that the goodness of a hymn can only be known in the action of singing with a particular group of people at a particular time.

Mary starts the essay in complete command of the historical and textual details. She moves to a related but new idea, returns to the original at a different angle, and ends in another new place. As a logical argument, it fails. As an almost picaresque narrative, moving around the landscape of Mary's mind and heart, it enchants. Her stories engage in a way that arguments do not, and along the way a lot of information is also communicated.

Mary's relationship to cultures is a persistent theme. From childhood she has negotiated the social meanings of her North American Mennonite culture in her encounters with many other cultures. The (Old) Mennonite culture of the early twentieth century and at Goshen College valued plain dresses and head coverings. Mary resented how her clothes set her apart from her public school friends. Her clothes made her feel embarrassed about her body. Her struggle to justify the pursuit of music and visual art studies was a cross-cultural negotiation between values of her (Old) Mennonite culture and the secular academic world. Through her studies she found language to reshape her religious understanding, which provided a way for her to remain Mennonite. Playing cello with a head covering at a Sunday afternoon symphony concert located her at the intersection of these distinct cultures.

By studying the relationships among musical and visual arts and architecture within a historical context, she gained perspective on how the arts reflect cultural understandings and how those understandings change over time. Her discovery of the original texts and tunes of hymns that she knew well helped her see how they were shaped by political, social, psychological, and theological forces.

Work on *The Mennonite Hymnal* set her cultural experience as an (Old) Mennonite teacher and musician in a new relationship with the General Conference Mennonite experience. By the late 1950s some (Old) Mennonite congregations had begun to introduce organs or pianos into their churches, to enhance their singing. But the hymnal committee work brought this significant area of cultural adaptation into sharper focus. The cultural climate of the (Old) Mennonite Church, including its singing practices, changed quickly during the 1960s.

The cultural differences between North American Mennonite society and African society were much vaster than anything Mary had experienced prior to 1969. But by now she had decades of practice at negotiating her identity in different contexts. Her studies of music and visual arts created a way for her to enter a new culture, to make personal contacts with musicians, and to learn the deeper unspoken assumptions of African life. The skills she developed for understanding one culture gave her confidence to enter other cultures. But then, for a time, it seemed to be difficult for Mary to be as generous and open toward people whose culture was similar to her own as she was toward people of more distant cultures. Her tensions with Goshen College and with the hymnal project in the 1980s can be seen as strained cultural negotiations.

Teaching in Taiwan presented significant barriers, because Mary did not know Mandarin Chinese. She could participate in many activities but could not understand the subtleties of the culture. In conversations with students and teachers who spoke English, she learned aspects of their home culture, but because her students came from around the Pacific region, the knowledge she gained was not specific to Taiwan.

Mary wrestles with what it means to be from a country that actively promotes globalization. She knows that for more than a century North American and European missionaries suppressed musical expression of African and Asian cultures. She has seen how "global" economics and marketing, controlled by Western interests, are replacing vibrant local economies. Africans and Asians reaching uncritically for Western lifestyle sadden her. In the months after 9/11 Mary watched British Broadcasting Company news reports and listened to National Public Radio news when she was home in Goshen, and she listened to Cable News Network (CNN) newscasts when she was in Taiwan. These news sources presented different interpretations of United States interests in the world. She again feels at odds with the dominant culture of the United States, which seems disinterested in the perspectives of other people around the world.

In the spring of 2005 Mary was asked to identify several global songs that would be appropriate for United Methodist women's groups to sing during their regular meetings. She struggled with this invitation for several weeks. The term *global* got in her way. As always, her response was thoughtful, but it raised more questions than it answered. She encouraged the United Methodist women to try to learn songs from other cultures in any way they could, preferably from a native of another culture who lives in their community. Whether or not they succeeded in their singing of another culture's song, the effort to learn something from another person's culture in itself would teach them valuable lessons. To fail at singing someone else's songs could teach them humility about living in our culturally diverse and complicated world.

Lively, astonishing, stimulating, fresh, remarkable, lovely—words of surprise, revelation, epiphany, presence. Conversations with Mary are peppered with these words. Experiences that deaden the spirit—dull, not worthwhile, not uplifting—she judges harshly. She thrives on the energy felt through connecting with other people, engaging with them in things that matter. It is not surprising that Mary would be drawn to the arts, because engaging any type of art demands undivided attention. We must be present to the art as the work is present to us. As a learner, a teacher, and a music leader, Mary lives in the immediacy of the moment.

In *Real Presences*,[79] comparative literature specialist George Steiner makes the case that art created with integrity expresses a real presence through sound, image, movement, word. The power of this presence can be felt in the embodied moment of drawing, painting, sculpting, singing, playing, dancing, or speaking. It can be known in the moment of contemplative gazing or careful listening. Steiner claims that experiences of this presence are moments of epiphany: something mysteriously hidden is made manifest. And these experiences change people.

---

[79] George Steiner, *Real Presences* (Chicago: University of Chicago Press, 1989).

As a young woman doing doctoral work, Mary studied aesthetics in hopes of finding a language to describe what was going on in the relationship between a work of art (music or other) and the person performing or listening, creating or observing. Something powerful was occurring, and she struggled to find words for what that something was about. Through a number of presentations, she tried to articulate her aesthetic understanding and to argue for why the arts should matter to Mennonites.

(Old) Mennonite Church culture in the early to mid-twentieth century was dominated by concerns for right living. Ethics, personal discipleship, and communal holiness were seen as sacramental signs of God's presence in the believer's life. Mennonites had not developed a strong theology of grace-full beauty, joy, and truth that can find expression in the physical dimensions of life. For generations, Mennonites have found it difficult to explain or enjoy grace as a gift from God, seen in part in the created world and in the works of human beings created in God's image. Mary and other Mennonite artists felt stranded without ways of speaking about how serious works of art have opened revelatory experiences for them.

At some point after completing her doctorate, Mary dropped her project of seeking to justify the arts by aesthetic means. Through work on the hymnal and later through her experiences in Africa, she began giving herself to the moments of singing, of teaching, of conversation. Over time she has increasingly developed a spirituality of the present moment. The Spirit that broods over the earth with ah! bright wings[80] is known in the moment of performance.

Mary was once asked which hymn is her favorite, to which she replied, "The next one I'm going to lead." She frets in preparing songs she has led many times before, but when the singing starts, her anxieties float away. "Something happens to people when they sing. They are transformed for a moment."[81] They sing better together than they could sing alone. They feel the power of breathing together. They feel their bodies resonate with others'—they know they are not alone.

---

[80] These images come from Gerard Manley Hopkins's poem, "God's Grandeur," a favorite of Mary's.
[81] Susan E. Janzen and Mary E. Klassen, *The Mennonite*, 12 May 1998, 5.

Mary rarely speaks of her relationship with God, yet she freely chooses others' words and images that demonstrate her beliefs. She delves into a hymn text, musical work, or visual image, gaining remarkable insights. In the immediacy of her discovery she is astonished. Her great gift as a teacher is drawing people into the astonishing truth the art can reveal.

As Mary has composed her life over eighty years, a number of loves have emerged with clarity. She holds dear the Mennonite Church; music and visual art that demonstrate honesty and integrity; people singing together; questions that expand commonly held beliefs or understanding; art that encourages exploration in freedom; probing conversations with people whose experiences are different from her own; teaching that frees the intellect and imagination of her students; learning that challenges and broadens her perceptions; freedom and spontaneity to be in the immediate presence of others; friendships that are honest, transparent, and forthright; family, and friends she claims as family; all life-giving things that are interesting, astonishing, lively, remarkable, fresh, and stimulating; the quest for interrelationships among things; and comparisons that lead to experiences of wholeness. These loves have increasingly shaped her choices—her letting go of responsibilities that threaten to distort these passions, and her acceptance of invitations and opportunities that deepen these commitments.

Appendix: Three Versions of Charles Wesley's "O for a Thousand Tongues"

Wesley's original (1740)

1. Glory to God, and Praise and Love
   Be ever, ever, given;
   By Saints below and Saints above,
   The Church in Earth and Heaven.

2. On this glad Day the glorious Sun
   Of Righteousness arose,
   On my benighted Soul he shone,
   And fill'd it with Repose.

3. Sudden expir'd the legal Strife,
   'Twas then I ceas'd to grieve,
   My Second, Real, Living Life
   I then began to live.

4. Then with my Heart I first believ'd,
   Believ'd, with Faith Divine,
   Power with the Holy Ghost receiv'd
   To call the Saviour Mine.

The Church Hymnal (1927)

The Mennonite Hymnary (1940)

5. **Glory to God and praise and love**
   Be ever, ever given
   By saints below and saints above,
   The Church in earth and heaven.

1. O for a thousand tongues to sing
   My great Redeemer's praise,
   The glories of my God and King,
   The triumphs of His grace.

2. My gracious Master and my God,
   Assist me to proclaim,
   To spread through all the earth abroad
   The honors of Thy name.

3. Jesus! The name that charms our fears,
   That bids our sorrows cease,
   'Tis music in the sinner's ears,
   'Tis life, and health, and peace.

---

1. **Oh,** for a thousand tongues to sing
   My **dear** Redeemer's praise,
   The glories of my God and King,
   The triumphs of His Grace!

2. My gracious Master, and my God,
   Assist me to proclaim,
   To spread thro' all the earth abroad
   The honors of Thy name.

3. Jesus! The name that **calms** our fears,
   That bids our sorrows cease—
   'Tis music **to my ravished** ears,
   'Tis life, and health, and peace.

---

5. I felt my Lord's Atoning Blood
   Close to my Soul applied;
   Me, me he lov'd – the Son of God
   For me, for me He died!

6. I found, and own'd his Promise true,
   Ascertain'd of my Part,
   My Pardon pass'd in Heaven I knew
   When written on my Heart.

7. O for a Thousand Tongues to sing
   My great Redeemer's Praise!
   The Glories of my God and King,
   The triumphs of his Grace.

8. My gracious Master, and my God,
   Assist me to proclaim,
   To spread thro' all the Earth abroad
   The Honours of Thy Name.

9. Jesus the Name that charms our Fears,
   That bids our Sorrows cease;
   'Tis Musick in the Sinner's Ears,
   'Tis Life, and Health, and Peace!

Wesley's original

10. He breaks the power of cancell'd Sin,
He sets the prisoner free:
His blood can make the foulest clean;
His blood availed for me.

11. He speaks; and listening to His Voice,
New life the Dead receive,
The mournful, broken Hearts rejoice,
The humble Poor believe.

12. Hear Him ye Deaf, His Praise ye Dumb
Your loosen'd Tongues employ,
Ye Blind, behold your Saviour come,
And leap, ye Lame, for joy.

14. See all your Sins on Jesus laid;
The Lamb of God was slain,
His Soul was once an Offering made
For every Soul of Man.

The Church Hymnal

4. He breaks the pow'r of **reigning** sin,
He sets the pris'ner free;
His blood can make the foulest clean:
His blood availed for me!

The Mennonite Hymnary

4. He breaks the power of **reigning** sin,
He sets the prisoner free;
His blood can make the **sinful** clean;
His blood availed for me.

15. Harlots, and Publicans, and Thieves
In holy Triumph join!
Sav'd is the Sinner that believes
From Crimes as great as Mine.

16. Murtherers, and all ye hellish Crew,
Ye Sons of Lust and Pride,
Believe the Saviour died for you;
For me the Saviour died.

17. Awake from guilty Nature's Sleep,
And Christ shall give you Light.
Cast all your Sins into the Deep,
And wash the Ethiop white.

18. With me, your Chief, you then shall know,
Shall feel your Sins forgiven;
Anticipate your Heaven below,
And own, that Love is Heaven.

Part 2

WAYS OF LOOKING

Encounters in the Life of Mary K. Oyer

Praise God from Whom All Blessings Flow

Praise God from whom all blessings flow,
Praise Him all creatures here below,
Praise Him above, ye heav'nly host,
Praise Father, Son, and Holy Ghost.

Swahili
Watu wote duniani,
Mwimbieni Mungu wetu,
M-cheni na kumsikia,
Njoni kwake na furaha.

Maasai
Esisa olOmaiyian iyiook,
Intai pooki li abori,
Esisa Papa te keper,
O Jesu, o lTau Sinyati.

Chinese
讚美真神, 萬福之根,
世上萬民讚美主恩,
天使天軍讚美主名,
讚美聖父聖子聖靈.

Chapter 3

TEACHING A WAY TO LEARN

James Miller

During our junior and senior years at Goshen College, my roommate, John Weber, and I went regularly on Sunday mornings to Mary's home, where we pretended to study a Sunday school lesson. It was a non-threatening and more desirable venue for our wayward thoughts, or so we thought they were at the time. Actually, in retrospect, they were not all that revolutionary.

An amusing incident took place on a choir tour in the spring of my freshman year, when I was but sixteen years old. It was the basement of Wayland (Iowa) Mennonite Church that witnessed this event. I was standing with one foot on a bench during an intermission, and another male member of the choir managed to push me in such a way that the seat seam of my trousers ripped. It would have been unseemly for me to return to the stage in this condition. Mary, our conductor, found needle and thread, and I bent over a bench as she made some temporary repairs.

In her academic role Mary was the most significant mentor I ever had. Like most of the Goshen students, I was a rural, sheltered Mennonite boy of little sophistication. She was not trying to teach sophistication but sensitivity; this she did by example and by preparing us to encounter writings on aesthetics and on critical listening and performing. In her legendary fine arts class, we all began collecting postcard sized reproductions of great works of art. Many of us discovered later that we had formed a habit of accumulating these reproductions. Mine served me well for years.

I remember visiting Mary at Aspen, Colorado, one summer when she was studying there. Miriam and Lowell Byler and John Weber and I drove from Denver and were introduced to quite another musical world. And then a couple years later, again largely because of her influence, I went on to graduate school at Michigan, where she had led the way. There I discovered why she was so enthused about classes taught by Hans David. And her openness to learning showed me the way to learn in the big university.

I have been retired for some years now but have returned to teach full-time this year, and not many days go by but what I think of ways her influence has been important to me. On many occasions I have told friends and students (sometimes they are the same) that until I was well into graduate school, Mary taught me everything that was important to me. She also laid the groundwork for what I learned later. She was so generous with her time and so patient with all the bumpkins who came out of the woods each fall to study at Goshen College, and all was done in her inimitable style and with grace. We all, as they say today, owe her big-time.

Chapter 4

REMAINING OPEN TO CHANGE

J. Harold Moyer

My direct contacts with Mary were primarily during the years 1957–69. In the fall of 1957 I joined the music faculty at Goshen College, having just completed a PhD in music composition at the University of Iowa. My teaching duties included music theory and piano. Mary was department chair, and she had a positive reputation as a teacher, particularly in a general education course relating to the arts and in teaching music history. In the area of public performance she was best known as director of the Motet Singers, a select vocal group that toured regularly and performed music in a wide variety of sacred and secular idioms.

The late 1950s was a period of change in Mennonite Church (MC)[1] music practices. Having grown up as a General Conference Mennonite, I was accustomed to the use of pianos or organs for worship services, including hymn singing. The Mennonite Church had a long tradition of only a cappella singing during worship services, but a few congregations were beginning to incorporate keyboards, at least for prelude music and for weddings. I remember one MC congregation that kept its piano in a side room and rolled it out for weddings. Mary supported creative change but did not want to lose the strong a cappella hymn-singing tradition. I observed Mary as an excellent director of congregational singing. She has a strong voice for leading vocally and has the ability to creatively teach a new song to the congregation.

Mary is a fine cellist, with a doctorate from the University of Michigan. She found herself at odds with those MC traditions that

---

[1] The Mennonite Church was sometimes referred to informally as the (Old) Mennonite Church.

assumed that Christian musicians should express themselves primarily with verbal vocal music, and instrumental music should have only a minor significance for them. With Mary's encouragement, some of us thus engaged in studying music aesthetics in some workshops and publications. An influential book was *Philosophy in a New Key*, by Suzanne Langer. We developed a more articulate appreciation for the significance of nonverbal artistic expression.

Mary was sometimes frustrated by some patriarchal MC church practices. Among some more conservative churches there was resistance to having women actively involved in conference committees, congregational leadership roles, and family structures. Oft-quoted biblical passages about women being submissive to their husbands were especially annoying for a single woman. I recall her remarking, "Who am I supposed to be submissive to?"

I appreciated Mary's encouragement to compose some pieces for the Motet Singers. Acquaintance with this fine choral group gave me some new insights into creating unaccompanied choral music. It was also a pleasure to compose a sonata for cello and piano. Working closely with her in creating the cello piece expanded my knowledge and skill in writing for string instruments.

I left Goshen College in 1959 to take a similar position at Bethel College. Within a couple of years my path crossed Mary's again, as we were both appointed to a joint hymnal committee given the daunting task of leading the preparation of a new hymnal, revising the then-current hymnals of the Mennonite Church (*Church Hymnal*, 1927) and the General Conference Mennonite Church (*Mennonite Hymnary*, 1940). Each conference had begun preliminary committee work, and these committees were already sharing material. The decision to combine the efforts into one new hymnal occurred in 1961. As the committee responsibilities evolved, Vernon Neufeld was chair, I served as vice-chair, and Mary Oyer as executive secretary. Lester Hostetler and Walter Yoder were named co-editors, both bringing experience in editing hymnals. There were also joint text and tune committees. For the next five years the joint committee had at least two weeklong meetings each year. Our family spent several weeks in Goshen during the summer of 1965, as Mary and I worked diligently with the later stages of the project.

Mary assumed her role as executive secretary with dedication and seriousness. The field of hymnology was somewhat new for her, as she and the rest of us gathered a library of hymnals and standard reference works. I appreciated her efforts to obtain the original text of a hymn wherever possible. She spent her 1963–64 sabbatical year in Edinburgh, Scotland, searching for the original form of the text and tune of many hymns, guided by the internationally recognized hymnologist, Erik Routley. This immense amount of research gave the committee a firm basis for the final editing process. I have mental images of Mary's work area in her Eighth Street house, piled high but neatly with material related to this project.

Because we were combining two groups' traditions, it was inevitable that our new book would be quite different from either of its predecessors. Mary was sensitive to the various groups within our conferences as they brought concerns about which hymns they thought it essential to retain. Someone has said that for a worshiping congregation the hymnal is next to the Bible in importance. We gradually evolved a list of "must retain" hymns from each of the traditions. We were amused by a letter from a person who listed four or five favorite hymns and asked whether we could keep the same hymn numbers for these in the new book!

While respectful of concerns for continuity, Mary helped move us into including some new areas such as plainsong and a few hymns from other cultures. We also followed the practice found in other hymnals of printing some hymns without meter signature. Aware that this might be confusing for some, Mary initiated some hymnsings in several churches and included some new hymns we were considering including in the new book. When she introduced some nonmetrical hymns, she noted three types of reactions. Well-trained musicians had no problems with it. People with very little musical training didn't notice a difference. The people who expressed concerns were local amateur song leaders who were uncertain about how to conduct without a regular meter.

Though we had many decisions to make, the hymnal committees' interactions generally proceeded satisfactorily. People often displayed good humor. Eventually we ran out of anecdotes from our past experiences with hymns and hymn singing, and we began repeating ourselves.

After *The Mennonite Hymnal* was published, congregations that had recently purchased it often asked Mary to introduce the hymnal. For a variety of reasons, publication of a companion handbook to the hymnal was delayed for several years. It eventually was printed in two volumes: *Exploring the Mennonite Hymnal: Essays*, by Mary Oyer, and *Exploring the Mennonite Hymnal: Handbook*, by Alice Loewen, Harold Moyer, and Mary Oyer. Here again I had many opportunities to interact with Mary. Her *Essays* book has a creative, unusual format.

I learned from Mary the importance of being open to change and growth in my music career. Hymnology had been a secondary interest for her, but she developed a respect for it, encouraging me in the same direction. She also helped me gain insights into some indigenous music she has studied in eastern Africa. In our Western culture it is assumed that a legitimate composition needs a beginning, middle, and end. I learned from Mary that in some African cultures music has a cyclic form, and this repetition can be a valid musical expression.

It has been a privilege to work with Mary as a colleague through the years, and I appreciate her many contributions to the Mennonite Church and to Mennonite higher education.

Chapter 5

AN INSTRUCTOR INSIDE
AND OUTSIDE THE CLASSROOM

Robert L. Weaver

I remember Mary Oyer as a gracious and warmhearted mentor. She had compassion for her students and a keen intellect, and she guided us with a thoughtful and caring hand. She prepared me well for my life as a graduate student and as a teacher.

During my Goshen College days (1954–58), Mary, in addition to teaching, worked on her Doctor of Musical Arts degree. She took a sabbatical leave during my sophomore year. In the following two years, I often heard her playing Beethoven's cello sonatas in the basement of the Union Building (then home of the music department), in preparation for her required recitals. Mary was among the first to earn this degree at the University of Michigan.

Already in my freshman year she began to prepare me for graduate studies. Her thorough and careful instruction in tonal harmony and composition permitted me to satisfy with ease the University of Michigan's entrance requirements in this subject. She had her students do homework for a period of two hours, rather than expecting us to complete a set number of exercises: we worked according to our abilities. (This pedagogical method I did not forget as a teacher.) During my junior year she advised me to develop a reading knowledge of French and German before I graduated. This counsel served me exceptionally well both in my first graduate course in research methods and bibliography of musicology, and later at Syracuse University in an art history seminar where we had no textbook but only a resource volume—in French.

Her attentiveness also improved my writing style, shaping a tool of inestimable value for my work as a student and later as a teacher. When she asked me to bring a term paper I had written for a senior history course, she took out her red pencil and kindly suggested alterations for clarity of emphasis and stylistic enhancement. That session, though somewhat embarrassing for me, taught me several points that I have never forgotten: to look for redundancies and to use active rather than passive voice.

As I recall my preparations for graduate study, I remember that Mary—in exchange for my giving her rides to Ann Arbor before I enrolled at the university—took time from her busy schedule there to introduce me to some of her colleagues. She also helped me with the practical details of finding a room and showed me places to eat on a budget. In these ways, too, she proved to be a wise and thoughtful teacher, concerned for my future.

Two classes, "Introduction to Fine Arts" and "Analysis of Musical Forms," shaped my later studies and my career as an instructor perhaps more than any others. Mary's ideas about parallels between art and music motivated me to choose a doctoral program at Syracuse University. For the degree, I posed this question: What was the effect of the Reformation on the arts? To develop this theme, I selected classes and seminars in history, art history, and music history from medieval times until about 1750, the time of the death of J. S. Bach. These classes provided necessary background for my dissertation topic, "The Motets of Hubert Waelrant (ca. 1517–1595)." Because I had read that this Antwerp composer might have been an Anabaptist, I had occasion to look at his texts and examine them in the light of the history of our church and its theology.

In her fine arts course, Mary's hands-on exercises—on perspective, creation of space and volume, and expression, given by different types of lines and combinations of colors—enhanced my study and understanding of style elements in the visual arts. Descriptive features of different epochs acquired a richer meaning. Similarly, in music, Mary's advice to read Susanne Langer's *Philosophy in a New Key* brought me to the realization that music communicates more than emotion and can express, by its shape, intellectual properties through sounds. One practical outcome I gained from this idea was Mary's use of listening guides for teaching in her classes. Having learned the basic vocabulary of musical notation during our first semester in her fine arts class, even the non-musicians could read enough musical notation to follow melodic patterns and rhythms and to discover their expressive purposes. Another way the intellectual element of musical form served me later was that of convincing colleagues in other disciplines that music conveys more than emotion. Once at an informal faculty gathering, to demonstrate the point I gave a lecture recital, "Why Study a Sonata at a Liberal Arts College?" in which I performed and discussed a Beethoven sonata.

Mary's classroom persona, thorough and earnest, took on a different character when she invited our freshman harmony class to her home for lunch. She became our friend and hospitable servant in true Mennonite fashion. Her bearing on this occasion embodied an ideal that I have used in my own work to bridge the gap between student and teacher.

Mary met us not only in the classroom but also in chapel and church services. Her role as a song leader always brought great assurance as she hummed the opening chord without the pitch pipe and then led us with sure gestures. She also introduced me to Mennonite hymn writers. We often sang from the *Church Hymnal* (1927) J. D. Brunk's setting of "Great God, Indulge My Humble Claim." (These were the days before Mary became associated with "606.") I still enjoy singing Brunk's Scottish Psalter–style hymn, "Before Jehovah's Awful Throne," especially because I have spent thirty years working and living in a Presbyterian milieu. Regarding the study of hymns, I am indebted too for her leading me to the writings of Erik Routley. For all students, Mary's Motet Singers provided inspiration both by the wide selection of types of sacred music and by the high standards of performance she maintained. Those who were in the group had a rare privilege in their college careers. But perhaps most impressive was her commitment to taking time out of what I would now consider an impossible schedule to teach a Sunday school class. Her example encouraged me to participate fully in the life of a church—to be a church organist and a member of the session and the worship committee.

How do I remember my teacher Mary Oyer? She taught me to be a tolerant, friendly, and forgiving teacher. She taught me to be a scholar: to love a discipline and to be organized and ardent in its pursuit. She taught me to extend my academic discipline beyond the classroom, especially to share knowledge and performance ability in the spiritual and cultural life of my community.

Chapter 6

LESSONS FOR LIFE

Philip K. Clemens

It was a Tuesday night. Along with about thirty other Goshen College students, I was in Mary Oyer's fine arts class on the third floor of the arts building. I had chosen to take the course, which met one night per week that semester. But a significant problem arose for me on that particular night, when—faced with what I considered an enticing opportunity—I made (literally) a sophomoric decision. That same night the athletic department had scheduled a home basketball game against Ohio Northern University. During the scheduled break of our extended class period, another student and I slipped out and went to the game.

Little did I anticipate the consequences of my choice. Did I not know who was teaching the course? Obviously not. Oh, I was acquainted with Mary Oyer, but I did not yet understand the depth of her interest in teaching the particular student, and I had not adequately absorbed her profound understanding of what it meant to learn.

When I was a student at Christopher Dock Mennonite High School in Lansdale, Pennsylvania, Mary had come to our home. I don't think Goshen College thought of her visit in terms of recruitment of students, but it made a lasting impression on me and influenced my decision to attend the college. Mary and my mother knew each other, and it felt natural for her to visit us and to play Brahms piano duets with me on our living room grand.

Later, too, as a high school senior, I had a series of wonderfully helpful interviews with three church leaders from Goshen College and Goshen Biblical Seminary, including Mary. First, J. C. Wenger spoke in a chapel service at Christopher Dock, urging students to consider attending seminary. That afternoon, in conversation with Wenger, I made the decision to go to seminary, and therefore dropped my plans to major in music during college; I thought the two were not compatible.

But the decision weighed on me, and that spring, when our high school choir traveled to Goshen, Indiana, I found my way to Miss Oyer's office on the third floor of the arts building. After hearing my story, Mary was encouraging and suggested that it would be fine for me to major in music in college and then attend seminary. To confirm her recommendation, she picked up the phone and dialed H. S. Bender, dean of Goshen Biblical Seminary, who invited me over for a chat. Bender agreed with Mary and saw no reason why I should not major in music and then come to seminary.

Yes, I was acquainted with Mary Oyer, but I really didn't know her—until after that momentous Tuesday night. Without delay, I was summoned to Mary's house. Little did I know what was in store for me, but I certainly found out—and I am grateful to this day. In no uncertain terms, with focused energy and a touch of sadness, Mary told me that she had devoted the second half of the class period on that Tuesday night to exploring the Catholic mass. Although this subject was an element of every fine arts course she taught, Mary had me in mind, specifically, as she had prepared the presentation for that night. She taught with individuals in mind, not generically. Attuned to my passion for music and the church, she had been eager to pass on to me the significant role of the mass in both fields. And I had skipped class! I could not have felt more penitent.

I'll never know what I missed because I skipped the second half of class that night, but I learned that teaching is more than passing along facts. I learned that good teachers invest themselves in students. I learned that good professors teach with purpose. I learned that it is important to be direct, instead of beating around the bush. And I learned that there is no substitute for being present in class.

I also came to learn that lasting friendships grow when teachers and students together are faithful to the teaching and learning process, whether in classroom discussion or ensemble performance. Besides enjoying Mary's courses in music history, church music, and forms and analysis, I also was privileged to sing as part of her Motet Singers, and later to play keyboard continuo alongside her superb cello continuo in such masterpieces as J. S. Bach's *St. Matthew Passion.* Her vivid example was musically formative for me and a lesson in commitment.

Later, when I joined the Goshen College music faculty, our relationship became that of colleagues, and I gradually became comfortable calling her "Mary," rather than the accustomed "Miss Oyer." Those were good years, and as I matured as a musician and a teacher, I never stopped learning from my former professor. She offered me the courtesy of regarding me as a professional co-worker.

What a great environment. Take, for example, the interest Mary showed in my efforts to establish and direct the Goshen College Jazz Band. She was delighted with the improvisation involved, and pleased that a wide variety of students took part. Instead of expressing concern that jazz may not belong in the fine arts tradition, she welcomed the non-Western elements that are so much a part of it. Instead of defending the Western practice of isolated performers playing to a quiet audience, she was pleased that jazz performance invites a lively audience into a kind of village dance.

By that time Mary's eager and thorough absorption in the music of Africa had become a love that affected her whole life. And as that passion intermingled with her passion for hymnody, we all stood to benefit from her considerable legacy. Hymns are folk songs of the people, whoever the people may be. No individual song from around the world is by ethnic origin or style more acceptable than any other song. Singing or playing music from diverse cultural backgrounds enriches people's lives and brings them together in mutual and vitalizing relationship. And as I've come to interpret it, participating in one another's music is an enjoyable and genuine way of experiencing the body of Christ.

One of the continuing gifts Mary Oyer brings to all of us came to light for me after my landmark Tuesday night. Mary takes interest in every person she meets—student, colleague, friend, neighbor—at home or abroad. She sees each person as a gift and values what can develop between herself and another. During my teaching days at Goshen College, I remember a particular student who came with hardly any formal music background and became a music major. He showed interest in music history, but, for example, pronounced Richard Wagner's last name not as "Vahg-ner," but as "Wag-ner." He was almost entirely self-taught.

Mary saw the intelligence and desire that lay just below his inexperienced surface and took a special interest in him. He improvised well on the bass guitar. At Goshen he learned to play the double bass and became an extraordinary bassist in the jazz band, continuing on with jazz performance after graduation. I wonder how many times Mary's attention and involvement has made such a difference in someone's life. We can only imagine.

Thank you, Mary, for your wonderful gift. As your student, colleague, pastor (for a time), and always as your friend, my life has been enriched deeply because of who you are!

Chapter 7

PASSION CULTIVATED

John Enz

> In the beginning,
> Coming to Goshen
> Senses athletic
> Naïve to Eden's fruit
> (Sighting GC's potency)
> Innocence unconscious
> Expressing by instincts of ear and eye
> Cellist's mannerisms abound
> Feeling the power of expression
> Though undisciplined, diffuse
> Unchartered to be sure.

Enter: Mary Oyer

Medium for cultivation: To focus our senses via presentation and the art of questions.

> Historically we find that people have done…
>> What lines of continuity do you find?
>>> The creative change then continues the lines?
>>> Or deviates from the lines justifiably?
>>> Or do we have trouble?
>>>> *Are we judging?*
>>>> *Oh, dear!*
> What is the phrase?
>> How is it developed?
>>> Do you hear this … or this?
>>>> *"Do you hear what I hear?"*
>>>>> An artist's Thoreau at expression

Are you getting enough sleep?

How is the theme related to the whole?

Are you balanced?

Performance practice historical?
Performance practice contemporary?
Performance practice in the piece?
Five epics old!
Are you practiced?!

What is your answer?
On a good day—"That is so interesting!"
On a great day—"That is so fascinating!"
Every day found constructive encouragement.

Velocity of knowledge went supersonic
as concepts of process went subconscious

Tooled for service … service for culture … Culture for Service

Thank you, Mary Oyer
Mentor of Expression
Cultivator of Passion

Chapter 8

A MENTOR FOR FUTURE TEACHERS

E. Douglas Bomberger

As I was preparing to enroll at Goshen College in the fall of 1977, my father gave me some useful advice on choosing courses. He asserted that the quality of the teacher was much more important than the subject matter of the class. I have repeatedly found this observation to be true, but perhaps never more so than when I took music history with Mary Oyer.

Music majors normally enrolled in this class as juniors or seniors, after completing two years of music theory, but rumor had it that Professor Oyer would be on sabbatical when I needed the class. Consequently, I signed up for music history in my sophomore year and found myself in the company of much more experienced students. Near the end of the first semester, Mary called me into her office and let me know the jig was up: "If I had known that you did not have the prerequisites, I never would have allowed you to take the class, but since you are doing well, I will have to let you remain in the course." My little deception—although exposed—had worked, and it turned out to be one of the most important decisions of my professional life.

The class was inspiring on a number of different levels. On the one hand, it exposed me to the field of music history, one that I found so congenial that I have devoted my career to it. On the other hand, Mary's teaching style was so inspiring that her techniques and perspectives are never far from my own classroom. Clearly I was not the only one inspired by her teaching. Though I do not have a list of my classmates from that memorable course, I am certain that at least six of us, of a class of ten or so, went on to earn doctorates in music and teach at the college level.

What made her such an effective teacher? In his book *Masters: Portraits of Great Teachers*, Joseph Epstein states: "What all the great teachers appear to have in common is love of their subject, an obvious satisfaction in arousing this love in their students, and an ability to convince them that what they are being taught is deadly serious."[1] Mary's teaching was far too subtle to break down to specific techniques, and undoubtedly my classmates' memories would be different from mine, but five things in particular meant a lot to me and continue to shape my teaching.

From the first weeks of class, Mary communicated an unusual passion for the subject matter. Whether she was introducing the intricacies of plainchant, helping us feel the emotions of a Monteverdi madrigal, or dissecting the structure of a Brahms symphony, she had a way of making each day's topic seem vitally important. Surely she could not have been equally excited about every composer and historical era, but she managed to generate an enthusiasm that made me believe that the subject matter of each day's class was a special interest of hers. As one example, she so impressed me with the rarity and significance of the pile of aging copies of the *Liber Usualis* locked in a cabinet in Room 36 of the music building that I began a quest to find a copy for myself. My search ended with another locked cabinet in a monastery in rural Haiti, where the wizened monks were simultaneously pleased and puzzled that someone still cared about the liturgy that had been rendered obsolete by Vatican II.

Her enthusiasm for the material did not mean that she was a mere cheerleader, however. Coupled with this excitement was a second attribute—a factual precision that was daunting for some students and motivational for others. Her tests demanded an impossible command of overarching ideas and minutiae. She admitted freely that her exams were difficult by intention, so that she would have a better idea of how much each student understood. In her view, an exam that allowed anyone to score 100 percent was too easy.

This factual precision—which was not limited to the classroom—is a part of Mary's personality that has always impressed

---

[1] Joseph Epstein, *Masters: Portraits of Great Teachers* (New York: Basic Books, 1981), xii.

me. Friends and colleagues experience it in perhaps a tempered form, but her critical faculties are never entirely shut down. Former students, of course, can expect no less. After completing my master's degree and joining the Goshen College faculty in 1983, I had the opportunity to take over the music history classes on Mary's retirement. She was very kind in helping me make the transition; she shared books, records, and advice. But as we talked, I happened to use the term "sonata-allegro form," which brought her up short. "You should use that term carefully," she told me, "because not every sonata form is in allegro tempo." Very true, and I am grateful that her attention to detail kept her from ignoring my imprecision.

The Mennonite church benefited most tangibly from Mary's attention to detail through her work on *The Mennonite Hymnal* of 1969. She insisted that selecting and printing hymns was not enough; the hymnal committee also bore responsibility to document in exhaustive detail the sources for every hymn. This feature gives this hymnal a historical authority that has seldom been matched. This attention to origins also makes a statement about a church that has prided itself for centuries on remembering where it came from.

A third hallmark of her teaching was her ability to place music in cultural context. She seldom spoke of music in isolation from the other arts, and connections with literature, art, and drama permeated every lecture. Musicologist Paul Henry Lang sums up this view in the introduction to *Music in Western Civilization*:

> Every civilization is a synthesis of man's conquest of life. Art is the ultimate symbol of this conquest, the utmost unity man can achieve. Yet the spirit of an epoch is reflected not in the arts alone, but in every field of human endeavor, from theology to engineering. Nor must we take it for granted that there is a uniform spirit of the age which is invariably expressed in every phase of art, and which transmits to us the same content and meaning in each. Rather, we find what we are seeking in the sum of the meanings of the various arts, which taken thus in conjunction form the essence of the artistic spirit of the age.[2]

---

[2] Paul Henry Lang, *Music in Western Civilization* (New York: Norton, 1941), xix.

These interconnections infused her other signature course, "Introduction to Fine Arts," in which she confronted students from all backgrounds and academic disciplines with the vital role of the arts in society. Her virtuosity at incorporating meaningful and relevant examples from all the arts serves as inspiration for my teaching, as I strive to bring the same interdisciplinary approach to my students. I would find it unthinkable to discuss a composition such as Bartok's *Allegro Barbaro* without first introducing primitivism in the visual arts (for example, Picasso's *Les Demoiselles d'Avignon*, which I first learned to know in her classroom) and the role of the Golden Section and the Fibonacci Series in Bartok's formal structures.

A fourth insight that I gained from her teaching was that performance may serve as an adjunct to teaching. When I took her class, I was spending many hours a day in the practice room, honing my piano skills and preparing solo repertoire for performance. She demonstrated that performance is more than an end in itself, as she daily used her voice and sight-reading ability at the piano to make her points. I have never met another teacher who could so seamlessly sing or play a phrase in the middle of a lecture to illustrate the idea under discussion. Her absolute pitch and clear voice made her vocal examples models of perfection. Her ability to sit down and play a complex piece like the D-sharp minor fugue from Bach's *Well-Tempered Clavier: Book 1* was astounding to me as a piano major. Often she would let us in on tricks of the trade that gave us insight into her mental processes without completely demystifying them; it turns out that she used an edition of the *Well-Tempered Clavier* in which the fugue was printed in the enharmonic key of E-flat minor, slightly easier but still no mean feat for this tricky piece. She also told us once that the weather affects her sense of absolute pitch, and she must make slight adjustments in inclement weather.

Finally, and perhaps most important, is a quality that permeates all aspects of her varied professional life: intellectual curiosity. Unlike some teachers who become set in their ways, and who save time and energy by becoming satisfied with their knowledge and abilities, Mary has continued to grow. Her interest in exploring new ideas, repertoire, and cultures has kept her vibrant and engaged, while her passion for sharing these discoveries has kept her classroom lively.

My first encounter with Mary came years before that class at Goshen College. In the early 1970s I was living with my parents in west Africa when she visited us during her sabbatical. She was discovering African music for the first time, and even as a preteen I could not help being impressed with her excitement at the daily insights she gained from contact with African musicians in their home countries. That someone of her knowledge and experience could be so eager to start from the beginning in a new field impressed me deeply. Meeting her again in 2004, I was struck by this same spirit of curiosity and discovery, as she described her experiences in Taiwan and led a group of musicians through some of the multicultural hymns from *Hymnal: A Worship Book*. If anyone is entitled to rest on her laurels, it is Mary Oyer, but she clearly does not intend to stop exploring just because she has passed the age of eighty. I believe that her own eagerness to learn and grow was a key ingredient in making her students so eager to learn.

These five qualities of Mary's personality sum up for me her effectiveness in the classroom. When I think back on my years at Goshen College, I realize that Mary's guidance and interest were crucial for my own development as a teacher. Her commitment to her students was not a matter of blind affection or doting pride— she demanded our very best and expected that we would meet her standards. This combination of genuine caring and high expectations made her a remarkable mentor whose influence extends far beyond the confines of her classroom.

Chapter 9

A LEGACY OF LIFELONG LEARNING

Jean Ngoya Kidula

Mary Oyer stands out as one of the few people outside my family who have profoundly influenced my life and work. She has affirmed, confirmed, and challenged me as a person, a musician, a Christian, and a student—as a whole package. To date, only two other people outside my family have had such an impact on me.

I met Mary Oyer when I was a student at Kenyatta University in Nairobi in 1980. The nine students in our class were in our final undergraduate year, preparing to join the workforce as teachers. In some ways we felt prepared, but after starting class with Dr. Oyer, we realized just how much more we needed to know, and as a result of her teaching, all of us became students for life. My fellow classmates and I agree that Dr. Oyer brought an excitement to European music history that we had not hitherto experienced at the university. At the same time, this North American professor opened our eyes to an appreciation of the rich African heritage that we had taken for granted. In addition to teaching these classes, Dr. Oyer gave lessons to piano and voice students.

The subjects that Dr. Oyer taught were not necessarily new to us. It was her approach that made a big difference in our understanding of the subject matter. She for some reason decided to approach our survey of Western music history through hymns. Because Western missionaries had initiated most of the schools in Kenya, hymns were normal fare for a majority of Kenyans twenty years and older. They were familiar territory for all of us, but we had not studied hymnody as part of the history of Western music. In starting with hymns, Dr. Oyer led us, using familiar tools, to faraway continents (Europe and the North America) and distant histories (medieval onward), to bring home cultures that had grafted themselves onto our histories.

But she also incorporated the architecture, painting, literature, and poetry of those times and places. Some of this art, architecture, and literature was present in our countries—for example, in our cathedrals and in texts we read in our English classes. She helped us picture how these structures were related to, reflected in, and contrasted with the music structures of similar periods. I came to understand the kind of vocal production needed to sing a cantata aria of the baroque period when I saw the kinds of buildings in which these sounds were produced, how the sound echoed in the arches, and so on. My performance changed as I recognized the ways people in different times and cultures have adjusted their performance styles to the environment (buildings and outdoor spaces) they find themselves in or create for themselves.

Dr. Oyer's teaching not only opened my eyes to European music history and its canonic embeddedness through a variety of circumstances, but it also opened my eyes to European music as a type of culture. That culture was different from what I had grown up with; it could be learned, in the same way that someone from outside could learn my culture. Dr. Oyer opened our understanding of music, as an art and culture in its own right, but also as an art related to other arts, reflected in or reflecting other arts, existing in time and space and often transcending time and space.

While Dr. Oyer may not be aware of this fact, some of the hymns that she introduced in our classes are sung in Kenya today by our students and by their students. Some that have made the rounds most include "When All Thy Mercies, O My God" and "Praise God from Whom All Blessings Flow." In the process of sharing her musical knowledge, Dr. Oyer also shared her faith, her gifts, and her talents. As my understanding of the subject grew under Dr. Oyer's tutelage, my teaching methods and approaches changed. One of the most interesting things about hymn singing is that it is mostly a communal art. Through her use of hymns as a starting point for moving into Euro-American music history and analysis, we got involved in the music. We possessed the instruments needed for the performance. The style was manageable for my whole class, and we bonded in the class because of rehearsal together and working to interpret the material as historical material and in contemporary space.

For many of my classmates who met Euro-American music history for the first time in college, when Dr. Oyer used material that was part of our language, the foreign became familiar. When we moved on to other genres and forms, we had already established an approach that made the foreign accessible and opened channels for exploration of new material. In my discussion with my classmates, they all agreed that it was not just the passing on of new material but also the way that material was passed on that made a difference, so that they went from having failing grades in the previous year to getting good grades the following year.

Dr. Oyer also prepared us for tests in ways that were non-threatening. In Kenya, students usually sit for a major exam at the end of the semester or year. By the time we were sitting for our final exam, most of us only had exam fever, not a fear of the exam itself. We were confident about our grasp of the material and our preparation for the test. It was not that the exam was easy but that we were well prepared.

I would probably not have become as involved in African music as I am now if it were not for Mary Oyer. I was a piano and voice major, and at the end of my undergraduate year, Dr. Oyer asked me if I would consider going to study piano pedagogy at Goshen College. During that year, I had also begun to study African music outside Kenya. Because my family could only afford the airfare, Dr. Oyer supported me and found some funding for me for tuition and accommodations. It was my first time on an airplane, and my first time out of Africa. This experience opened tremendous opportunities for me, and for my students and my family.

I enrolled at Goshen College and studied piano pedagogy but also took classes in anthropology and did independent studies of African music. One of my assignments included transcribing African music from tapes and LPs. I compared notes with colleagues and discovered that while we agreed in general about the rhythmic structures, we could not agree on meter. I realized that the best way to get at meter is to watch musicians: their bodies tell us something of the strong and weak beats and of the relationships among the body parts and among the instrumentalists and vocalists. In the process, I found myself rethinking my definition of music, to include more than just sound. Dr. Oyer challenged me to expand my definition, and my new awareness in turn expanded my view of dance (another art form) and its history and intersection with music.

It was also during this time that I met and performed with Ephat Mujuru and gained firsthand experience of music of Zimbabwe. What a long way to come to experience it! I was introduced to African musicians and scholars while at Goshen College, and this encounter opened my eyes to the vastness of the field—so much that I decided that I wanted to study African music in graduate school. Dr. Oyer's approach was not just to introduce African music with audio recordings; in the early 1980s she found film footage that made the work come alive. Then she challenged me to teach an African dance to a group of non-African students. The students were diligent, and some danced even better than some of my colleagues in Kenya did. The experience was holistic: I read, listened, watched, sang, danced, and interacted with African musicians and people with interest in African music. At Goshen College, I also got to watch how the academy interacted with the immediate community and the world at large. This opportunity allowed me to see ordinary students moving beyond their borders and resources. I was inspired to encourage my students and others not just to think about what they have or don't have but to share what they have and what they learn—because this sharing makes us richer and creates room for the emergence of new things.

While at Goshen College, I applied and was accepted at University of California, Los Angeles. I could not afford the fees and went back to Kenya, but my eyes had been opened to a wealth of knowledge. As Dr. Oyer had inspired me (and others) to do, I continued to be a student of African music and European-American music.

Although I was in Kenya, Mary Oyer continued to mentor me. She made sure I got information on what was happening in the music field, in terms of materials and discussions. When she came to Kenya and was invited to present a paper on African music, she included me. Eventually I did return to the U.S. for graduate study, first at East Carolina University and later at UCLA. The first person to read my draft of a dissertation manuscript at UCLA was Dr. Oyer. I had been working on it for about a year when she came to visit and to read my work. She so encouraged me that within four months of her reading, I submitted the dissertation and graduated.

Dr. Oyer has continued to encourage and mentor me, and in the process to affect my students and therefore their students. When I started working at the University of Georgia, Dr. Oyer came to visit. She talked to my classes. My colleagues were amazed that she could play African instruments, particularly when I mentioned that she is a cellist by training. They all wanted to know how old she was when she started to study African music. She has continued to open doors for me. I would definitely not be where I am if I had not met Dr. Oyer. Maybe God would have found another way, but I am glad and grateful that God opened this path for me through Dr. Oyer.

Chapter 10

A MODEL OF SOLICITUDE FOR AUTHENTIC EXISTENCE

Justus M. Ogembo

The differential distribution of gifts and talents imposes on each individual the onus of relating her measure and degree of endowments to her everyday life. As is implicit in Jesus' parable of the talents (Matt. 25:14-30) and St. Paul's exposition on spiritual gifts (1 Corinthians 12), it is the degree to which an individual accomplishes this task that stamps her existence with a specific character. Happy are they who have come into the sphere of influence and have learned from a specially gifted individual, as I was under the tutelage of Professor Mary K. Oyer.

Professor Oyer's style of teaching the music that she knows, learning the music she does not know, and relating with other people all bespeak a philosophy of life that should be expounded if only to appreciate the measure and quality of her influence on those who have come into contact with her. As her student and later collaborator in lectures to the Goethe Institute in Nairobi,[1] I learned from her that gifts and talents should be appreciated as means by which to understand the world and positively relate with others in their situatedness. I have seen her use her aptitude for music to explore and uncover the essential features of exotic music so as to capture the cosmology, faith, and corporate life of a community.[2]

---

[1] Mary K. Oyer, "Hymnody in the Context of World Mission," in *The Hymnology Annual: An International Forum on the Hymn and Worship,* vol. 1, ed. Vernon Wicker (Berrien Springs, MI: Vande Vere Pub., 1991), 68, 72.
[2] Ibid., 52.

There is a distinction between a talent and a gift. Although popular discourse uses these terms interchangeably, their connotations are not identical. *Talent* has come to refer not just to the natural endowments of a person but also more specifically to a special (often) creative or artistic aptitude. It suggests a marked natural ability in a given domain that needs to be developed. *Gift*, on the other hand, is not just a notable capacity, talent, or endowment for a particular social function; its association with voluntary transfer of something by one person to another without compensation gives it the special meaning of miraculous favor by God or nature, the possession of which accounts for charisma. Professor Oyer is a musically gifted and talented person. Whatever the measure and degree of her endowments, it is important to know *what* she has done with her aptitude for music, for society, and for the students she has taught, both in their intellectual quest and in their social being—and *how* she has done it. This short paper will deal with these matters.

Professor Oyer arrived at Kenyatta University when the music department was being reorganized to meet Kenya's need for formal music education at all levels of education countrywide. I was one of the twenty-five musically inclined primary school teachers who were selected from across the country to be specially trained for this purpose. Professor Oyer was assigned to teach musicology, piano, and choir training to this group of undergraduate majors in music education. Within a short time, she won the affection and respect of students, fellow lecturers, and the university administration, for her exemplary teaching and personal deportment. In fact, so beloved and respected was she that she was persuaded by the university administration to chair the music department. As time has gone by, I have come to understand in retrospect the possible source and strength of her charisma.

As a nontraditional student studying music education, philosophy, and religion, I was privileged to study musicology and piano with Professor Oyer. In musicology she structured the material in a way that accentuated the distinctive features of various musical genres and periods with which she was familiar—from the Renaissance, Baroque, Classical, and Romantic periods to American Blues. She came to class armed with well-ordered notes, cassette player, taped musical excerpts, and sometimes her cello, to play illustrative examples of the kinds of musical elements we needed to note and remember. By the end of the course, students were able to listen to and talk about music much more intelligently than they could have done had they not taken the course with her. Indeed, not only did the hitherto uninteresting classical music begin to make sense, all music began to make sense.

This approach to musical knowledge reinforced an orientation I was being exposed to in the philosophy of education: the rationalist tradition of inferring the general from the particular, the essential from the phenomenal, and the necessary from the contingent. It should be remembered that the greatest rationalist, G. W. F. Hegel, had tried to construct a science of truth by which he hoped to instrumentally reduce the phenomena of human experience to a manageable number of ideas, forms, or contents of thought. He believed that if he discovered these categories of being and their relations, rules of combination, oppositions, and dialectic, he would construct a formal system for the rigorous description and prediction of cosmic evolution, an evolution he equated with the life of absolute spirit. How would musical knowledge and experience relate to such a formal system?

Professor Oyer's approach to musicology may have enabled her students to appreciate the various genres of music in terms of such universal elements as melodic and rhythmic structures, tonality and dynamics, but it also raised questions. If the discipline of music discloses any essential features of human existence, what are these features and how do they relate to the features disclosed by other disciplines? Is there an essential correspondence between an acoustical order of a given piece of music and a biological order of human emotions? Or is the description a mere subjective expression of the speaker's impression at the moment? If the description captures an essential link between the acoustical order of musical sound and certain emotional responses, what is the general principle by which this correspondence comes about?

These kinds of questions continue to intrigue and fascinate her students in various ways. As thorny as the questions may seem, Mary's contribution toward a possible formulation of a Hegel-like alethiology,[3] by which they could be appropriated, even if in small steps, is the training of a coterie of students, many of whom have acquired doctorates in various fields and from various universities in the world and are in a position to broadcast her legacy far and wide.

The cognitive component that Mary helped develop in her students is never disclosed to us in isolation from the affective and emotional components that make up the core of our humanity. When listening to Mozart's *The Marriage of Figaro,* for example, my developed ability to analyze the opera does not preclude my disposition to be pleased or not pleased by the opera as a whole or certain of its arias, duets, recitatives, etc. Neither does it preclude my disposition to react to it in a certain way—laugh at certain scenes and be revolted by certain scenes, for example—even if some of these reactions may be modified later. Further, my enjoyment of the opera does not lie in my taking in each rhythmic or melodic motif separately from the rest of the elements, any more than breathing in oxygen and hydrogen can quench my thirst. Rather, the beauty of the music hits me in its harmonious whole in the same way that my drinking of water, the compound H_2O, quenches my thirst.

Thus, my sensitivity to and perceptiveness of the world in its manifoldness is always a wholeness that consists of my current level of understanding of my world, and my moods about it. I call *situatedness* the convergence of personal, social, cultural, and historical factors on an individual at a given time in a given place. Because each individual is reared at a given period in a family that lives in a given community that occupies a certain territory in a certain nation, the individual's situatedness will be unique to herself and to her community in certain respects and common in others. If our developed ability to analyze and appreciate music enhances our understanding of musical creativity, it also by that very act influences not only our attunement to our world but also our responses to it. It is in this second area of attunement and response to our world that I wish to recall Mary's contribution: modeling a solicitude that fosters authentic existence.

---

[3] Alethiology is the science that deals with the nature of truth and evidence.

Professor Oyer went about her musical career on the premise that "the hymnody of a given people grows out of that group's mode of perceiving and responding to God and to the Good News of Jesus Christ."[4] To grasp her style of acting on this premise, we should note several points about the premise. First, it is founded on the gospel commission to Christian believers, "Go therefore and make disciples of all nations, baptizing them in the name of the Father, and of the Son and of the Holy Spirit" (Matt. 28:19). Clearly, this commission rejects the treatment of our fellow human beings instrumentally, as means to our ends. Second, it recognizes and appreciates the different situatedness of each person. This recognition and appreciation, too, rejects one individual using another instrumentally. Finally, it presumes that any given people's "mode of perceiving and responding" to the world in its manifoldness—to divinity ("God"), to information ("the Good News of Jesus Christ"), to creativity ("hymnody")—is discoverable, communicable, and describable. Taking the same posture, St. Paul asks rhetorically, "But how are they to call on one in whom they have not believed? And how are they to believe in one of whom they have never heard? And how are they to hear without someone to proclaim him?" (Rom. 10:14).

For the time she taught us at Kenyatta University, I never heard Professor Oyer mention the name of Jesus Christ or God either in class or out of it. Yet her everyday demeanor exuded a charismatic serenity that seemed to buoy her spirits above the vexations of everyday pettiness and to betray a connectedness with transcendence. Her presence in or entry into class purified from the lips of the usually jocular and boisterous students every trace of superficiality and vulgarity. Once during choir practice, she played Bach's "Jesu, Joy of Man's Desiring" on the piano while Anita Miller conducted the choir. The tender and soothing message from the keyboard touched our hearts. The fragmentary impressions of her everyday demeanor that had formed in my mind seemed to converge on her at this moment as she sat by the piano. After the choir practice I went straight to her and asked her if she was a product of Christian upbringing, and if so, in what denomination. She knew

---

[4] Ibid.

exactly why I was asking and, without disguising her affiliation with the Mennonite Church, tried to disabuse me of my subservience to denominations. In a nuanced way, she urged me to stay in whatever denomination I was in but at the same time to plug into and exploit my measure of endowments. "The kingdom of God is among you" (Luke 17:21). When I cast my mind about, I saw the truth of her exhortation: there are many acquaintances and friends who do not profess any religion at all but whose gracious goodness to others and to posterity is unmatched by anything that I know of in Christian circles.

Professor Oyer's keen awareness of the differential distribution of endowments, of the differential awareness of this fact, and of the differential actualization of the endowments has a counterpart: some social institutions could frustrate or stand in the way of one's right to actualize their measure of endowments. This is not to say that she advocated the destruction or rejection of institutions. Rather, with an awareness of the dialectical relationship between individuals and the institutions and societies to which they belong, she seemed to advocate taking stock of the possibilities and limitations inherent in one's institutions and society and then projecting personal possibilities into the future by actualizing one's own endowments. She therefore avoided letting her own voluntary institutional affiliations (such as her commitment to the church) come between herself and her students. She never wore her religion on her sleeve, as the popular phrase goes. Instead, she "set the believers an example in speech and conduct, in love, in faith, in purity" (1 Tim. 4:12).

Her students were not aware of their own ethnocentrisms. In fact, it is difficult to completely come out of one's cultural way of seeing and interpreting the world, but Mary consciously let students and locals bring out their own perceptions of the world. When some Western professors tried to collect and compile into books indigenous music from students, Mary was turned off. She made it known that the best way to go about such matters is to help students and locals write their own indigenous music. She seemed to believe, as I do, that what is wrong with ethnocentrism is not so much its one-sidedness as its attempt to promote its one-sidedness to the level of sole truth. This brings us to the third element in her approach to music, namely, people's modes of perceiving and responding to the world in its manifoldness (to God, nature, etc.).

Professor Oyer's solution to this problem is in line with the aims of existential phenomenology: try to see God from the perspective of those you intend to proselytize. There is greater power in well-lived principles than in mere preaching, disengaged from everyday life, as long as the principles privilege the well-being of every person. In a word, live out the truth you wish to preach, and do it so faithfully that those you wish to proselytize will seek it out of their own accord. Her entry point is hymnody,[5] mainly because it brings out a group's perceptions of and responses to divinity without the lenses of rationalization or justification. In the context of the gospel commission (what she refers to as "world mission"), hymnody breaks down the comfortable security of ethnic or national understandings and calls for reflection on how hymns convey meaning from one society to another.

The text and music of the hymnody, she says, can open the door to a group's cosmology, its attitudes toward time and space, life and death, the ancestors and the unborn, revealing the group's unique thought processes and its choice of themes that capture the meaning of the group's faith and corporate life.[6] If the text and music of their hymnody disclose this much about a people's meaning system, then they are symbols and therefore require a hermeneutic that presumes a correspondence between thought processes and musical organization, a correspondence that becomes communally distinct as one moves from one group's hymnody to another.

There surely must be such a correspondence, but whether it is the result of a discoverable socio-psychological mechanism is a complex matter, given the complexity of our being-in-the-world and the creative flexibility of the individual musician within a given community. Whatever the case, the musician becomes impressed by some aspect of his or her situatedness and transforms that impression into a musical rendering, a hymn, which communicates a message of existential import. Where do the musician's impressions come from? Mary does not address this question, because she is more interested in the forms and styles of the hymnody of

---

[5] Ibid.
[6] Ibid.

various groups. Because the musician's enactment of personal impressions in the hymn finds society-wide (or even worldwide) acceptance, the impressions and their origin must have widespread appeal and relevance. They are worth looking into.

Professor Oyer is a musically gifted and talented teacher. As a Christian who adheres to the gospel commission to spread the good news of Jesus Christ to the entire world, she has chosen to use music as gateway by which to understand a people's ways of perceiving and responding to divinity. To spread the gospel message, she prefers to live the truth rather than to talk about it. In this, she has been successful, because of her awareness of diversity and its inherent pitfalls and strengths. By this strategy of respecting the perspective and integrity of the other, she has reached and touched many music students, many of whom have achieved doctorates and are teaching in universities around the world. She has modeled a solicitude for authentic existence.

Chapter 11

AN EXCEPTIONAL COLLEAGUE
AND FRIEND

Luzili R. Mulindi-King

Mary Oyer and I met in Kenya almost twenty-five years ago, when I was teaching at Kenyatta University, near Nairobi, Kenya. I had been working on a Mozart operetta *(Bastien and Bastienne)* with my students, directing the singers from the piano during rehearsals. We anticipated that a Russian colleague would provide the piano accompaniment for the actual performance, although I had never heard her play. When we got close to the date of the performance, somehow she developed an injured finger that was heavily bandaged. Gradually it dawned on me that she had no intention of playing for this production. A desperate search for a substitute accompanist yielded Mary Oyer. She turned out to be not just a wonderful accompanist but much, much more.

It was not long before Mary joined the music department at Kenyatta University and got a taste of the inner workings of such institutions in the Africa of the 1980s. Musically, she was an immensely talented pianist, cellist, singer, and choral director. These musical abilities were matched by a great insight into all aspects of Western music. But what was totally unexpected was her knowledge and appreciation of African music. She not only had a vast knowledge of the music, she was conversant with and appreciated the principles behind its performance. There just aren't many people with this range of musical attributes. We were indeed privileged to have her in the department.

It happened that as soon as Mary joined Kenyatta University, she was hoisted into heading the department. And somehow she asked me to work with her as joint head. I sensed that it was

129

not her lack of expertise or experience in doing this kind of work but rather that she recognized that, having come into a new culture, she needed someone to work alongside her who was more at home in this culture. Her request was a sign of exceptional humility—something very few expatriates would have done at the time. The assumption was that anyone coming from Europe or America automatically knew better what was needed than any indigenous Kenyan did, and the notion that academic pursuit had anything to do with culture was a totally alien concept. As a result, most expatriates paid scant attention to what Kenyans had to say. Anyway, we worked together, and I think that her presence was one of the high points of that department.

The humility with which she approached heading the department was also evident in the way she treated the students. She respected them, and her cheerful disposition made her one of the most loved and accessible lecturers in the department. Consequently, she could impart great truths to the students without intimidating them. Her standards were exceptionally high, but she was much more than a mere lecturer or a performer. Her teaching methods were unique and ultimately inclusive, because she could approach a musical problem from a wide variety of angles.

Most students regarded her as a learned friend and considered it a tremendous privilege to have met her. Many visited her at the United Kenya Club in Nairobi to discuss their projects and research findings. Her interest in African music was especially significant, as few students would hitherto have met highly trained Western musicians who would have considered African music worthy of serious study.

Under her guidance, several outstanding musicians came to perform African music for the students, and Mary always held these visiting performers in high esteem. I recall the visit by Joseph Kizza from Uganda—quite a coup! We had not heard much authentic Ugandan music, in spite of having at least two lecturers of Ugandan origin on the staff. He taught several dances, including Baksimba, and led some dazzling xylophone (Amadinda) ensembles. He created a terrific buzz in the department, which encouraged more students and staff to consider studying African music at an advanced level. Mary's gift for appreciating a wide range of musical styles enabled us to collaborate on activities both within and outside the department. Certainly the department saw marked improvement in individual performances; meanwhile the university choir flourished.

At about this time the late Professor John Blacking was the visiting external examiner. He had researched the music of the Venda of South Africa, and his book *Venda Children's Songs* had already been published.[1] Another of his books, *How Musical Is Man?*[2] encapsulated some of his musical thinking, which in turn had been informed by his research in southern Africa. My encounter with Mary Oyer and John Blacking encouraged me to enroll for a course in social anthropology (ethnomusicology) at Queen's University of Belfast, where Professor Blacking was head of the department. I worked on the music of the Logoli, a subgroup of the Luhya people of western Kenya. My main interest was in how children acquire musical skills and the role of their music in Logoli culture.

It was just after I finished my course at Belfast in 1984 that Mary invited me to Goshen College to co-teach a course in African arts to a group of twenty-five students. About a third were of African descent, and the rest were mainly North American. It was an intensive course covering a wide range of disciplines, including literature, material art, music, language, and religions. Mary's knowledge of this field was astonishing, and her lectures were so fascinating and stimulating that although I had gone as a co-teacher, I came away saturated with more knowledge and enthusiasm than I could have thought possible. The students were encouraged to keep a journal of the course, and judging by what they wrote, the class was a life-changing experience for a significant number of them. They also produced outstanding written and practical work.

During my stay I was also able to watch Mary in a completely different context, leading Mennonite congregational hymn singing before worship on Sundays. Her sense of humor and musical talent coaxed out of that congregation such accomplished hymn singing

---

[1] John Blacking, *Venda Children's Songs: A Study in Ethnomusicological Analysis* (Johannesburg: Witwatersrand University Press, 1967; repr. Chicago: University of Chicago Press, 1995).

[2] John Blacking, *How Musical Is Man?* (Seattle: University of Washington Press, 1973).

as I had never heard before or since from a nonspecialist group of singers.

She maintained that her knowledge of the music of other cultures had enhanced her knowledge of her own music. This was an outlook that some other members of her department did not seem to share or accommodate; they appeared to support the theory that involvement in other music somehow compromised one's grasp on Western classical music. In this respect Mary stood apart as one who did not pursue performance for its own sake but as something that has the power to enhance the social and spiritual well-being of those who take part.

Although she aimed at high standards, other people's shortcomings did not inhibit her desire to share musical experiences with them, and everyone was allowed to give according to his or her ability. This approach accords with my understanding of musical performance in Africa, where everyone shares in performance regardless of ability, and those with exceptional talent take charge of the more challenging aspects of the music, such as singing the solo part, which requires a better than average memory, sense of pitch, tempo, and style, as well as the ability to improvise. If you are an excellent performer, everyone is happy, and if you are not so brilliant, everyone is happy provided you don't bite off more than you can chew.

The idea of performance calls for integrity when evaluating one's own and others' abilities to perform at all. This observation calls to mind an incident that occurred when I was doing a field recording with a group of pupils at Kapsambo School in Maragoli, Kenya. The session came to an abrupt end when the children rose to chase a boy across the field. They later explained that the boy in question was ruining the song. I took their explanation to mean that this child was not yet capable of executing the role he had elected to take on, and his chosen way of participating was having a detrimental effect on the performance as a whole. The incident was not dissimilar to that of the colleague who failed to play for our production of *Bastien and Bastienne*. But only Mary could solve this problem when later, as head of the department, she gave this colleague a private audition that proved conclusively that she was not a pianist! Mary's courage and tact was a great inspiration to all. In a way, she used the same principle as that used by the children to get at the truth. Thus she saved generations of students from receiving fake piano lessons from our colleague.

When we both returned to Kenya in the mid-1980s, we collaborated on a series of lectures for the annual "Know Kenya" course, organized by the Museum Society in Nairobi. We developed a style of delivery that focused on and fully engaged the audience. We delivered our lectures in the form of a conversation generated by a series of questions and answers. In this way we were able to juggle our knowledge of African and Western music and leave the audience feeling able to understand some of the instruments, sounds, and rhythms that they might encounter in Kenya. We did not read from a script, which meant that we maintained eye contact with the audience at all times. Although the delivery seemed easy and relaxed, we actually spent a fair amount of time in animated discussion to prepare the lecture, which we then condensed using a spider diagram. We always got the audience involved in performance, which ensured an animated presence. This lecture was one of the highlights of the "Know Kenya" course; it was so successful that it ultimately became the culminating event for that series. After Mary left Kenya, I carried on until I too left in 1991. Although the audience was always responsive and enthusiastic, I greatly missed Mary's input.

Mary's knowledge of many musical styles makes her a potential friend of people from all walks of life. For this reason her life in Kenya was perhaps more exciting and fulfilled than that of her compatriots who were not so adventurous in their musical tastes and, by extension, in their social interaction. She was once quoted as saying, "I am a class above or below them, I don't know which!"—a phrase that gradually became a favorite quotation with our family. Because she was at ease with a wide range of people, Mary could be found enjoying teaching with Justus Ndungu's family in the slums of Kawangware or with one of the well-to-do families in the leafy suburbs of Nairobi. I mention Justus here because he was a taxi driver and one of the most intelligent, wise, and knowledgeable people in Nairobi. She became one of his most loyal customers and a good friend of his family. What a way to get to know a country!

Our connection with Mary as a family friend gave us a privileged share of her company. We had an agreement that she should turn up at any time, with or without warning. We did not need to evacuate children's toys and other paraphernalia before she arrived, and she could eat whatever we had cooked that day. This informality made her one of the most welcome and enjoyable guests in our home. She took a lively interest in our two girls and would play for them on a quarter-size violin, sing, or tell them stories. When they got older, she sent them a tape and book of Sunday school songs for children. She was one of the instrumentalists accompanying the singers on the tape. Another prized possession was a beautifully illustrated African tale, *Mufaro's Beautiful Daughters.*[3] The story deals with a common theme in African stories and songs: physical beauty must always come second to beauty of character. Of the two beautiful daughters, Nyasha ends up marrying the king, because she had a kind and generous spirit, unlike her sister Manyara, who is unkind and self-centered.

Aside from her musical genius, what I value most about Mary is this beauty of her character and especially her sense of humor. It is a wonderful privilege to call her my friend. The same goes for my family, who arrived on the scene long after I met her. I used to think that Mary had been born on the wrong continent, that really she should have come out of Africa! Now I think differently: more people of her caliber should born in all places. Then more people will have a friend or colleague such as I have in Mary Oyer.

---

[3] *Mufaro's Beautiful Daughters: An African Tale,* illustrated by John Steptoe (New York: Lothrop, Lee & Shepard Books, 1987).

Chapter 12

Making Music with Mary in Nairobi

Julia Moss

Mary Oyer first came into our Nairobi musical world around 1979. She had been in Kenya for some time before that, but in mid-1979 she felt like joining forces with the musical fraternity in the city. Here she found a flourishing amateur symphony orchestra, Nairobi Orchestra, and an assortment of chamber music groups. For the next twenty years she was in and out of Kenya for a multitude of reasons, but she always included some music making in her plans. We locals viewed such visits as highlights in the calendar and arranged to use Mary's talents to the full while she was around. Not only did she play the cello well (we never had enough first-rate players), but her indomitable personality always raised our spirits. She was unfailingly friendly, cheerful, positive, enthusiastic, helpful, candid, musical, and questing.

So there she was for the first time in the ranks of Nairobi Orchestra on 28 October 1979 in Nairobi's National Theatre playing Brahms's Academic Festival Overture, Mozart's Piano Concerto in C Major, Schubert's Fifth Symphony, and Elgar's Pomp and Circumstance no. 1, under the baton of Nat Kofsky.

Thereafter, whenever she was Nairobi based for any length of time, she graced the cello section, often in the principal chair. Her influence was such that she was voted onto the committee in early 1986 and was rapidly promoted to chairperson later that year. During her "reign" she instigated a "Do It List," which tabulated the multifarious tasks that must be completed in the run-up to each concert, with a column indicating the name of the person designated for the task. This pro-forma is in use to the present day.

But of course, Mary's first love in classical music is chamber music, so with a handful of like-minded string players, domestic sessions flourished during the first half of the 1980s. The purpose of these get-togethers was to indulge in the sheer pleasure of making intimate music within that most balanced and blended of all groups, the string quartet. Mary insisted that it was preferable to play for our own satisfaction and not for public performance (performing always put special strains on the personalities in the ensemble). In fact, on the only occasion that a serious performance was mounted, a farewell concert for the ensemble's leader of the early days, James Fenton, differences of opinion arose to mar the serenity of the enterprise.

Mary was not averse to playing gigs where the casual atmosphere didn't exert much strain on the players. As long as the quality of music was good, the players congenial, and the meal that usually followed was up to standard, she didn't think it too degrading. And of course several of these concerts raised money for charity.

One evening in late 1980 we played at the Norfolk Hotel in Nairobi and received vouchers for dinner at a date of our choosing. Mary didn't want to use hers and urged us to take them up before the expiry date of 31 December of that year. On New Year's Eve we debated about whether to go out and celebrate on these vouchers but were too comfortable at home. That evening a terrorist bomb destroyed the Norfolk dining room, and because Someone was looking after us all, Mary was spared having our deaths on her conscience.

The last time we played together in public was in 1995 in Arusha, Tanzania, as a prelude to the annual Black and White Ball, an event on the calendar of the Safari company Abercrombie and Kent.

Chapter 13

A PROFESSOR WHO PERFORMS PASTORAL MINISTRY

Lu Chen-Tiong

Mary Oyer made a good impression when Dr. I-to Loh first introduced her to us. She was approachable, and she got so close to us that we grew accustomed to calling her "Mom." She is an authentic, humble, and patient teacher. She is well qualified and competent in many fields. Moreover, being her student for two years, I found that she is not just an ordinary academic teacher; she plays the role of pastor as well.

Respectful Teacher

Mom Oyer respects students who have different talents and abilities in the class. She is patient with those who have little knowledge of English, and she never turns down any student's work. Instead, she helps the students by giving them a second chance and offering her time to guide them. She reminded us to be ourselves, and that counsel helped us be aware of the fact that we are created in the image of God. Individually, we are unique and special, and each one of us had her or his role to contribute in the class.

Honoring Teacher

It is quite difficult for me, like many Asians, to honor other people's works. It is from Mom Oyer that I learned this important lesson, as Paul urges us to "outdo one another in showing honor" (Rom. 12:10). She always appreciated and complimented the good aspects of our work and performances, and only then did she give us comments on areas that could be improved. We were affirmed and encouraged to press on.

Caring Teacher

Mom Mary is a caring teacher. She cares for the students, not just for their academic achievement. She extends her care to the felt needs of the students. Students from other countries sometimes have financial needs, and she helps them by promoting their works. That is to say, she makes use of their music and gives them a certain amount of cash to help them buy books or other needs. In this way, she makes the students feel that the money is a reward for their own work and helps the students cultivate the habit of laboring for a reward. Her caring aids the students financially, and at the same time she nurtures the students' self-esteem and dignity.

Responsible Teacher

Mom Mary has been teaching for more than fifty years. However, she prepares her teaching lessons a week ahead. She surveys the venue and tests the equipment before classes. She is a very responsible teacher, and her spirit motivates me in my teaching and pastoral ministry to be a responsible person, to be prepared, and to keep up-to-date.

Learning Teacher

Mom Oyer's spirit of learning is unceasing. She is interested in Asian music and arts. She sat in on our class, "Seminar on Asian Music," and she studied with us. Later, she made a strong statement to me: "Music is not a universal language," as people from one culture might not understand the music of another culture, just as she does not understand much of the Asian musical languages.

Creative Teacher

Mom Oyer's creativity always inspires me. I learned from her creative choir teaching and vocalization as I translated for her during choir rehearsal. She knows exactly the style and character of the music that she teaches and that was educational to me. Her lovely singing voice and inspiring conducting gesture always kept the students in oneness, and they always looked forward to the next rehearsal.

In "Hymn Pedagogy" class, she gave me many insights and possibilities for teaching hymn singing and singing hymns creatively. The three-minute preparation to teach a hymn during the examination was a challenge to us. In church, too, the musician may be asked to teach the congregation a new song without being informed beforehand. The practice Mom Oyer gave us in class enables us to remain calm and respond promptly to unforeseen circumstances that may arise in a worship service.

The "Arts and Symbol in Christian Worship" class was fascinating. She took us to visit the Taipei Palace Museum. There we were asked to observe the Chinese artwork, including painting and ceramics, and make analysis of them. Our horizon of artwork appraisal was broadened in the visit. Her teaching was also practical and contextual. She encouraged us to create artworks and symbols that are related to our own culture and to integrate them in our worship.

We also learned to make a musical instrument from another culture: an African musical instrument called a mbira, in the class on African music. This was a fantastic experience that meant a lot to us: we made the instrument with our own hands and then learned to play it. We rejoiced and valued this great musical experience, and one of us even turned a mbira into a diatonic instrument!

Writing a journal after reading is another experience that we learned in her class. This helped us think and reflect, and it enabled us to remember for a longer period. Apart from the class work she assigned, she also exposed us to the practical field. She asked us to plan and lead worship and songs, and to conduct music at the end of the semester in relation to the subject she taught and in worship services.

Conclusion

Mary Oyer is a professor who teaches not just knowledge. She teaches through her life, a life that inspires others' lives, a life that speaks the glory of God. This role is a kind of pastoral ministry. Personally, I benefited not only from her teaching but also from being nurtured spiritually by her. She gave me many new insights, which are helpful in my present ministry. Praise God for bringing her to us. May the gracious God continue to bless her, use her, and speak through her.

Part 3

AH! BRIGHT WINGS
Selected Writings from the Life of Mary K. Oyer

God's Grandeur

The world is charged with the grandeur of God.
   It will flame out, like shining from the shook foil;
   it gathers to a greatness, like the ooze of oil
Crushed. Why do men then now not reck his rod?
Generations have trod, have trod, have trod;
   And all is seared with trade; bleared, smeared with toil;
   And wears man's smudge and shares man's smell; the soil
Is bare now, nor can foot feel, being shod.

And for all this, nature is never spent;
   There lives the dearest freshness deep down things;
And though the last lights off the black West went
   Oh, morning, at the brown brink eastward, spring—
Because the Holy Ghost over the bent
   World broods with warm breast and ah! bright wings.

Gerard Manley Hopkins, 1877

From *Poems of Gerard Manley Hopkins,* ed. Robert Bridges (London: Humphrey Milford, 1918).

Chapter 14

A Philosophy of the Use of Music in Mennonite Meetings

Mary K. Oyer

Mary Oyer spoke on "A Philosophy of the Use of Music in Mennonite Meetings" at the First Mennonite Musicians' Meeting (Chicago, March 1955). Mary was thirty-one and nearing the end of her doctoral studies. Her purpose was to outline a philosophy of music capable of building "a richer group approach to worship." In this and several other presentations Mary explored the nature of beauty and its theological significance. At heart, she argues, music making is rooted in love. Here she asks many questions intended to stimulate discussion among the musicians about the philosophical ideas of beauty, truth, and love, as they relate to Mennonite music practices in worship.

The topic suggests investigation in two directions: what practices have we inherited from the past that might constitute a philosophy, and what should be the nature of our developing philosophy?

I. What practices have we inherited from the past that might constitute a philosophy?

A. Introduction

The Mennonite Church has maintained a tradition of singing since its infancy. Worship for the Anabaptists included songs with texts recalling the martyrdom of their members

---

[We have elected to print this piece in essentially unaltered form, retaining features that date it, including masculine language for humanity and quotations from the Revised Standard Version of the Bible.—Eds.]

and with music taken from the folk music and chorales of their time. The generations since the sixteenth century have carried on the tradition of singing, suiting the type of music they used to the temper of the times.

The present music situation in Mennonite meetings is perhaps not so much a philosophy that has grown out of a creative search into a uniquely Mennonite approach to music, as a set of practices that the group as a whole has learned to appreciate. They are traditions that our church has found useful and helpful and usually worth defending.

B. Specific practices

1. Congregational singing

At the time of Luther's break with the Roman church, sacred music had reached a high level of beauty and refinement. It was too difficult, however, for the layman to sing; performance was left to choirs. Luther held a strong conviction that the congregation should participate actively. In his effort to provide music suitable for the entire group, he created the Protestant chorale, a simple, straightforward type of hymn. Whether or not the Anabaptists accepted congregational singing through direct knowledge of Luther's position we do not know. However, they held firmly to this wholesome principle until the present time, and this remains the foremost characteristic of our music.

2. "Special music"

Practices differ on the use of "special music" and perhaps the justification for its existence is less clear-cut than that of congregational singing. Some congregations and church leaders develop church choruses to encourage better congregational singing. Quartets and choruses are asked to sing sometimes to create variety in the service, though we rarely plan consciously a sequence of worship experiences—a liturgy—that has sound aesthetic value. Undoubtedly some groups exist simply because they enjoy singing and they welcome social relationships within their congregations. "Special" groups generally sing the type of music that the congregation could, and possibly should, do themselves. However, some choruses are investigating the possibilities of longer and more difficult works that are beyond the performance level of the congregation.

3. Absence of musical instruments

The pattern in our branch of the Mennonite church is that of a cappella singing; instruments are not admitted. Our reasons for maintaining this position vary. Some members feel strongly that there is scriptural evidence condemning instruments. Others feel that it is expedient to keep the a cappella tradition because it demands active participation from the congregation rather than dependence on an instrument. Still others recommend the use of instruments for certain situations—for the performance of "special music" that may require an accompaniment or for use in mission stations or in very small congregations where a cappella singing may not be practical or helpful.

C. The need for reexamining our position and developing a philosophy

These three principles form the basis for our present practice. However, we are living at a dynamic time in the history of our church. We are interested more and more in examining and challenging our traditional practices on many issues rather than accepting them without question. In recent years we have been forced to clarify our thinking on the problems of the Christian's position in society—particularly in the area of peace. Some leaders in our group are formulating a more concise theology. The very existence of this conference on music, which includes a few topics suggesting a philosophic approach, shows this trend at work in the field of the arts. Perhaps we are ready to reexamine our practices in music to see if they express our faith as effectively as we would wish. Perhaps the time is ripe for us to share our personal philosophy of music with one another in order to build a richer group approach to worship.

The increase in music education in our church forces us to look at our practices in a new way. The number of college graduates majoring in music is increasing rapidly. A rather large percentage of these Mennonites have taken or are taking graduate work toward master's and doctor's degrees. The level of music performance is rising; we have singers and instrumentalists who are no longer amateurs. Most of these people want to remain in the church and contribute actively to its music program, but they will have difficulty finding a sympathetic place in our brotherhood unless we are constantly open to reevaluating our purposes. What are we saying, beyond the words, in congregational singing? Is there anything beyond the words? What are "spiritual songs?" What can we offer the instrumentalists among us? Have we biblical directions for the character of worship? What did Christ say?

II. What should be the nature of our developing philosophy?

I would like to suggest areas in which, because of our present church development, we will be forced to work out a philosophy—to clarify our reasons for using the arts as a part of our worship. I will present these questions under two headings: can beauty be a part of Mennonite worship, and can the Christian express Christian truth through music?

A. Can beauty be a part of Mennonite worship?

1. Philosophic aspect

a. The nature of the aesthetic element in worship

Is there a vital place for the aesthetic emotion in the Christian life? Our use of hymns in the worship service is primarily verbal; we wish to concentrate on the concepts—on the meaning of the words. How often we are encouraged by the leader of a meeting to think of the words, because the meaning of the song lies there; but there exists a whole world beyond that of words. Words form only one of our varied means of communication and expression. Beauty also has meaning. It is true that many hymns lack beauty in either words or music, and the most significant meaning resides in the concepts, but for the good works—the hymns that at least approach the level of art—beauty becomes a prominent factor.

The poem "Jesus Thou Joy of Loving Hearts," by Bernard of Clairvaux, for example, is so full of imagery that it evokes an emotional response of which ordinary prose is hardly capable.

> We taste Thee, O Thou Living Bread,
> And long to feast upon Thee still;
> We drink of Thee, the Fountain Head....

This stanza in a concentrated way expresses ideas that are far from factual—closer to ecstatic. It functions to make one man's intimate experience available to others. Although the poem was undoubtedly better in its original language, the very sound of the words contributes further to beauty. They ebb and flow in rhythmic patterns. Their arrangement in a balancing rhyme scheme gives the whole poem dignity and a sense of fulfillment, which are emotional meanings. The words are there as symbols of concepts, but they are shaped to create beauty of form, also.

Music apart from words contains meaning, too. The beauty of the pure music of the Passion Chorale [HERZLICH TUT MICH VERLANGEN] has a great deal to do with the content of the hymn, The contour of its melody is arranged in balancing patterns: the first and third phrases begin low and are balanced by the higher second and fourth phrases, with the feeling of question and answer:

$$\overset{\frown}{1^{st} \& 3^{rd}} \quad \overset{\frown}{2^{nd} \& 4^{th}}$$

The last half of the hymn reverses the process, creating the effect of one large upward sweep, which is balanced and completed by its falling complement:

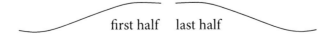

first half   last half

The harmony is so tastefully arranged that all the chords create tension until they come to rest at the cadence of each phrase, producing a continuous ebb and flow in the piece. Each of the four voice parts has melodic beauty—always shifting in an unexpected way—sometimes moving with another part, sometimes against. It is an imaginative piece of music—always moving rather than static, always full of sensitive change.

In order to communicate a point to you, I have attempted to define a few of the beautiful aspects of a hymn text and a chorale. An artwork may lose some of its freshness when it is translated in this way into words of explanation. A work of art speaks best to us directly through its particular medium—as long as we remain open to the possibilities of beauty. John Keats described vividly a specific aesthetic experience that came to him when he first read a translation of Homer by Chapman:

> Then felt I like some watcher of the skies
> When a new planet swims into his ken.

Should Christians not know the experience of seeing "new planets swim into their ken," of being swept away by the beauty of a religious expression? We seem traditionally to fear such an approach. The question that I hear most frequently when I talk of art and faith in my classes is this, "Are you not afraid that the aesthetic emotion will be mistaken for worship?" My answer is, "No, not if we belong to Christ." All things are ours when we are his. Christ was consistently silent on specific means of worship. He gave the basic principle that we must worship God in spirit and in truth, but not the specific means. Can we learn anything from his acceptance of the worship of the woman who anointed his feet with precious ointment? Our problem is to live as creatively as we can—to find among the infinite possibilities for worship as many as we can comprehend.

We dare not pinch ourselves into tight molds that make us afraid to learn what possibilities God has created for us. We must have the spiritual freedom to explore and discover and mature continually. The experience of beauty has rich potentialities for enhancing our worship.

b. Beauty of nature a gift of God to fulfill man's need

Beauty is a part of God's plan for us. He created us with an aesthetic need—a need that craves satisfaction through beauty. It is not as obvious a need as our physical wants—we die when we lack food—but it exists nevertheless. The second chapter of Genesis hints at one provision that he made to fulfill that need: "And out of the ground made the LORD God to grow every tree that is pleasant to the sight, and good for food."

We usually ignore the "pleasant to the sight" clause as useless, but it is there. God might have supplied our physical needs through a nature that was uniform and monotonous, but our world is incredibly varied and beautiful. Every tree, even within one genus, is different. No two leaves, even on the same tree, are alike. Every snowflake has its own individual pattern—never recurring in another. No sky is ever static: always there is some subtle nuance in its color or its clouds. God did not have to create such beauty to supply our physical needs. His love and his desire for our pleasure are its only excuse. We misunderstand an important aspect of the very nature of God, that is, the expression of his character and love through beauty, when we do not accept beauty as valid. Furthermore, we are created in his image. If we choose to be ascetic, we negate an important part of our nature—a part that functions in a spiritual way and confirms the presence of God within us. Our lives would be infinitely richer if we were to accept nature as an expression of love rather than an impractical or peripheral area of experience.

c. Art a reflection of God's creative love

I submit to you the concept that the finest works of art spring from this same motivation. They are expressions of love. They are weak and human, and yet they reflect the truth that their creators were made in the image of God. Gerard Manley Hopkins wrote a sonnet to a bird, "The Windhover." The poem makes no mention of Christ at all; it simply describes the beauty of the bird and of nature. But it has a remarkable subtitle, "To Christ our Lord." I puzzled over the relevance of this dedication for years before it made any sort of sense to me. That was before it occurred to me that, whenever I play a great piece of music on the cello—Bach, Beethoven—its inevitable subtitle must be "To Christ our Lord," or perhaps "To the Glory of God." Should not the Christian church welcome into its service the works that are directly inspired by the love of God as well as those that exist on a spiritual level compatible with Christian experience?

d. Spiritual nonconformity in the arts

I would like to suggest further that, in our selection of works of art for our services, we practice spiritual non-conformity—that we learn to recognize the difference between surface beauty and spiritual, or non-material, beauty. A few examples from visual art may help us. Alan Gowans, in reviewing a book of religious paintings in the *Christian Century*, makes these generalizations:

> A Christian artist cannot treat the supernatural spiritual world as if it were unimportant or non-existent.... An art which is "photographic" to the extent that it represents the world entirely in terms of material laws, depicting only the external aspects of things—light shadow, three-dimensional form, perspective space, and so forth—is unChristian, no matter whether it deals with "Christian" subject matter or not. Such an art cannot avoid giv-

ing a presentation of Christianity distorted and biased on the materialistic side.

We have come to accept Leonardo da Vinci as a Christian painter. His *Last Supper* sells well among us. But Leonardo's subject is only incidental to his surface beauty. He is much more concerned with showing depth in space than with interpreting the meaning of the scene. He loved to paint people in delicate half-shadows so that their gracefulness would be emphasized. Herein is much beauty. However, he was a skeptic and had no particularly spiritual concern for his subject. Christians may read their own meaning into the work; they may certainly enjoy its artistic worth; but Leonardo did not intend to express profound Christian truth—perhaps not even spiritual truth.

Rembrandt, on the other hand, rejected the world of surfaces and painted with a deeper reality. In his *Jeremiah* he caught the pensiveness and depression of Jeremiah by focusing the small amount of light he used on the posture and gesture of the prophet. Rather than emphasizing glamorous details, which appear here in deep shadow, he encourages us to reflect on the spiritual significance of Jeremiah. Even his portraits, which are not directly Christian—such as *The Old Man with Red Hat*—show little sensuous beauty of color; contours of the figure are swallowed in deep shadow. But he makes clear that the physical world is not the only fact that man can know. The spiritual world is inviting and overpowering.

Rouault's figure of Christ has a surface ugliness, at least on first sight; but he too cared less for surface beauty than for spiritual reality. He says, "I do not believe in what I touch or what I see. I believe only in what I cannot see and what I sense." With the color and black outlines of medieval stained glass he paints so intensely that he compels the perceiver to consider the work. With bold simplicity he paints a humble and submissive Christ and suggests the brutality and horror of sin. This is a painter whose chief ambition is to paint a picture of Christ so moving that those who see it are compelled to believe in him.

In the medium of music these opposite poles exist, too, but they are probably harder to crystallize. The words do not form the ultimate spiritual reality of a work (though they certainly have a contribution to make; one should use words that he believes—that express his faith—for worship). The words combine with poetic sound and form and with the meaning of the music to create either a work that has beauty and integrity or one that is haphazard and trite. Can we recognize the spiritual reality in our musical expressions?

May I use the hymn "O Happy Day" as an illustration? The basic concept of joy through rebirth and baptism is good, and this hymn has had rich meaning for a number of people. However, I suggest that its value comes from the experience that the believer reads into the hymn rather than from the hymn itself. The text is mediocre, lacking in imaginative suggestion. The music is far more empty. The rhythm pattern ♩ ♩ ♩ ♩. is repeated sixteen times in one verse; after five verses the chief subject of the song becomes monotonous rhythm. The melody is repetitious, the harmony unvaried, the form too obvious to be challenging. Only music devoid of spiritual overtones would be used by the secular world for a drunkard's song. The music is really more suitable in the secular setting. The Passion Chorale could not be abused and degenerated in this way because it is inherently spiritual.

2. Practical implications

If we are to embrace beauty within our worship, certain questions inevitably arise as we reconsider our present traditions.

a. Congregational singing

What should we sing? Is there virtue in simplicity of music? Are we keeping up with the level of the music appreciation of the congregation with the songs we use? What is our responsibility to the growing number of laymen who can grasp and appreciate chamber music, symphonies? For whose taste do we plan—the simplest possible or the more complex? The teacher must face the same problem. He will have both A and F students and all kinds in between. Is it his responsibility to teach the F student first of all? the A? How do we make clear to the congregation that beauty is a part of God's nature and man's need? How can we encourage one another to worship more fully in the best way each person can find? How do we recognize spiritual values in art? Are we justified in using poetry and music in our worship without examining their methods of communication?

b. "Special music"

Is it right that a "special" group should sing the same music that the congregation could, and probably should, sing? What is the responsibility of college choruses when they come to sing for congregations? What should the church expect of them? What is the responsibility, the privilege of a church chorus? Is there not a place for presenting new and fresh works too difficult for congregational performance? What should be our plan for the education of tastes? Must we believe that highly specialized art should be questioned and folk art embraced? Dare we believe that corporate and functional art has more significance for the Christian than individual expression?

c. Absence of musical instruments

How important is the medium? Does four-part unaccompanied singing have spiritual meaning in itself? It is a wholesome medium which makes active demands on the congregation and has fine possibilities. However, is it the medium itself that is significant? Is there virtue in preserving a unique medium? I personally do not want to see us lose a singing emphasis. The problem of education of tastes for organ (or piano) music would be extremely difficult, and for us our medium is rich and worthwhile. But I seriously question our maintaining so rigid an attitude toward instruments that we are unable to perform some of the greatest music. *The Messiah,* for example, was never meant to be sung without accompaniment or with a piano. The instruments are as important as the voice parts in creating the whole work as Handel conceived it. Some of the works most compatible with Mennonite piety are unavailable to us because they are accompanied. For example, Bach has written over two hundred cantatas of the most profound devotional character in which the instruments are an integral part of the whole.

What is our attitude toward those who play musical instruments? Do we recognize that they have a contribution to make to our music program, or are we afraid that they will destroy our traditions? I am convinced that the instrumentalists have a good deal to teach us about the expressive element, because they deal continually with pure sound apart from words. They are forced to recognize expression of a musical sort. Do we want them to help us? Do we really believe what Paul tells us about the nature of the church in 1 Corinthians 12—that it is made up of differing members with varying contributions? Do our instrumentalists feel that they are on the fringe of acceptable Mennonite activity? Is our vision broad enough to accept the concept of a "call" to the instrumental field? Do we use the people who are musically trained in the most creative way we could?

B. Can the Christian express Christian truth through music?

1. Re-creative nature of music

Music is a re-creative art. The composer tries to capture his musical ideas in notes in order to communicate them to anyone else; but no matter how accurate his notation, he is finally at the mercy of a performer who translates his notation into live sound. The performer will try to understand the composer's intention, but he cannot escape from a kind of creative and independent process somewhat similar to that of the composer: he must have a grasp of the total work and put it together logically and feelingfully, much as the composer does originally.

2. Possibility of performing more than technique and notes

We are concerned here with the performer's expressive possibilities. Can he be totally objective and reveal only the notes of the composer without expressing his own convictions? What can he communicate? We usually limit the answer to words, but there is much more. Words in speech have varied meanings dependent on the particular inflection, the intention of the speaker, his spirit. With music, too, there are many sources for the meaning, dependent on the performer. One can sing profound words but miss completely their significance. One can convey boredom, criticism, or hatred with perfectly wholesome words. Whether we realize or not, we are expressing a good deal of our philosophy of life, of our faith, whenever we perform music in any medium. Performance is a mirror of our life—of our belief.

I was jolted into realizing this when I first studied cello in graduate school. My teacher told me early in my study that he could tell from my playing that I was a Christian. In a kindly way, he suggested that if I wanted to be a musician I should probably give up Christianity because it was too limited and unimaginative. Unfortunately, he had encountered only unimaginative and repressed Christians. But I, too, was unimaginative and limited. I had grown up not knowing that music aside from words communicates a great deal. I had never imagined that playing had anything to do with faith.

I have learned more about communication from two other persons. One is a warm-hearted minister, who convinces me, no matter what his sermon topic, that he understands forgiveness—that he forgives. It is not the words he says but his spirit that convinces me. The other is the most remarkable song leader I know. He so identifies himself with the congregation in a loving way that the group is transformed into one body. His technique is fine, but his spirit exerts an even stronger influence.

So it is in music: each time we perform, we say something besides technique or notes. In this rather intangible area lies music's greatest spiritual reality.

3. *The unique expressive possibilities for the Christian musician*

a. *Individual expression*

The problem of the Christian musician is to discover the unique expressive possibilities for Christians. What do Christians have to say in performance that only they can say profoundly? The answer to this depends on the answer to another question. What are the unique experiences of Christianity? I suggest that above all, Christians know love in a remarkable way. Christ gives love as the first commandment for moral action—as the basic principle in Christianity. Love should be the overpowering motivating force in Christian performance. Paul makes this clear in 1 Corinthians 13:[1]

> Love knows no limit to its endurance, no end to its trust, no fading of its hope: it can outlast anything. It is, in fact, the one thing that still stands when all else has fallen.

> For if there are prophecies they will be fulfilled and done with, if there are "tongues" the need for them will disappear, if there is knowledge it will be swallowed up in truth.

The relevance of this passage to the Christian musician is unmistakable. Knowledge and technique—which are so important for any performance—will be unnecessary at the end of time; the need for them

---

[1] Quoted from J. B. Phillips, *Letters to Young Churches: A Translation of the New Testament Epistles* (London: G. Bles, 1947).

will disappear. Our struggle to attain them is a sign of our humanity and imperfection. Only love has eternal value. Love can and must be the undercurrent of any performance with Christian significance.

b. *Group expression*

In any performance involving a group of people, there is an unusual possibility for the expression of the fruits of the Spirit. Singing or playing together can bring out the worst in people. I have sung and played with groups where there was a good deal of hatred expressed, simply because in a group situation involving the creation of beauty, relationships are touchy. Occasionally, I have had choruses who sang the right notes at the right time—who reached a fairly high level of polish and refinement, yet who hated, who were hyper-critical and uncharitable, in small details of living together as well as large. I am sure that such groups could say nothing profound and spiritual, regardless of the words they sang. But a chorus experience can also bring out the finest in people; they can learn to forgive in a remarkable group way. I have had other choruses who recognized the sensitive group situation of intimate working together and who were willing to work creatively to produce a Christian result.

4. Summary of principles for Christian performance

Ultimately a chorus or any "special music" group must recognize and cope with the following two principles in order to create a spiritual end:

a. *Differing personalities each have a place*

A chorus is composed of all kinds of personalities and many degrees of musical understanding and technical proficiency. This is the situation of the church—the body of Christ, as Paul describes it in 1 Corinthians 12. Its members are as varied as the organs of the human body, but each is as important, too. Each member must be accepted with his peculiar contribution and all reckoned equally indispensable in fulfilling their roles. The miraculous element of Christian group activity is that Christ joins into one body widely differing individuals. Inasmuch as they maintain their individuality but give themselves they contribute to a unified whole.

b. Love is the uniting principle

In practical terms love means forgiving one another and praying for one another. May I read you a paraphrase of 1 Corinthians 13 that we have used as an interpretation of the principle of love in my chorus at Goshen College:

> Though we sing with the voices of the Shaw Chorale or even of a choir of angels, but have not love, we are become as robots or a lifeless machine. And though we should have the gift of artistic insight and understand the musical heritage of man as well as God's laws of order and design, and though we should have such faith that we could overcome any technical problem, but have not love, we are nothing. And though we dedicate all our Sundays to program performance, and though we waste away in our zealous effort to promote the music of the church, but have not love, it profits us nothing.
>
> Love endures tedious practices patiently and is constructive; love accepts its own limitations gratefully; love is neither anxious to impress nor does it cherish inflated ideas of its own importance.
>
> Love is courteous, and sensitive to the needs of the group above its own; it is not easily annoyed nor is it prone to concentrate on the weaknesses of others. It finds such joy in that which is true and right and beautiful that by its very attitude the haphazard and dishonest are outlawed.
>
> Love knows no limit to its endurance, no end to its trust, no fading of its hope: it can outlast

anything. It is, in fact, the one thing that still stands when all else has fallen.[2]

A Christian chorus is a laboratory or workshop where we have the privilege of working out the practical problems of getting along with one another. The experience of expressing Christian love and fellowship along with beauty is so rich that the latter alone seems pale by comparison. The expression of beauty and of Christian truth are each valid alone; when they are combined, they create a powerful expression. Could not a church chorus be a cell of active love that makes love and fellowship so clear to the congregation that their example becomes contagious for other types of groups? In the final analysis, what people are and believe most firmly is what they express through music. The greatest reality of a performance lies here rather than in surface expression and values.

For the entire congregation, love should be the motivating force for singing. Singing is expressing. Spiritually it means unmasking ourselves, accepting and embracing one another in a common fellowship. Every song could be an expression of communion—of remembering Christ and his commandment that we share with one another. Each song could be the humbling experience of washing one another's feet.

Can beauty be a part of Mennonite worship? Can the Christian express Christian truth through music? As we grow in our understanding of the relevance of love for the Christian musician, these things are possible, in fact, imperative.

---

[2] Ibid.

Chapter 15

A CHRISTIAN VIEW OF THE FINE ARTS

Mary K. Oyer

> *In "A Christian View of the Fine Arts," presented at the Eleventh Conference on Mennonite Educational and Cultural Problems in 1957, Mary Oyer explores the questions that shaped—or perhaps haunted—her doctoral work, and she lays out her thinking on faith and the arts as it had developed over the course of several years. She blends theological and philosophical perspectives to shape a respectable apologetic and concludes with reflections on the vocation of the Mennonite artist. Love appears again here as a reason to create art.*

Introduction

A broad definition of art includes man's skillful and tasteful participation in almost any human activity. If the term is narrowed to the so-called fine arts, only those areas emerge that are set apart from a practical function. Music, poetry, painting, sculpture are isolated from other human activity by their insistence on the quality of beauty and their relative disregard for the ordinary level of existence. Artistic values are their raison d'être and not merely by-products of an otherwise acceptable activity.

["A Christian View of the Fine Arts" is reprinted from *Proceedings of the Eleventh Conference on Mennonite Educational and Cultural Problems,* Bethel College, North Newton, KS, 6–7 June 1957 (N.P.: Council of Mennonite and Affiliated Colleges, 1957). Council of Mennonite Colleges (1956–1967) Collection, Mennonite Church USA Archives–Goshen, 1700 S. Main St. Goshen, IN 46526. Used by permission. We have elected to include this piece in essentially unaltered form, retaining features that date it, including masculine language and quotations from the Revised Standard Version of the Bible.—Eds.]

For centuries Christians have questioned the validity of the arts (the term will be used in its more restricted sense throughout this paper). Art has often been associated with the "world" of the New Testament or with pagan cultures. Christians observe that Christ never discussed the arts; his mention of the transitory character of the temple appears negative: "As for these things which you see, the days will come when there shall not be left here one stone upon another that will not be thrown down." John cautions the Christian disciple in similar terms: "Do not love the world or the things in the world.... All that is in the world, the lust of the flesh, and the lust of the eyes and the pride of life, is not of the Father but is of the world. And the world passes away."[1]

But the basic problem does not stem from explicit New Testament statements about art; rather, it seems to lie in the existence of a tension between Christ and any aspect of culture. On the one hand, the Christian is placed under the Lordship of Christ; on the other, he finds himself bound to a temporal world and a cultural framework which demand of him certain types of commitment and submission. For some Christians the demands of the spiritual and temporal worlds present an almost irreconcilable opposition, and life consists of a continuous struggle to resolve the tension. Mennonites traditionally have recognized the opposition and have often chosen to isolate themselves as much as they can from prevailing cultural practices in order to escape compromise and to maintain the life of the group. Thus, with few exceptions, the arts—along with politics and a few other fields—have remained outside of the center of Mennonite culture.

Tension arises perhaps most severely between Christ's soteriological plan and art's peculiar character. Christ's teachings point toward the redemption of man; Christians are commissioned to make disciples of the world. Art cannot redeem; at best it only prepares man to see himself in the light of his destiny. Therefore some Christians maintain that the realm of the arts is peripheral to the Christian life and cannot be considered a legitimate vocational field. Although this view often is not articulated consciously

---

[1] 1 John 2:15-17.

among Mennonites, the attitude of suspicion of the values of art predominates over a positive view of acceptance.

It is the purpose of this paper to present bases for the Christian's acceptance of the arts and to point out a few of the implications of such acceptance in Mennonite higher education.

It will be necessary first, however, to make more precise the boundaries of the word *art.* Certain similarities among the various media make possible grouping the arts together. In addition to their concern with beauty and organizational relationships, the arts are alike in functioning non-discursively. Susanne Langer points out that they lie "within the verbally inaccessible field of vital experience and qualitative thought";[2] much of their significance lies in their power to present insights inexpressible through language. They are as direct as possible as they stand; they do not become clearer through translation into another medium nor through verbal interpretation.

Yet the peculiar characteristics of each medium demand individual treatment for each art form. Although the ultimate significance of poetry is non-discursive, its material—language—is discursive. It is capable of specific subject, of complicated ideas, of extensive thought. Its meaning resides in the union of discursive and non-discursive elements. Painting and sculpture generally use nature as their point of departure. They, too, have subject, though their deeper content is something quite different. At any rate, their meaning stems from the combination of representational and intuitional factors. This paper will lean toward the abstract arts —instrumental music and non-objective painting and sculpture—in part to limit the scope of an otherwise far too extensive subject, in part to exclude moral problems that arise out of subject rather than aesthetic content, and finally to stay closer to the bias and training of the writer.

Bases for the Christian's Acceptance of the Arts

1. Art, as an aspect of culture, is the privilege and responsibility of man. Since the creation of the world, man has been compelled to relate himself satisfactorily to his natural environment and to

---

[2] Susanne K. Langer, *Philosophy in a New Key: A Study in the Symbolism of Reason, Rite, and Art* (New York: Mentor, 1948), 210.

other men. He has continually explored the world and attempted to overcome its destructive features. He has constantly sought to refine and conserve values that he has inherited or discovered. He has molded temporal and material means of every sort to create culture.

Culture in turn places certain claims on man. He cannot isolate himself completely from the heritage that he knows, from the institutions that have risen to enrich his existence. He must make some sort of response. Christ also lays claims on man's loyalties. He appears to ask man to leave family and work, to view cultural achievements lightly, to live with the future world as the truest reality, in order to become his disciple.

H. Richard Niebuhr, in *Christ and Culture*,[3] points out five characteristic responses to the apparent conflict between opposing claims. At one extreme lies the rejection of culture in clear cut either-or form. Tertullian preached separation from the culture of the world in the second century. The medieval monk isolated himself from the prevailing culture by setting up a distinct and differing plan. Niebuhr considers the Mennonites the purest example of this strain in the present world. The opposing extreme accepts Christ and culture as standing in complete agreement; Christ is the hero and fulfillment of culture.

Three intermediate views recognize the tension but suggest resolutions. Thomas Aquinas believed that Christ participates in and fulfills cultural aspirations and yet lives above it—transcends the earth-bound limits of culture. Luther taught a dual approach, accepting the authority of both Christ and culture. Existence on earth always involves subjection to both moralities; resolution and justification come only beyond history. The final view acknowledges Christ's power to convert culture. Augustine and Calvin taught that God continues to work creatively and redemptively in the present. Man finds God within society, not apart from it; he must accept culture as a value that can perpetuate God's work.

Niebuhr's five characteristic responses to the problem could be multiplied by innumerable variations and nuances of meaning.

---

[3] H. Richard Niebuhr, *Christ and Culture* (New York: Harper Brothers, 1951); views summarized on 40–43.

Each finds at least some support in the Bible. Differences arise out
of disagreements in epistemology and theology.

The problem involved in the Christian's acceptance of the arts
is basically this larger issue of his attitude toward culture. If the
arts are to be pursued fully and creatively, it is essential that the
Christian assume a positive attitude toward culture. He must accept responsibility for its perpetuation and for the quality of its
direction. He will consider his capacity to understand, to make
discoveries, to grasp relationships, a gift of God, the natural expression of which is cultural activity. Through culture he will be
fulfilling God's commission to have dominion over the earth and
subdue it. Leon Wencelius explains that "Culture is ... the accomplishment of the creative will of God. It is the way in which man
has been called to achieve his dominion on the earth and to re-
plenish it. As man had to plough the ground in order to receive its
fruits, man has to plough his mind in order to give birth to Art,
Science, Philosophy, which are the fruits of his culture."[4]

The Christian will observe also that, although many of Christ's
statements taken in isolation are uncompromisingly anti-cultural,
yet his incarnation is an affirmation of cultural values. His message was spiritual, and yet Jewish culture was its frame of reference. He did not attempt to reform Jewish cultural life; yet he built
his message with Jewish language and symbolism. The symbol of
the lamb, for example, became a profound and meaningful reality
when the Lamb of God died. He made no attempt to replace Jewish symbols with his own; he intensified and fulfilled rather than
destroyed his cultural heritage. He gave no pertinent rules to the
artist for artistic morality, but he spoke with artistic integrity in the
colorful language of the parable.

Two corollaries accompany the premise that the Christian
should positively perpetuate culture as a responsibility ordained
by God. In the first place, he embraces the commission in the context of sin and redemption. He recognizes the presence of tension
between Christ and culture but realizes that the tension is created

---

[4] Leon Wencelius, "The Word of God and Culture," in *The Word of God and the Reformed
Faith*: Addresses Delivered at the Second American Calvinistic Conference, Held at Calvin
College and Seminary, Grand Rapids, Michigan, June 3, 4, and 5, 1942 (Grand Rapids:
Baker's Book Store, 1943), 161–62.

by sin. Man may view culture as the final cause of existence and separate himself from God, or he may turn it toward ends that violate the will of God. Culture belongs exclusively to the realm of human achievement; and, because man is a sinner, culture is inevitably imperfect. It is redemption that reconciles. The Catholic philosopher Jacques Maritain explains it in this way for the arts: "Is not art pagan by birth and tied to sin—even as man is born a sinner? But grace heals the wounds of nature."[5]

Redemption heals and reconciles because it enables the Christian to see the wholeness of life, even though through a dark glass. It makes him view any aspect of culture in the perspective of truth as Christ reveals it. If all else is equal, the Christian can produce an artwork of truer reality than the non-Christian. The nonbeliever will reveal glimpses of truth, but in fragmentary form.

The Christian with a positive approach to culture will be a kind of Christian humanist. He will value man's achievements because he recognizes the dignity of reborn man. He will welcome the artist's serious statement because he is thoroughly aware of the possibility of redemption for any and all men. He will explore the whole range of human experience as it is expressed in culture and specifically in the arts. His approach will not be dilettante but a sympathetic sharing in the family of man.

The second corollary insists that the Christian accept the autonomy of each distinct area of culture. The ultimate end of all man's activity and creation is the glory of God. The arts, if seriously treated, present a kind of homage and praise. The *Soli Deo Sit Gloria* appearing at the end of most manuscripts of Bach's music, and Gerard Manley Hopkins's "To Christ Our Lord"—which forms a subtitle for his poem "The Windhover"—consciously articulate this possibility.

However, each discipline operates under its own laws of rightness, which are determined by the nature of each discipline. Music, for example, belonged to the Quadrivium during the Middle Ages because it was basically number. Its numerical relationships were far more significant than its sound. With the increasing differentiation of areas that came with the Renaissance, music broke away

---

[5] Jacques Maritain, *Art and Scholasticism* (New York: Scribner's Sons, 1930), 53.

to the realm of aesthetics. In the twentieth century it is impossible to lump mathematics and music together; each has its own material, methods, and cultural ends.

The most serious violation of autonomy occurs when an artist tries to justify his artistic end by a forced relationship to the ultimate cause, that is, the glory of God. He may sacrifice artistic principles in order to articulate some Christian doctrine. This is the sickness that pervades most of the art Christians accept as sacred. The artist may even try to impose subject or representation on an abstract art medium in order to vindicate himself morally. A composer, for example, may resort to a whole series of clichés of organ church literature in order that the listener associate a "religious" mood with his music. Such manipulation is immoral. God created the laws for each discipline in the sense that they are inherent within each medium. Thus the artist who would glorify God with his work must thoroughly understand and respect his medium. Maritain's views in this case are pertinent:

> If you want to produce a Christian work, be a Christian, and try to make a work of beauty into which you have put your heart; do not adopt a Christian pose.... Do not *separate* your art from your faith. But leave *distinct* what is distinct. Do not try to blend by force what life unites so well. If you were to make your aesthetic an article of faith, you would spoil your faith. If you were to make your devotion a rule of artistic operation, or turn the desire to edify into a method of your art, you would spoil your art.[6]

2. Art, as it is identified with beauty, glorifies God. Beauty, which is defined for this paper as the quality of perfection in the sensible world, was closely bound to the theology of the Christian church until the Renaissance. "The heavens declare the glory of God, and the firmament showeth his handiwork" was a kind of motto for the Middle Ages as Europeans viewed the material world. All corporeal existence pointed somehow toward the incorporeal. The result was a deeply Christian aesthetic—one that acknowledged God as the Source and Cause for all beauty and

---

[6] Ibid., 54.

the church as the instrument through which its laws were understood.

Such a complete union between beauty and theology was possible, however, largely through Neoplatonic epistemology, which, with the exception of occasional periods of recession, dominated the church from the time of St. Augustine. Neoplatonism influenced the aesthetic directly. Plato had taught that truest reality lay in the spirit, mind, Idea. Nature was one step removed from the Idea, or a shadow of reality. Art, which in a sense imitated nature, was another step removed and merely a shadow of a shadow; it could never reveal the truth of an object. His views were introduced into the church by Christian Neoplatonists—especially Pseudo-Dionysius and St. Augustine. Boethius's three categories of musicians express the Neoplatonic hierarchy; knowledge was superior to practice. The true musician was the theorist—the philosopher who dealt only with the concepts of music, acoustical relationships, theological implications. The composer was on a lower level. He actually dealt with the sensible medium, but he, too, might arrive at the basic laws through instinct and inspiration. The performer was the lowest in value. He handled only the material and did not comprehend the metaphysical aspects of his art.

Matter was made acceptable to the medieval church only through an elaborate Neoplatonic symbolism based on the belief that matter aspires toward spirit. John Scotus Erigena taught that all beauty is a theophany. Things are beautiful in the measure in which they manifest unmistakably the perfection of absolute Beauty. For St. Bonaventura, who culminated the Neoplatonic aesthetic in the thirteenth century, all matter had a double aspect—a physical and a spiritual existence. Symbolism was the key to his Christian aestheticism.

Throughout the Middle Ages the octave, for example, was valued for its simple numerical relationship—2:1. Mathematics formed a link between God and the world; it had power to influence the soul. The octave came to symbolize rebirth and the whole mystery of redemption because it was an acoustical beginning again. Its merit as beautiful sound was quite incidental to its symbolic worth.

Light, also, had rich symbolic connotations. It was responsible for the sensible value of jewels and colored glass, and it was the cause of visibility in the sensible world. But, more significantly, it symbolized the illumination of truth. Because it was visible and yet penetrated matter, it served as the most direct bridge possible between the material world and the spiritual. Otto von Simson explains the metaphysical aesthetic of light: "Light is conceived as the form that all things have in common, the simple that imparts unity to all. As an aesthetic value, light, like unison in music, thus fulfills that longing for ultimate concord, that reconciliation of the multiple into one, which is the essence of the medieval experience of beauty, as it is the essence of its faith."[7]

Neoplatonic views of matter brought serious conflicts to the greatest artists of the Renaissance. Early suggestions of the problem appear in Petrarch's writings. On one occasion, when he climbed Mont Ventoux, he was overwhelmed with the view. However, he felt that he must read St. Augustine's *Confessions* to counterbalance his intoxication with the material world. He was angry with himself that he still loved earthly beauty, for "no thing is admirable besides the mind; compared with its greatness, nothing is great."[8]

In Michelangelo, a member of the Florentine Platonic Academy, the conflict became sharply focused. Early in his life he painted and carved idealized figures to express man's creation in God's image. As time went on he longed to express more fully the truer reality of the spiritual world. His figures were less refined and polished, expressive of man's inability to reach perfection in this world. One of his last sonnets reveals his disillusionment after a life of working in artistic media:

> In a frail boat, through stormy seas, my life in its course has now reached the harbour, the bar of which all men must cross to render account of good and evil done. Thus I now know how fraught with error was the fond imagination which made Art my idol and my king, and how mistaken that earthly love, once light and gay, if now I approach a twofold death. I have certainty of the one and

[7] Otto von Simson, *The Gothic Cathedral* (London: Routledge and Kegan Paul, 1956), 54.
[8] Translated in Ernst Cassirer et al., *The Renaissance Philosophy of Man* (Chicago: University of Chicago Press, 1948), 44.

the other menaces me. No brush, no chisel will quiet the soul, once it is turned to the divine love of Him who, upon the cross, outstretches His arms to take us to Himself.[9]

Three changes in thought reached their culmination in the sixteenth century and made—are still making—a direct relationship between beauty and glorifying God impossible. They created the impasse that Michelangelo discovered. First, Neoplatonism faded. In the thirteenth century Thomas Aquinas had advocated an Aristotelian acceptance of the sensible world, but his emphasis did not become dominant until the late Renaissance. This change lessened the urgency of justifying the material world with symbolic association. The rejection of Neoplatonism was significant also because it made way for the Hebraic-Christian attitude toward matter. God created the world and declared it good. He confirmed this truth by the Incarnation. The meaning of redemption was clarified when God became man, when spirit and flesh were combined. There is nothing in the Bible to indicate that the Christian should debase matter and expect that truth resides only in spirit. Total truth unites flesh and spirit, just as Christ became flesh.

Along with the waning of Neoplatonism came the emergence of aesthetics as a distinct area of experience, governed by its own laws. Theology no longer determined the laws of beauty. Artists and critics developed theories of judgment, based often on the pleasure that the material world might stimulate in the perceiver. Art moved from a didactic to a purely artistic function, and thus its immediate ability to convey Christian dogma was weakened. It existed now for man's joy and contemplation.

The third significant change of the sixteenth century was the divorce of art from the church. The Reformation finally severed the medieval synthesis. Leslie Spelman[10] believes that Calvin completed the divorce of art and the church and forced the artist into the secular realm. This has the advantage of compelling the Christian artist to work creatively in his day to convey truth aside from sacred subject and symbol. However, few artists since the Reformation have devoted their finest efforts to sacred art, and the loss

---

[9] Anthony Blunt, *Artistic Theory in Italy*, 1450–1600 (Oxford: Clarendon Press, 1940), 80.
[10] Leslie Spelman, "Calvin and the Arts," *Journal of Aesthetics and Art Criticism* 6 (March 1948): 251.

is severe for the Protestant church. Spelman holds, too, that Calvin did a disservice to art by ascetically declaring it a waste of time and condemning it because it appealed to the senses. Perhaps this latter view is the Protestant version of Neoplatonic rejection of matter. It is a factor in the Mennonite view of the arts.

In our day art glorifies God primarily because it confirms man's creation in the image of God. The character of God's creation is beautiful. Its organization and unity, its rhythm both in time and space, its unending variety and freshness, its consistency give man his concepts of beauty. The artist imitates—not God's material world, but his act of creating. Thus, whether consciously or not, he praises God because the basic power to create reflects God's likeness. The artist reflects at least dimly God's perfection. Wencelius holds that artists "are the continuators of creation, of which they have realized the inner dynamism." They are co-workers with God.[11]

3. Art, by its nature, is a unique vehicle for stating truth. In order to see the place of art as a vehicle for the expression of truth, it will be profitable first to examine certain facets of the nature of art and then to try to define ways in which art may deal with truth.

Inherent within art is the possibility, first, of articulating concepts and realities that language cannot make clear. Art's non-discursive character complements discursive methods of communication in extending the gamut of man's understanding and insight. Quite in contradiction to Plato's view of art as a "shadow of a shadow" of reality, the twentieth century recognizes art as the most direct and immediate means for making its own kind of statement. It can reveal reality in the form of insights, intuitions, intimations, which language cannot touch. Its imaginative character frees it from the conventions of the fixed symbols of language.

In the second place, the element of beauty in art makes it a suitable vehicle for truth. Its striving toward perfection lifts it above casual and ordinary experience. Emil Brunner explains that "art intensifies and elates, it brings order to the chaotic, gives form

[11] Wencelius, "The Word of God and Culture," 161–62.

to the casual and shape to the shapeless, it exalts and ennobles the material reality to which it gives form."[12]

Third, art functions in the realm of contemplation; it is not a stimulus for action. It does not contribute to the preservation of life or the fulfillment of physical need. This quality has been the source of much suspicion among Christians. St. Bernard's complaint about elaborate church buildings represents the attitude of Christians over many centuries: "The church is resplendent in her walls, beggarly in her poor; she clothes her stones in gold, and leaves her sons naked; the rich man's eye is fed at the expense of the indigent. The curious find delight here, yet the needy find no relief."[13] Yet, because art is contemplative, it is peculiarly qualified to deal with the truth that lies at the roots of immediate problems such as preservation of life and fulfillment of physical need.

What is the truth with which art deals? As has been pointed out earlier, art's meaning defies translation into words. It suffers severe loss through attempts to explain and interpret. Its force and impact lie in the success with which it can communicate directly through its own peculiar character. One can only suggest indirectly something of the nature of its deepest content.

A great work of art may reveal most crucial problems of existence—the relation of God to man and man to man. Its meaning is broader and deeper than simply an intellectual or rational concept. It conveys wholeness of experience in a spontaneous and immediate way. It strikes man with a freshness of insight which he cannot know outside of the arts. In its own way it has the capacity to help man sense ultimate relationships of life, to see truth—perhaps even to see Christ, the Word of John 1—less dimly.

The artist dare not force his medium to reveal truth. He does not set out as an evangelist to convince man of his sin and urge recognition of Christ. His work achieves such an end only if he possesses three important qualifications: he is the master of his technical equipment, he searches to create a work of beauty and integrity, and he has struggled with the most basic problems of

---

[12] Emil Brunner, *Christianity and Civilization* (New York: Scribner's Sons, 1948), 74.
[13] G. G. Coulton, *Life in the Middle Ages,* vol. 4 (Cambridge: Cambridge University Press, 1930), 173.

existence so earnestly that an attempt to isolate them from his sensible expression would be false.

Rouault has made the curious statement that his chief ambition is to paint a head of Christ so convincing that all men will believe. He could gain his redemptive end much more directly with words, particularly with the words of the Gospel, which clarify the redemptive plan; but there is the strong implication that artistic integrity can reveal something of ultimate reality through means other than verbal.

There is no basic difference in content between a Rouault "Christ" and a late string quartet of Beethoven. Both are unconsciously testimonies of faith; both are serious statements concerning man's situation and destiny; both exist on a level compatible with the great issues of life; both bear witness to the deepest realities.

Implications for Mennonite Higher Education

A Mennonite liberal arts college needs to examine carefully its excuse for being. Is Niebuhr correct in judging the Mennonites anti-cultural? Is a positive view of the liberal arts possible within the present Mennonite tradition? What was the attitude of the sixteenth-century Anabaptists—of the New Testament church? To what extent are their views applicable in the twentieth-century Mennonite situation? The faculty and administration must consider seriously questions of this sort before they can solve the specific problems in the fine arts. A Christian college must clarify its underlying philosophy of culture before it can hope to act positively in implementing details within a liberal arts program.

If a positive view is feasible, the teacher of the fine arts should encourage both passive and active participation. All students in a liberal arts college should be exposed to the relatively passive or "appreciation" side of the arts. They should encounter the great minds of a civilization and have the opportunity to profit from the accumulation of insight that has come to men in many generations. Often students will feel that the Christian had best approach the arts as a harmless diversion—as a leisure time activity; a more serious participation might be involving. But the teacher must have the freedom to deal with the central and compelling aspects of art. He must make clear art's capacity to function as a vehicle for statements of truth.

Students should know also the active, creative level of participation. An amateur acquaintance with an art medium can help a student develop a sympathetic understanding of an artist's handling of that medium. In the Renaissance a man such as Leonardo da Vinci could master the knowledge and traditions of several fields—painting, sculpture, engineering—within his lifetime. The accumulation of knowledge since the sixteenth century makes such an accomplishment almost impossible in the twentieth century; men are forced into highly specialized areas in order to be able to operate creatively. Amateur participation at least makes room for a more genuine understanding of art than does a purely spectator view.

The most problematic area for Mennonites participating in the arts is serious study that leads to an art vocation. The arts do not fit into the traditional Mennonite concept of service vocations. The specialized, professional artist becomes almost inevitably isolated from the Mennonite community because there is little place for his contribution. Gifted students often are made to fear that serious involvement with the arts will threaten or even replace their faith.

Students with creative ability must learn that all they do is a witness to their faith. It is essential that they master their art medium in order that they be capable of "speaking" with integrity. The Christian dare not be shoddy in his expression; his command of technical phases of his medium must be as thorough and complete as is humanly possible. Because he loves God and his neighbor he is compelled to equip himself fully if he deals with any art seriously.

The creative student also needs encouragement to work freely within his medium. An artistic expression is an individual rather than a group statement, and the individual must be free from group pressures in order to make new and pertinent statements about reality. St. Augustine's advice to the Christian artist is applicable to the twentieth-century situation: "Love God, and make what you will." It is the artist's relationship to God that frees him; love controls his desires and molds the inner content of his work. The Christian teacher can help a student deepen his concept of

God, and he can train him to respect and master the medium. But the student must be free to determine the specific content and expressiveness of his work.

Students should be helped to sharpen their powers of discrimination and judgment. Christians tend to judge moral worth in art by the existence or absence of Christian subject or symbol rather than by the artistic integrity of the total work and the quality of its Christian insights. Students must learn to discriminate between great art and hackneyed clichés; they must prefer fresh insights to facile and superficial expressions. They must know the difference between stating truth as an honest and urgent necessity and attempting to moralize.

Art has a peculiar pertinence for the Christian, which Mennonites—most of Christendom, for that matter—have hardly tapped. We will have to choose between the negation and the acceptance of culture—between deserting the field to the non-Christian and embracing the arts for the glory of God.

Chapter 16

THE CHURCH'S RESPONSIBILITY
FOR ARTISTIC DISCRIMINATION

Mary K. Oyer

> *"The Church's Responsibility for Artistic Discrimination" is an outline of a presentation Mary gave at the Mennonite Graduate Fellowship, 2 January 1959, in Columbus, Ohio. She lays out a rationale for aesthetic judgment that sounds somewhat elitist. In this presentation she does not consider how a work of art functions within the context of a human community. Aesthetic virtues seem to reside in the work itself without relationship to the culture or people that create and use the art. In the decade to come, Mary's work on* The Mennonite Hymnal *and her experiences in Africa would radically change her views on these matters.*

Thesis of the paper:

1. The church has a responsibility to make careful judgments in the arts, because it incorporates them in worship, it uses them in communicating Christian reality to the unbeliever, and it accepts them as an enriching element outside of worship context.
2. Artistic criticism depends on a thorough acquaintance with and experience of the nature of art—its unique potentialities and its limits.
3. Christian discrimination in the arts is the serious responsibility of Christian artists, who know both the reality of the Christian experience and the value and power of artistic expression.

[We have elected to include this piece in essentially unaltered form, retaining features that date it, including masculine language for humanity and quotation from the Revised Standard Version of the Bible.—Eds.]

If the church accepts artistic discrimination as its responsibility, it faces an elusive problem. Meaning in the arts, at its deepest level, defies definition. It cannot be described; rather, it is recognized through intuition or sympathy and known by those who become involved seriously with its means of expression and the significance of specific works.

Nonetheless, one can describe in a given work certain aspects that contribute to meaning:

1. Technical manipulation of materials can be verbalized. This is the basis for much teaching in the arts. One can describe, for example, the nature of the violin—its possibilities and limitations, its unique contribution among instruments, the character of idiomatic writing for the violin, etc.

2. One can describe to some degree the nature of the aesthetic experience, at least pointing up distinguishing characteristics. For example, the aesthetic experience:
   a. belongs to the emotional realm. It is not a description of one specific emotion or mood but a revelation of the nature of emotion—of patterns of feeling; it reveals "how feelings go."[1]
   b. belongs to the realm of imagination and illusion, separated from experience of other disciplines—science, theology, philosophy, discourse. This aspect of its nature compels contemplation, reflection.
   c. reveals experience uniquely, newly; it provides insight unavailable by other types of thought or exploration.
   d. reveals wholeness and completeness (cf. nature of the human organism).

These aspects of art will be vital considerations in art criticism. Judgments must be built on a thorough knowledge of the field. They will center around questions of this sort:

1. What are the artist's premises? (example in music: premises in terms of style, length, gamut of contrasts, rhythmic, melodic, harmonic materials, choice of instruments). Has he convincingly achieved the ends that logically follow his premises?

---

[1] See Susanne K. Langer, *Philosophy in a New Key: A Study in the Symbolism of Reason, Rite, and Art* (New York: Mentor, 1948).

2. Has the artist convincingly and truthfully laid the groundwork for aesthetic experience (as distinct from scientific, religious, etc.)? Has he:
   a. revealed the nature of the emotional world?
   b. separated himself sufficiently from sheer imitation of nature that his work has a life of its own?
   c. presented his experience of life with newness and originality?
   d. revealed the experience of wholeness?

But there are virtually no reliable verbal criteria for making the value judgments suggested here (i.e., convincing, truthful, significant, meaningful). A judgment is finally a personal statement made in response to an experience with a given work. Its validity depends on the breadth and depth of the critic's experience—his understanding of the nature of art, his ability and willingness to become involved with specific artworks, the bases for his authority. We accept the artistic judgment of another person to the extent that we respect the validity of his experience with the arts.

Christian judgments are shaped by the believer's acceptance of Christ as the source and revealer of meaning (Col. 1:15-17). This should not imply that the need for artistic mastery is lessened or that purely artistic values can be slighted. It means rather that, if one really believes Christ to be central to meaning and significance in life, judgments in this discipline will be influenced—not in ways that submit to dogmatic rules, but in an approach to life that permeates every judgment. We accept the Christian artistic discrimination of another person to the extent that we respect both his artistic experience and his integrity as a child of God.

The Mennonite church could well reexamine its practices in artistic discrimination. The following areas need urgent attention by the Mennonite Graduate Fellowship:

1. A consideration of music, poetry, and visual media as art forms, rather than simply as didactic instruments.
2. An encouragement of active involvement in the arts in order that valid judgments may be possible.
3. An insistence on proper documentation in writings that appear in official church papers and in policy-making groups in the

church. Documentation from the arts must include above all direct experience with the arts.

I would suggest that a way to more valid judgments than we have made in the past might lie in a more wholesome relationship between Mennonite artists and the rest of the church. If the artists could be accepted for what they are and encouraged to function in an advisory capacity in artistic matters, the life of the [Mennonite Church] fellowship could be enriched. Until this is done, the artists will of necessity continue to separate their art from their church life. If Mennonite artists could study together the church's use of the arts and explore the educational implications, the quality and effectiveness of our art could be vastly improved. Perhaps the church should include artists among the apostles, prophets, evangelists, pastors and teachers of Ephesians 4, to whom were give gifts "for the equipment of the saints, ... to the unity of faith and of the knowledge of the Son of God, to mature manhood, to the measure of the stature of the fullness of Christ."

Chapter 17

QUESTIONS THAT ARISE WITH THE CONSIDERATION OF INSTRUMENTS IN MENNONITE WORSHIP

Mary K. Oyer

For the General Conference Hymnal Committee, also charged with studying "the organ question," Mary Oyer created this list of questions arising from consideration of the use of instruments in Mennonite worship. The occasion was a consultation on instruments held at Laurelville Mennonite Church Center in September 1959. The list's six subsections illustrate Mary's typical multifaceted approach to treating a topic, and her capacity for viewing an issue from a variety of angles and at varying levels. The questions reveal the complexity of the issue; few of them admit of easy answers.

A. Does music have meaning?

If so, how can that meaning be defined?
How does it differ from meaning conveyed by words?
Does the music influence the meaning of our hymns?
Are there varying levels of involvement with music?
How do the following differ:

1. using music for therapy
2. valuing music for its recreational possibilities
3. accepting music as a serious means for communicating experience

---

[We have elected to include this piece in essentially unaltered form, retaining features that date it, including masculine language.—Eds.]

Which is the more significant in conveying meaning—the medium of performance or the total combination of elements that make up the music?

B. What is the role of the performer of music?

What is his relationship to the composer?
What equipment (understandings, skills) does he need?
Can any two performances be alike?
What might be the performer's motivation?
How might he relate to the congregation?
How do live and recorded performances differ?

C. What are the values and limitations of four-part, unaccompanied congregational singing?

Is there any approach that would invite a more active participation?

Does size of congregation or its sociological background offer problems?

> Is our practice adequate for a city mission?
> What should be our approach in a foreign culture?

Are there dangers inherent in a move toward listening rather than actively participating?

What are the expressive and communicative limitations of four-part, unaccompanied congregational singing?

> What great musical works are not open to us?
> Are length and scope of hymns limiting?

Is there value in a performance that achieves a refinement beyond an amateur level?

Is it possible that an approach become too important?

> Might it obscure the end desired?
> Could the urge to preserve our method thwart our discovery of meaningful ways to praise and worship?

May the uniqueness of an approach be a danger?

D. What are the reasons for the apparent desire among many church members to expand their church music experiences—to choirs, recorded music, live music for listening?

Are Mennonites' musical experiences outside of the church expanding and deepening?

Might there be an honest and deep-seated need to bring more fullness and depth of experience to the worship experienced?

If so, are we meeting this need by a serious exploration of the field of a cappella music?

Are there evidences of blind imitation of worship patterns of other churches?

E. Are some instruments more suitable for use in worship than others?

To what extent do tradition and the development of music within Western culture influence the answer?

Why is the pipe organ the most significant church instrument?

Are any other instruments possible? What church music exists in the piano literature?

Are we prepared to evaluate a good instrument in contrast to a cheap imitation?

Why is recorded music inappropriate?

F. Are we interested in securing serious players who might contribute positively to the worship situations?

Where will organists come from?

Have we good players now in the church?

What are the demands of the instrument?

Are we prepared to accept among us a member who submits to the rigors of learning to play?

Are we prepared to pay an adequate salary to an organist whose profession is church music?

How might we win the respect of the young Mennonite musicians to the extent that they would bring their musical gifts to the church?

Chapter 18

THE LIFE AND METHOD OF MUSIC

Mary K. Oyer

Published in Mennonite Life, *January 1965, "The Life and Method of Music" illustrates Mary Oyer's ability to translate her technical skills in music analysis into images and ideas that could connect with an educated but amateur reader. At this time the committee work on* The Mennonite Hymnal *was nearly complete. This piece displays the value Mary has come to attach to the purely musical meaning of a tune paired with a text—a dimension of the experience of singing that Mennonites had frequently overlooked. Mary uses a variety of visual images to help the reader sense how a Western hymn tune could convey meaning without words.*

Most Christian groups find that music is a basic means of expression. They have grown up singing hymns, and they assume that music contributes something to the texts. However, when the texts are removed, the music becomes a bit more mystifying; and when a composition extends to twenty minutes in length, it leaves the realm of the "useful" and "practical." If it should include harsh and strident combinations of sound, questions of its validity may arise.

Is music a valid part of the Christian's world? Does its significance go beyond the role of supporting a text? An examination of a simple hymn tune could point to some basic characteristics of music:

[*"The Life and Method of Music" is reprinted by permission of the publisher, from* Mennonite Life, *January 1965, 30–31. We have elected to include this piece in essentially unaltered form, retaining features that date it, including masculine language.—Eds.]*

TALLIS' ORDINAL was written for a specific text, but for nearly four centuries it has been used as a "common tune"; it appears with a large number of different texts in common meter—eight syllables followed by six with a second pair of eight and six. In spite of its simplicity and brevity, it has maintained its interest throughout the years and appears now in many hymnals.

The tune would usually function as a vehicle for the text. It would likely support pairs of phrases and the rhyme scheme of the poetry. But beyond that, it would "say" something in itself—something nonverbal. Just what its message is can hardly be captured in words. We can only see some of the ways in which the music "speaks."

It consists of four phrases which group in pairs. The rising first phrase is answered by the second, which reaches the highest point of the tune. The third begins again as the first and is answered by the fourth, which is parallel to but lower than the second. Phrases one and two form the first member of a pair which is completed by three and four.

The word *answer* suggests a parallel with speech. In a sense the melody is like a conversation in which questions or statements are presented and answered. In this case the questions are identical except that one comes after the other. Phrase three is asking the same question, perhaps more emphatically; it receives a related, yet different, answer. The first answer, phrase two, reaches to the highest point and pulls the farthest away from the low keynote (F) on which the tune begins and ends. The second answer, phrase four, has the same shape as the first. But this time it ends on the keynote and makes a more convincing conclusion—a more decisive answer to the question.

The tune also reflects basic movements in nature. Question and answer pairs appear in many things that move; time with alternating day and night, tides with their ebb and flow, and breathing are a few of the clearest examples.

The low keynote presents a kind of pull not unlike a gravitational force. It is an insistent note that creates tension whenever any other note is sounded and constantly urges the melodic line back to itself. We respond to the pull with a sense of relief and satisfaction when we arrive at the last note.

The repetition of a pulse, similar to a heartbeat, characterizes the tune. But the monotony of too much repetition is broken by the always-changing direction of the melody which the rhythm supports. The presence of both repetition and change, interacting on each other, reflects one of the most basic characteristics of the created world. The leaves on one tree are similar but never identical; they are always varied. Clouds appear frequently enough that we recognize and identify them. However, the sky never appears exactly the same. It is always shifting, both in cloud formations and in light effects.

The tune is related also to human experience. It touches the emotions in some way. Tension, relief, and satisfaction have been mentioned already, but these are quite general emotions that would characterize the large majority of musical works. The smooth movement of this particular melody might suggest an overall effect of calmness and peace, with one active, stretching spot in phrase two. It is probably fairer to say, however, that a specific emotion can hardly be identified. Rather the listener encounters a combination of emotions—perhaps opposing ones appearing at the same time, much as joy and grief, for example, may appear together in an actual situation. The hymn tune presents emotions, but they can be known better by direct experience than by attempts to verbalize them.

This brief tune is a miniature version of aspects of many long and complex compositions. The first movement of a symphony usually makes a statement, departs from it, and returns to a restatement in the original key. The statements and departure are of course expanded far beyond the limits of this hymn tune, but the basic principles of construction—the logic of the "speech"— are much the same.

Music, then, has a life and method of its own which in some ways parallels communication with language. It makes use of basic movements of nature and reveals areas of experience that cannot be captured by words.

The listener welcomes music because it expands his experience. It stretches his ways of knowing life and lets him share in the experiences of a composer who took the trouble to turn his insights into sound rather than speech. The listener can understand these insights providing he cares enough to follow as attentively as he would another person in conversation. Patient reflection will help him see why twenty minutes rather than two were needed to carry out a particular musical conversation in a logical way. It may show him how clashing, "ugly" sounds might be needed to make resolution clear. Music is as valid for the Christian as any serious attempt to communicate with another person—to share a significant area of experience.

Chapter 19

CULTURAL PROBLEMS IN THE PRODUCTION OF A MENNONITE HYMNAL

Mary K. Oyer

In 1967, at the time of her writing of "Cultural Problems in the Production of a Mennonite Hymnal," Mary Oyer would have been reading proofs and doing final editing on The Mennonite Hymnal. The committee work was completed. A forerunner to this paper she presented to ministers of the Indiana-Michigan Mennonite Conference. The paper has two primary parts, though the second part has several subsections. The first part sketches the larger cultural context of music performance and media options in which the production of a hymnal and congregational singing are located. Mary observes that "hymnody in large part is not keeping pace, but perhaps it cannot. Perhaps radical new forms and media must emerge to express the experience of faith in the 1960s."

Against this backdrop, the remainder of the paper discusses the cultural differences between the (Old) Mennonite Church and the General Conference Mennonite Church, with regard to their histories and practices of singing in

["Cultural Problems in the Production of a Mennonite Hymnal" is reprinted from *Proceedings of the Sixteenth Conference on Mennonite Educational and Cultural Problems,* Hesston College, Hesston, KS, 8–9 June 1967 (N.P.: Council of Mennonite and Affiliated Colleges, 1967). Council of Mennonite Colleges (1956–1967) Collection, Mennonite Church USA Archives–Goshen, 1700 S. Main St., Goshen, IN 46526. Used by permission. We have elected to include this piece in essentially unaltered form, retaining features that date it, including masculine language and quotations from the Revised Standard Version of the Bible.—Eds.]

> *worship. Mary also describes the hymnal committee process and the issues that emerged within it. Her conclusion, somewhat abrupt, is that despite the various problems that have been her focus in this presentation, "the committees have compiled what they unanimously believe will be a fine hymnal for Mennonites."*

Any church contemplating a hymnal revision in the 1960s faces serious cultural problems. These problems deal primarily with a search for hymns and tunes that are relevant in the contemporary world. In its music the church seems to have kept pace neither with the artistic world nor with the realm of mass communications.

The Need for Contemporary Texts

The need for contemporary texts, in the first place, is urgent. Since the change to the use of the vernacular in 1964, Roman Catholicism requires English hymns. The liturgy has been translated into contemporary language—using "you" rather than "thou," for example. There is no large body of English hymns to match this modernization. The suddenness of need for new texts is unprecedented in history, unless one might find a parallel in the outburst of Protestant hymnody in the 1520s and 1530s. It necessitates much translation from Latin, borrowing from Protestantism, and creating a new body of texts and tunes.

Although the need is not as sudden or striking in Protestantism, it exists. Varied translations of the Bible are causing a revolution in religious language and calling for fresh statements of faith. The King James Version, which lies at the heart of much hymnody, is no longer the norm for religious expression.

Professor U. S. Leupold, a Lutheran who is working on a revision of the 1958 *Service Book and Hymnal,* has articulated some of the problems in a paper presented to the Lutheran commission for planning the revision, February 1967. He points out that, not only are some of our religious words obsolete—"vouchsafe," "beseech," "eschew"—and images such as that of the shepherd have lost their cutting edge, but the whole realm of words is suffering an inflation comparable to the monetary inflation of the mark in Germany after the war:

I don't have to remind you how the modern mass media, commercialism, brainwashing, and political filibustering have contributed to this inflation of words. But I must stress the bitter cynicism and distrust of every form of verbal communication that they have engendered in the public. Our world has become deeply suspicious of words. And this affects us as church. For we have always boasted of being the church of the "Word of God." But often we only have rattled "words about God," instead of communicating the "Word of God." And so the great words on which Western culture is built, God, soul, freedom, love, righteousness, virtue, etc., have become paper money. They no longer buy anything. They are not covered by reality. The great claims of the Gospel are just as suspect to the ears of our contemporaries as the claims for patent medicines or political panaceas....

We Christians share in the inflation of words and have ourselves contributed to it. Of course in teaching and preaching we can seek to combat this erosion of Christian words, to re-interpret them, and to bring them back to the gold standard. But neither liturgy nor hymns are the place for interpretations or explanations. Here we must use terms that still are forceful and fresh, clear and cutting, biting and bright. We must seek to recover or recreate an idiom that will not muff or muffle the message, but will give it compelling strength. This is a task which will require all our patience and ingenuity.[1]

The Musical Situation

The musical situation is equally alarming. Neither the usual harmonic style nor the four-part congregational approach to singing reflects the musical world outside of the church. Throughout much of church history hymn tunes bore stylistic marks of the times. Musical styles are too complex today for congregational performance and perhaps even for congregational listening. Historically hymns were congregational; the people were the "performers." The role

---

[1] U. S. Leupold, "New Hymn Texts: The Present Crisis in Hymn Writing" (paper, February 1967), 1–2.

of the performer in recent years has shifted somewhat, however. A virtuoso technique is necessary to conquer the complexities of much of the new music. Amateur performance has diminished, and enlightened listening has gained prominence. Some recent composers ask the performer to improvise, to compose as he performs. Improvisation in the church could be an invigorating venture—comparable perhaps to speaking in tongues. But few church members at present would be willing or able to experiment. Other composers eliminate the performer altogether in favor of composing directly on magnetic tape with an electronic synthesizer. Is it possible that congregational—especially four-part—singing is outdated?

Basic changes are taking place in our ways of perceiving. Marshall McLuhan has been pointing out a shift from concentration on verbal communication, spoken and written, arranged in logical, consecutive order, to perceiving life through widely varied media. Television, he says, has revolutionized our attitude toward perception and our ability to perceive. Regardless of the content of the program, we are involved immediately in the medium of tiny dots which we must connect in our minds. We are drawn by sight, hearing, and motion, by understatements and momentary flashes which we must complete.

Television is a symbol of the variety of stimuli that bombard the contemporary believer. Hymnody in large part is not keeping pace, but perhaps it cannot. Perhaps radical new forms and media must emerge to express the experience of faith in the 1960s.

Leland Sateren, a composer of church music, who along with Dr. Leupold is working on a revision of the 1958 Lutheran hymnal, wrote this in a letter of March 1967: "I'm almost convinced that the day of the 'set' hymnal is over. That is, in many respects a hymnal establishes a worship 'environment'—and, as the life of a hymnal usually runs to about a quarter of a century, it 'set' it for a quarter of a century. It does this even though one augments it with other worship materials." And elsewhere, informally, "The 25-year hymnal we've known now in our churches is a thing of the past. Or, if it isn't, it should be. Things are moving so fast now that any 'conventional' hymnal we produce will be out of date by the time it is published. Same for the service-book. I'm convinced we must move to hymnals of what Erik Routley calls 'disposable music,' paperbacks which can be replaced with fresh material every 5–10 years."

There has been a great deal of experimentation in the last three or four years in new forms of music for the church. Jazz and folk idioms are appearing to replace the gospel song, with which they have certain points in common. Ballad-like texts seem to challenge poems in which dignity is a virtue. It is hard to know what the climate in Mennonite church music will be by 1969, when the *Mennonite Hymnal* is published; but in June of 1967 the experimental works seem to belong to the paperback editions Leland Sateren is advocating. They might be valid for a short time only. A standard hymnal seems to be a desirable repository of genuine expressions of Christians of the past, but perhaps by August 1969, the committee should be ready with a supplementary "disposable" hymnal to go along with the standard hymnal it has produced.

At any rate, the question of relevance to our times—relevance in an electronic age—is the basic problem for hymnal making. Specifically "Mennonite" problems in contrast seem far less significant. Yet, in the actual work of the committees, the large question was rarely faced directly, and the relatively smaller problems loomed large. Limits of time and perspective held committees close to immediate matters. The human process of arriving at unanimous decisions kept the tone of the work conservative.

Different Cultural Strands among Mennonites

The current hymnal revision is the work of two groups—the General Conference Mennonite Church (GC) and the (Old) Mennonite Church (OM). This fact was a source of enrichment to each group. Although the tensions between churches of the 1920s occasionally rose to the surface momentarily, and the urge to defend some practice of one group or the other emerged periodically, the working together was not a "problem." Differences on theological questions occurred between individuals or generations—almost never between the two groups. Differences in practice, however, became increasingly clear and problematic.

Cultural backgrounds vary from one congregation to another, but two primary cultural strands distinguish the two groups. Many General Conference Mennonites are German speaking or have immigrated recently from a German culture. The Lutheran chorale is a prominent aspect of their church music. The (Old) Mennonite churches have been established in America usually for a number of generations. The influence of American hymnody—and emphasis on the hymns of Watts in particular, along with men such as Wesley and Newton—has been strong. The singing school movement was an important influence; folk hymns and American tunes of composers such as Lowell Mason replaced the German chorale for many of these people from 1832 onward. Some of the congregations come from Amish backgrounds; the worship material then came from the *Ausbund* rather than the Lutheran chorales.

The hymnals of the two groups point in differing directions. The first English hymnal, 1847, was meant to be used with Joseph Funk's *Genuine Church Music*, 1832 (called *Harmonia Sacra* in 1847). This tune book, designed for singing schools, had a distinctly American flavor. A number of tunes were folk hymns, which were being notated in the early nineteenth century in Baptist hymnals and in singing school books. English and Scottish Psalm tunes and several chorales represented the European element in the tune book.

In 1890 the (Old) Mennonites produced a small collection, *Hymns and Tunes*. It perpetuated both texts and tunes from 1847 but had in addition a sizable number of works "by the Committee." A certain charm and distinctiveness characterize this book, in spite of the lack of scholarship and musical sophistication.

At almost the same time, 1894, a group of GCs published their first hymnal in English, *Mennonite Hymnal: A Blending of Many Voices*. They selected a suitable standard hymnal already in existence rather than compiling their own. They selected *Many Voices; or Carmina Sacra, Evangelistic Edition with Tunes*, prepared by DeWitt Talmage, minister of the New Brooklyn Tabernacle. This in turn was a revision of a standard hymnal of good quality, *Carmina Sacra, A Selection of Hymns and Songs of Praise with Tunes*, 1886. It was one of a line of fine hymnals published by A. S. Barnes and beginning with Henry Ward Beecher's *Plymouth Collection* of 1855. Mr. Talmage had included approximately forty gospel songs in his evangelistic revision of 539 hymns. The Mennonites made five changes of hymns, as far as I can see, and omitted one stanza of a baptismal hymn. The five changes were all P. P. Bliss tunes and three of his texts, so one rather suspects that the changes were made for reasons of copyright rather than because of doctrinal objections. (They substituted five other gospel songs.) Otherwise Talmage's hymnal remained intact.

This basic difference of approach has persisted up through the 1940 *Mennonite Hymnary.* The (Old) Mennonite hymnals represent a folk-like character and a less professional approach. The General Conference books have been closer to the mainstream of hymnody (including in 1927 and 1940 a number of German chorales); the collections have been more sophisticated and broader in coverage of types of works but are probably less distinctive. Both groups gradually absorbed a rather large number of Victorian works and gospel songs. More detail on differences between specific books would probably be fruitful, but suffice it to say that difficulties in understanding and accepting the integrity of both approaches probably lay at the root of some of the problems of making a Mennonite hymnal in the 1960s.

Not only are the selection of texts and overall tone of the hymnals different, but variations occur within materials we currently hold in common. "Crown Him with Many Crowns," for example, appears in the index for both *Mennonite Hymnary* and *Church Hymnal,* but the poems are not alike. One is Catholic, Matthew Bridges' original poem of 1851; the other is Anglican, Godfrey Thring's new version of 1882. Both hymnals have "Alas and Did My Savior Bleed." However, rather than using Watts's original line, "When God, the mighty Maker died," *Mennonite Hymnary* has "When Christ, the mighty Maker died," and *Church Hymnal* has "When God's own Son was crucified." Hundreds of instances of differences had to be reconciled. The use of the original texts was a boon to objectivity, but it was still difficult to move through fifty or seventy-five decisions in one day.

Frequently both hymnals have a text in common but use differing tunes. "Art Thou Weary" uses BULLINGER and STEPHANOS; "I Heard the Voice of Jesus Say," BRUNK and VOX DILECTI; "Christ for the World We Sing," KIRBY BEDON and MALVERN; "Give to Our God Immortal Praise," LASST UNS ERFREUEN and WARRINGTON. Scores of similar variations appear. The committees had to search for principles for decision making. The existence of a standard combination of text and tune among many churches, the actual usage of a given combination in either group, the effectiveness of each tune for congregational use, and the vitality of the musical expression for the twentieth century were some of the questions asked in making choices.

Worship practices, in addition to materials, differ. General Conference churches on the whole sing with accompaniment; (Old) Mennonite churches as a rule do not. However, since both groups sing in four parts, there was no significant handicap to either group; both need voice ranges that fit four parts and a simplicity of voice line to make congregational singing valuable. If either church had worked alone, however, there would probably have been slight differences in the number of hymns included for unison singing with accompaniment.

Many (Old) Mennonite churches read music more easily with shape-notes. These go back to the four note shapes of Little and Smith in the *Easy Instructor*, 1798. Joseph Funk used them in his 1832 songbook. The four expanded to seven in the 1840s. (Old) Mennonite hymnals have always been available in shape-note editions, using the shapes of Jesse B. Aiken since the 1890 *Hymns and Tunes*. The publishers have decided that the need is great enough for some congregations to warrant both shape- and round-note editions.

The groups differ in their use of musical aids to worship, such as sung Amens. General Conference churches tend toward their use; (Old) Mennonites do not. A limited number were included.

Committee Structure and Process

Committee structure presented "problems." It is hard to imagine a more complicated working organization. Each church had its parent committee from which three representatives were chosen to form a joint committee for carrying out the major work of the revision. Subcommittees on texts, tunes, and worship aids were responsible to the joint committee, whose members in turn were accountable to the parent committee, and by extension to the conference of each group. Co-editors and an executive committee of three officers from the joint committee had further responsibilities. But a careful balance of power gradually emerged, cutting off all possibilities for individual initiative and imagination and assuring the project of a group character.

Furthermore, consensus was the method of working within the joint committee, who stayed with most problems until agreement was reached. The process was painfully slow, but it achieved a satisfying result—the strength of committee support. The total revision, however, is for this reason conservative (term not used theologically here) rather than pioneering and imaginative.

Individuals and the various committees struggled often with the question of bases for decision. Were the members appointed or elected to represent the tastes of the groups whom they understood, or were they expected to move ahead in a role of leadership—to plot a direction in church music for the next generation? If the former, they needed, and found to some extent, ways of measuring the interests and needs of representative congregations. If the latter, they faced further questions: how can one know the needs of the future—by intuition or some kind of information? Can a group structured with careful checks and balances move forward aggressively?

Additional Variables

A number of additional variables affected the process of revision. Congregations vary considerably—quite apart from (Old) Mennonite and General Conference differences, which seem slight by comparison. A given congregation merges the cultural and geographic backgrounds of its members—German, Virginian, Western Canadian, etc.—with their theological orientations—orthodox, conservative, revivalist, Anabaptist, etc.—to form a unique group, unlike any other congregation anywhere. Each congregation has developed its own canon of hymns that suits its needs—its size, the education of its leadership and laity, its toleration for change and new expressions, the nature of its musical gifts, its musical resources, its residence—rural or urban—and thus its susceptibility to specific types of imagery. The list could be enlarged greatly. The committee would have been at a loss to describe the "typical Mennonite congregation." Rather, they tried to anticipate the needs of varied types of Mennonite congregations. They prepared an eclectic hymnal, which in its entirety would not appeal to any one congregation (no group sings 650 hymns; perhaps less than 200), but from which hopefully every congregation will be able to find its own significant collection.

Age span became a prominent variable occasionally in the committees. Inevitable differences in outlook came to light in matters of language and preferences in taste. Age span was an even greater problem in planning the contents of the hymnal. It is a rather sobering fact that the generation that will be the users of the hymnal in the next thirty years was hardly represented in a direct way. Most of the committee members were forty years old or above.

Interest in scholarly treatment of texts and tunes varied considerably. This revision represents a departure in procedure from previous Mennonite compilations. Past editors tended to choose their work from existing hymnals. They may or may not have been aware of the length and contents of the original poem or of the extent of alteration. The 1927 *Church Hymnal*, for example, illustrates a number of approaches to indicating alterations in text, depending on the editorial practice of the source hymnal. Markings for dynamics appear there occasionally, seemingly dependent on the treatment in the hymnal source.

Careful scholarship entered the present revision first as a practical solution to collating *Mennonite Hymnary* and *Church Hymnal* texts. With some members it became an approach essential to the honesty of the work. With others it remained unnecessary to the needs of the church and perhaps threatening to the work of the past. One committee member suggested that the hesitation is quite natural. Scholarship was accepted among us first in disciplines outside of the church. It came later with some difficulty in biblical studies, and it comes now with resistance to the materials used by the worshiping community. Whatever the reasons for differences in approach, the group as a whole moved in the direction of scholarship—not forging ahead with a pioneering spirit but simply catching up with trends of the last 100 years.

Not Just Problems

The assignment for this paper asked for a focus on "problems." It would be quite unfair to close without a statement that, in spite of problems and perhaps with their help, the committees have compiled what they unanimously believe to be a fine hymnal for Mennonites. They hope that congregations will share their growing appreciation both for the rich heritage of hymnody from the ecumenical church and for the specific values perpetuated within Mennonite traditions.

Chapter 20

Evolving African Hymnody

Mary K. Oyer

This 1990 essay on evolving African hymnody draws on material Mary Oyer had been working with for several years in different configurations. Here she discusses briefly some aspects of the historical development of East African hymnody and characteristics of the music. The primary focus of the paper is the performance practices of hymns and songs in the context of worship. The paper illustrates how Mary adapted her ability to derive performance practices from written musical scores—the focus of her work in graduate school—to analyze the significance of practices in specific cultural settings of performance. By this point, her identity as an ethnomusicologist is well established.

The hymnody of a people reflects that group's mode of perceiving and responding to God's person and acts in history. Both the concepts of the text and the character of the music reveal the particular people's view of life—their experience of time and space, of cosmic order, and of relationships among human beings and with the supernatural world.

Congregations seldom find a need to articulate the role of hymns in their worship. It is usually obvious. There is for individuals and for the group an inner recognition of the value of their tradition without rationalized explanations. When two diverse groups wish to meet, however, the traditions of worship of the one—in use of language and music—will not be immediately understandable to the other. In order to communicate, they will need to

"Evolving African Hymnody" is reprinted, by permission of the publisher, from *Mission Focus* 18, no. 4 (December 1990): 52–56.

197

learn each other's language and find some way to grasp the other's musical idiom.

Unfortunately, when missionaries went to Africa almost 200 years ago, they saw the need to study language, but they carried their own hymns and musical practices with them. They translated the texts into various vernaculars, even though the shape of the Western musical line violated the tone of the African language, and accents often fell on unaccented syllables of text.

We have the record, through oral transmission, of a remarkable exception to this general rule. Ntsikana, the first Xhosa Christian in South Africa, composed a hymn in his own idiom. The translation reads:

> He is the great God, Who is in heaven.
> Thou art Thou, true Shield.
> Thou art Thou, Stronghold of truth.
> Thou art Thou, Thicket of truth.
> Thou art Thou who dwellest in the highest.
> He who created life below, created life above.
> That Creator who created, created heaven.
> This Maker of the stars and the Pleiades.
> A star flashed forth, it was telling us.
> The Maker of the blind, does he not make them of a purpose?
> The trumpet sounded. It has called us.
> As for his chase, he hunts for souls.
> He, who reconciles flocks that fight with each other.
> He, the Leader, who has led us.
> He is the Great Blanket; we do put it on.
> Those hands of thine, they are wounded.
> Those feet of thine, they are wounded.
> Thy blood, why is it streaming?
> Thy blood, it was shed for us.
> This great price; are we worthy?
> This home of thine; are we worthy?[1]

The music consisted of one phrase, falling from its highest note to its lowest at the end of the phrase.

---

[1] *Lumko Song Book* (Lady Frere, Transkei: Lumko Music Department, 1984), no. 7.

Example 1. Elele

E - le - le   hom - na,   hom,   hom - na

Its shape is far more African than Western. European melodies tend toward an arch shape, with moderate rise and fall. The continuous repetition of that one musical phrase for the entire text was and still is an attractive form in traditional music, but it may have been one reason why Western missionaries neither understood nor valued this hymn. It is hard to imagine what might have happened to missions had Ntsikana's poetic and musical gifts been acknowledged and pursued, but Western hymns in translation prevailed in mission churches for nearly 150 years after his Great Hymn.

Early in the twentieth century, indigenous groups began to break away from mission churches, often following the call of a prophetic leader. The Harrists in Ivory Coast, the Kimbanguists of Zaire, and the Zionists in southern Africa, for example, all emerged in early decades of this century. In Kenya, secessions of new groups began in 1914, and by 1972 more than 150 distinct groups were reported in the *Kenya Churches Handbook*.[2] Many had thousands of followers. These independent or indigenous churches usually rejected the policies of the mission churches as well as their westernized modes of worship. They encouraged the use of traditional instruments, though they tended to make drums of their own design, size, and shape, in order to distinguish their use in Christian worship from specific roles in traditional society, for which specific drums functioned.

Mission churches throughout the continent had good opportunities to hear indigenous church singing. A number of congregations, such as the Africa Israel Ninevah Church of Kenya, often worshiped out of doors; services began and ended with processions to a drumbeat through the village or town. Each denomination, however, seemed to retain its own distinctive musical style, perhaps a bit like North American denominations and even congregations,

---

[2] John P. Kealy, "Catholic Progress with Traditional Music," in *Kenya Churches Handbook*, ed. David B. Barrett et al. (Kisumu: Evangel Publishing House, 1972), 67.

which can be recognized by the type of hymns they sing—perhaps German chorales, gospel songs, or prayer and praise types.

A significant breakthrough came with the Second Vatican Council, 1963–65. African Catholics were mandated to Africanize: "In certain parts of the world, especially in mission lands, there are peoples who have their own musical traditions, and these play a great part in their religious and social life. For this reason due importance is to be attached to their music and a suitable place is to be given to it ... adapting worship to their genius."[3]

The impact on the musical style of East African Catholics could not be instantaneous, but within a decade masses and hymns in the Kiswahili language and in African musical styles were spreading rapidly. At the same time, the Lutherans and Anglicans in Tanzania were experimenting with singing Christian texts to traditional melodies.

It may be valuable to try to identify the elements of an indigenous "African" style of music. Although each vernacular carries with it a unique music, one can make certain distinguishing generalizations.

1. Rhythm is basic to the musical texture. For some groups, the drum is essential to an African sound. Father Stefan Mbunga of Tanzania in a 1967 workshop presented a paper on "The Right Appreciation of Tanzanian Indigenous Music," urging the use of drums:

> You cannot prohibit African instrumental music or dancing without disturbing the soul's life. But you can give a new outlook and content to drumming and dancing through religious ideas and influences. The drum is not in itself a "heathen" instrument, but because it is used in many pagan contexts it had been regarded with suspicion.... In fact, it is the rhythm of the drums which "crosses" the rhythm of the song, and helps to create the interplay of rhythms which is the foremost distinguishing mark of African music.[4]

---

[3] John S. Mbiti, "Preface," in *Kenya Churches Handbook*, xviii.
[4] Stefan Mbunga, "The Right Appreciation of Indigenous Music" (workshop paper, Tanzania Conservatoire of Music, Dar es Salaam), 6.

For other people, a shaker or handclaps may have the highest priority. In any case, the texture will be dense—full of beats. There will be cross rhythms: two beats against three occur frequently. For example, Jean Kidula recorded the singing of SOLID ROCK among Pentecostals and Quakers of western Kenya. They altered the rhythm to accommodate faster tempo, then added two claps to each triple grouping.[5]

Example 2. Cross rhythms

My   hope   is   built   on   no - thing   less

Becomes:

Claps

2. The emphasis on rhythm draws out the dance. North Americans can sit very still while singing, using only the head. An African would involve the whole person, often allowing different parts of the body to pick up the varied lines of rhythm. The whole body is involved in praise when Africans use their own idioms. Languages reveal that dance is inseparable from music. English has two words, *music* and *dance*. *Ngoma* in Kiswahili could mean drum or dance or the entire musical event. That language would talk of music in isolation with a Western-derived word, *musiki*.

3. The predominance of rhythm minimizes melody and harmony. Western music emphasizes precision of pitch in order to be able to combine notes in harmony. The percussive sounds of rattles and shakers, which are always present in African style, diffuse the sound and reduce clarity of pitch. It may be more important for a melody to follow the tone of the vernacular language than to settle on pitches that can be identified by lines and spaces of Western notation. Melodies often start high and fall gradually, as in Ntsikana's

---

[5] Jean Kidula, "The Effects of Syncretism and Adaptation on Christian Music of the Logoli" (dissertation, East Carolina University, 1986), 117.

Great Hymn. They may cascade downward slowly in a shape that Curt Sachs, one of the earliest ethnomusicologists, claimed to be a common gesture in ancient melodies around the world.

Harmonies, which function to create tension and resolution in Western hymns, usually have a different role in African music, if they appear at all. A second voice—even third and fourth voices—may be added to a Western hymn, but the harmonies will probably be altered to adjust to African tastes. Opposite motion of parts, which Westerners value, may turn into parallel gliding lines that decorate a melody rather than providing clash and tension. Here is a phrase of parallel lines in "My Jesus, I Love Thee," which I heard Brethren in Christ Zambians sing in 1987:

Example 3. Parallel lines that decorate a melody

Choirs learn their parts in lines, one at a time, rather than by chords. The resulting sound is more linear than vertical and harmonic. Key changes may be avoided by eliminating accidentals.

4. The strophic form (the same music used for each stanza) of a Western hymn is not a lively African form. Much more common is a solo-response structure in rather rapid interchange. The response is frequently repetitious so that the group can learn it on one hearing and will have no trouble responding as needed. The length of the interchange is not programmed in advance. A given hymn may be brief one day and considerably longer on the next, depending on the leader's imagination and the energy with which the group responds. The solo-response form signifies an important relationship. Nathan Corbitt discovered in his work with coastal Kenyans that "without a leader, the song does not sing well." The leader must be able to "light the fire," to "fill the heart"

for the singers.[6] Solo and response make an inseparable pair, creating the complete expression.

An equally important structural characteristic is the cyclical repetition of a brief phrase (as in Ntsikana's Great Hymn). For my ears, there seems to be no strong forward thrust or sense of growth leading to a climax in much traditional music. Perhaps work songs influence this form. A work song regulates the speed of activity, keeping it uniform—neither too fast nor too slow. This evenness of flow in time strikes the Westerner as a unique African contribution to world music. It may symbolize an attitude toward time that accepts, rather than attempts to overcome, the natural regularities: day and night, the changing seasons, for example. Marwa Kisare, Mennonite Bishop in western Tanzania, commented in his autobiography on the cyclical effect of the music of the Luo drums played at his father's burial: "As Father's body was lowered into the grave, the drums began their rolling dirge—rising and falling like the ceaseless rolling of waves onto the lakeshore, sighing and moaning, representative of the ceaseless circle of life, birth, bloom, infinity, death, round and round, a dirge articulating the sorrow and despair deep in the souls of scores of people cut adrift by Father's passing."[7]

5. What makes a "beautiful" sound is determined by the ideals of a particular culture. The West over the centuries has cut out the buzzing sounds that are vital to traditional African music. An African university student told me that there is no emotion without a buzz. The sound of most instruments dies away rapidly. The sustained character of the imported organs must have shocked and baffled early African Christians, who were accustomed instead to fast reiterated sounds. In addition, much music making takes place out-of-doors. An enclosed space, so valued by Westerners since the first opera house in 1637, creates very different acoustical effects. Some Africans have learned to like it, but for many of them it is an acquired taste.

---

[6] Nathan Corbitt, "The History and Development of Music in the Baptist Churches on the Coast of Kenya: The Development of an Indigenous Music, 1953–1984" (dissertation, Southwestern Baptist Seminary, 1985), 156.

[7] Marwa Kisare, *Kisare, a Mennonite of Kiseru* (Salunga, PA: Eastern Mennonite Board of Missions and Charities, 1984), 34.

Within the past three decades the movement toward these indigenous African values has increased. I suggest four stages in that change of direction and will illustrate each with an example from the Mennonite Church in eastern Africa.

1. Continuing use of Western hymns in translation, though altered to fit local tastes.

2. Exploring the use in hymns of the innovations introduced by choirs.

3. Writing Christian texts for traditional tunes.

4. Composing new works in African styles.

The Mennonite Church in East Africa, like other mission churches, has been enlarging its vision of a hymnody in African style.

1. Western hymns in translation, especially in Kiswahili, are valued. A hymnbook, *Tenzi za Rohoni* (Songs of the Spirit) was published in 1968. The editors recommended using the tunes in the books they had drawn from for the compilation: *Church and Sunday School Hymnal,* 1902; *Church Hymnal,* 1927; *Life Songs [Number One],* 1916; *Life Songs Number Two,* 1938; and some British favorites, especially Sankey's *Sacred Songs and Solos.* The translators often encountered accent problems. For example, "How Sweet the Name of Jesus Sounds" is in iambic rhythm (alternating light, heavy). In translation it became trochaic (alternating heavy, light), which would suggest that the tune ORTONVILLE would not be suitable.

Example 4. Accent problems in translation

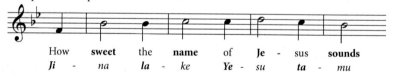

| How | **sweet** | the | **name** | of | **Je** - sus | **sounds** |
| *Ji* - | *na* | *la* - *ke* | | *Ye* - *su* | *ta* - *mu* | |

But congregations seem to be able to cope with what seems awkward to me. Perhaps traditional music of some ethnic groups has more rhythmic flexibility than is present in ORTONVILLE; accents may not be placed as strictly at beginnings of measures. In any case, Mennonite churches continue to use these translations. Congregations do alter some musical details of their favorite hymns, adapting the music to their own hearing and values. Half steps and leading tones are not a part of the musical vocabulary of some groups, so congregations will remove them, substituting other notes, as in "Rock of Ages" at ✳.

Example 5. Leading tone substitution

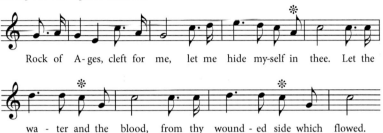

Rock of A - ges, cleft for me, let me hide my-self in thee. Let the

wa - ter and the blood, from thy wound - ed side which flowed.

Key changes may not appeal to them. The Nairobi Mennonite Church adds a second line to NICAEA, leaving out the accidental that pulls to a new key in the second phrase (see ✳).

Example 6. Avoidance of key change

Ho - ly, ho - ly, ho - ly, Lord God Al - might - y,

Ear - ly in the morn - ing our song shall rise to thee.

2. Innovations in hymnody have often come through the choirs. Bishop Kisare was supportive of choirs at a time when choirs were not permitted in worship in the missionaries' home congregations. He wrote in his autobiography: "I love music. Choirs are my delight. I try always to promote choirs. In our spiritual life conferences I give the young people a large part of the program for their choirs. Sunday morning worship is too dull if there is no choir to brighten the service. We all need each other in the church, each contributing his or her part according to the gifts and station which each has."[8]

I attended such a spiritual life conference at Shirati in 1972. At each of the sessions, all eighteen choirs who came sang several numbers. Two choirs stand out especially in my memory. The first

---

[8] Ibid., 99.

was a group of mature Luo women who sang in their vernacular rather than in Kiswahili. The resulting music could not follow Western rhythms or scales. The other choir of younger singers had the courage to add percussion: a metal ring struck by metal and a nail rubbed across the rings of a glass Fanta bottle. In both cases, the spontaneous response of the congregation was overwhelming, and high-pitched ululations broke out among the women in appreciation and approval. At my next visit to Tanzanian Mennonite churches in 1980, choirs were using drums and shakers as a matter of course.

That gathering of choirs in 1972 was characterized further by suggestions of dance. A number of them entered down the aisle to the platform with a rhythmic processional, until one of the worship leaders requested that they get to their special numbers with less expenditure of time. And the directors, with ornate batons, seemed to be dancing in front of their choirs; the usual Western role of keeping the group together was not needed because the singers listened to each other intently and stood close enough to their neighbors to feel their breathing.

3. Last August I visited a Maasai Mennonite congregation which met under a large fig tree near Ogwedhi, Kenya. They sang from a book of texts published by the Christian Missionary Fellowship, a group that values and respects the culture of the people with whom they work. Many of the songs in this hymnal, *Maisisa Enkai*, they recorded on tape and made available to Maasai. The Mennonites sang one in solo-response style, with this refrain.

Example 7. Refrain

One of the members, Joseph Sangale, told me that the melody is an old Maasai song for the worship of special, sacred trees or for unusually important people, such as the healer. The word *ho-la-le-yio*, he said, could not be translated; it is there like a "helping verb, to make the song sit."

The tune has characteristics similar to those of Maasai cattle songs: quick upward leaps at beginnings of phrases and a slower descent downward to a magnet-like lowest note. The fall of a fourth (as from *doh* to *sol*) is a typical Maasai cadence. In fact, it is quite characteristic of cattle songs I have heard from other Kenyan groups. The text fits Maasai experience, with its motif of sacrifice and mention of sacred trees and the fly whisk ("holy tail"), symbol of authority:

> *Refrain: Ehoo loomon holaleyio*
> > *Ashe naleng Enkai ai parmuain*
> > *To lasui lo Ikikau lino Yesu*
> > *Oinoti le Nkai ai kimug'iet lyie intaras.*
> > (Thanks be to God, who gave us Jesus,
> > the first-born, as a sacrifice, by his mercy.)

1. *Ayooki endaruna sirua pasae iruko enajo.*
   (I go in early morning. God hears me.)

2. *Intaiki ntomonok o ilewa olasar to Ikikau Yesu.*
   (You give women and me a sacrifice of first-born: Jesus)

3. *Inchoo enaisho o emukate meyaki empuan lelo.*
   (Let the wine and the bread bring life to them.)

4. *Oong' amu to Ing'ur le Yesu intaiki enashe Enkai.*
   (I receive the mercy of Jesus and give God thanks.)

5. *Enkai nasai atasaiyia tokordu maa kisai.*
   (God [to be worshiped], help those who pray to you.)

6. *Tokordu oloiruko oleitu eiruk meibung'a osotua ng'ejuk.*
   (Help those with faith and without —so hold the good news.)

7. *Osotua lo inoti Yesu eitukuorieki ilasarri.*
   (The peace of Jesus Christ is the one that washed away all other sacrifice.)

8. *Neari te msalaba neitajeu pookin osuj.*
   (He was killed on the cross and saves whoever follows.)

9. *Inyo tudumu inkonyek mirura olalashe ogol ong'u ening.*
   (Stand up. Open your eyes, you hard-hearted brother.)

10. *Inyo isoma Ilhebrania oolimu ematua e tomon.*
    (Stand, read Hebrews chapter 12.)

11. *Ajo eiting'o ilasarri le nkop liyieng'ie intare olmong'*
    (All sacrifices have ended, where you offer sheep and cows.)

12. *Eiting'o entasim olchani orok meekure ekutu toki.*
    (The idol of the tree doesn't value anything.)

13. *Osesen, osarge le Yesu, olasar lintaiki Enkai.*
    (The body and blood of Jesus is the sacrifice you give to God.)

14. *Eitanapa Yesu ilenyena nemaiyian ile keper.*
    (Jesus commanded his followers and blessed the heaven.)

15. *King' amunye olmumua sinyati olamal oiruko Enkai.*
    (We receive with a holy tail the team who believe in God.)

4. Occasionally an original work in an indigenous style emerges from Mennonites in eastern Africa. One that the 1978 *Mennonite World Conference Songbook* introduced to North Americans is *Hayye an ammanno.*[9]

// Let us praise him! Praise him!//
God the great Creator!
Let us praise him! praise him!

// *Hayye an ammanno,*//
Ilahi na untay
Hayye an ammanno.

---

[9] Clarence Hiebert and Rosemary Wyse, compilers, *International Songbook* (Lombard, IL: Mennonite World Conference, 1978), no. 1. Somali text by Adam J. Farah; translated from Somali by Bertha Beachy and adapted by the editors.

1. God Creator made us all.
   Ears and eyes and all four limbs.
   Over us he watches.
   Let us praise him! Praise him!

2. God Creator gave his word.
   Called us to obey him too.
   He will then reward us.
   Let us praise him! Praise him!

3. Those who on the Lord believe;
   He has made us each his child.
   God the Father loves us.
   Let us praise him! Praise him!

1. *Wu na egayayo*
   na ilaliyaye,
   Ilahi na untay
   Hayye an ammanno

2. *Indhihiyo dhegaha*
   iyo afarta adin
   Assaga na siyye,
   Hayye an ammanno.

3. *Inti eraygisa*
   adde'do rumaysa
   Wu u abalgudaye,
   Hayye an ammanno.

4. *Inti aminto dhan*
   inamu ka yele.
   Hayye an ammanno.

Example 8. Tune for *Hayye an ammanno*

The tune was composed by Adam J. Farah, whose early years were spent as a camel herder. An oral work such as this will have varying versions of pitch in notation. This version corresponds closely to the way he sang it at Wichita in 1978 and the way the believers in Mogadishu sang it in July 1986.

These four stages do not necessarily occur in chronological order from one to four; they may be simultaneous. The newer approaches are often additions to the continued use of Western hymns in translation, and they represent an enrichment of worship resources rather than a replacement of the earlier. However, the last two stages represent the more complete contextualization of musical style, and they offer enriching possibilities for the worldwide church.

Chapter 21

ON THE TABLE OF CONTENTS
OF A HYMNAL

Mary K. Oyer

> *During 1992 Mary Oyer was a regular contributor to the*
> *Trends in Music column in* Festival Quarterly, *often writ-*
> *ing on topics directly and indirectly related to* Hymnal: A
> Worship Book *This brief essay sets the organization of the*
> *new hymnal in relationship to the tables of content of other*
> *historic hymnals—Mennonite and non-Mennonite. As the*
> *last paragraph intimates, Mary was a bit skeptical about*
> *this way of organizing the hymns in* Hymnal: A Worship
> Book, *but as usual was willing to wait and see whether it*
> *would prove to be useful.*

One of the valuable features of the *Hymnal Sampler* and the new
hymnal to be published in June is the message they convey by their
format or organization of contents. Hymns as well as the spoken
resources are arranged according to acts of worship: gathering,
praising and adoring, confessing and reconciling, proclaiming, af-
firming the faith, praying, offering, witnessing, and sending. The
list suggests the progression through the service in an orderly, logical way. I believe that this approach, which the worship committee
of the hymnal project settled on early in their work, is unique.

The table of contents of any hymnal is a valuable window into
the book. Unlike the indices, which reveal details of various kinds,
it lets us see relationships within the book in one broad sweep and
often reveals the theology of the denomination producing it. In

---

order to understand the special value of the *Hymnal Sampler* approach, I offer the following brief survey of a few hymnal organizations in the past.

Probably the first hymnal whose table of contents expressed the theology of the group and its leader, John Wesley, was *A Collection of Hymns for the Use of the People Called Methodists*, published in 1779. Its five sections make a progression from the call to sinners to return to God, through descriptions of religion (both formal and inward), praying for repentance and recovery from backsliding, and living the Christian life, to living with other believers in the society meeting. It was a suitable format in which to present the evangelical hymns of John Wesley's brother, Charles.

The most important nineteenth-century English hymnal, *Hymns Ancient and Modern*, 1861, began with the hours of the day and the seasons of the church year. A large section of general hymns followed. Hymns for the sacraments and varied occasions—thanksgiving, times of trouble, for example—concluded the book. In the prominence of the church year (one-half of the hymnal) the table of contents reveals a desire to connect with the centuries-long liturgical tradition, perhaps in reaction against Methodist piety.

The (Old) Mennonite book *Hymns and Tunes*, 1890, does not have a table of contents. In its place, opposite the first hymn, is an index of subjects that functions to present contents. Subjects, twenty-seven in all, are arranged alphabetically. The committee made no attempt to relate subjects: the index is purely functional.

The *Mennonite Hymnary* (General Conference Mennonite), 1940, has a unique structure—a series of seven books. Book I, consisting of 402 hymns, begins with worship and proceeds with a structure that follows the creed, concluding with Special Services and Seasons. The remaining books are briefer: hymns for children, gospel songs, the church year in chorales, metrical psalms, responses and aids to worship. The gospel song and chorale sections exist because of their distinctive musical styles rather than the topics their words suggest.

The committee for the *Mennonite Hymnal*, 1969, compiled by two groups of Mennonites, agreed on a format based on the creed, ending with times and seasons. A separate gospel song section carried over from the *Mennonite Hymnary*, 1940. A section of choral hymns at the end attempted to sort out difficult hymns suitable for choir use.

The unique approach of the *Hymnal Sampler*, 1989, and of the new hymnal lies in its emphasis on acts of worship rather than topics or styles. In so doing it acknowledges that music as well as words enter worship through hymns. A gathering hymn, for example, invites people into worship not only with its words; the character of the music may draw them together. It can be exuberant in character, as in "Come We That Love the Lord," or reflective and comforting, as in "Come, Ye Disconsolate." The worship leader can try to capture in both words and music the ethos of the gathered group and respond to their spiritual needs at the time.

The emphasis on acts of worship may be a present trend that will fade soon, but it brings a freshness and breadth of approach to a new hymnal, and it serves a fine purpose if it raises musical consciousness among those who choose the hymns.

Chapter 22

"AH, HOLY JESUS" AND HERZLIEBSTER JESU

Mary K. Oyer

> *For one year (1993) Mary Oyer served as contributor for the Hymn Interpretation column that appears regularly in* The Hymn, *the quarterly publication of The Hymn Society in the United States and Canada. These incisive essays cover a good deal of territory and explore the historical context in which the text or tune was written, structural features of the text or tune, something about performance practices, and/or the experience of singing the hymn. This style of essay writing stands midway between the brief articles she wrote (along with J. Harold Moyer and Alice Loewen) in* Exploring the Mennonite Hymnal: Handbook *and the expansive essays written for* Exploring the Mennonite Hymnal: Essays.

The Passion hymn "Herzliebster Jesu" is one of those personal, intimate poems that emerged during the Thirty Years' War in Germany—1618–48. The devastation of the war, which together with a deadly pestilence wiped out two-thirds of the German population during that time, turned some of the hymn writers away from the confident, outward expressions of the sixteenth-century Reformation to inward, reflective meditation.

Johann Heermann (1585–1647) was such a poet, born in Silesia and pastor at Koben. In addition to the external chaos surrounding him, his inner battles with ill health and his wife's early death

---

Reprinted, by permission of the publisher, from *The Hymn* 44, no. 1 (January 1993), 37.
"Ah, Holy Jesus" is #254 in *Hymnal: A Worship Book* (Elgin, IL: Brethren Press; Newton, KS: Faith and Life Press; Scottdale, PA: Mennonite Publishing House, 1992).

helped shape the spirit of his work. Because he was familiar with Latin poetry—he wrote poems in Latin early in his life—he used a collection of *Meditationes,* at that time attributed to St. Augustine, as a model for "Herzliebster Jesu." He entitled it "The cause of the bitter sufferings of Jesus Christ, and consolation from his love and grace. From Augustine."

Heermann chose the sapphic poetic meter: 11 11. 11 5, a favorite form for early Latin poets. It harked back, in turn, to the lyric poetry of the Greek woman Sappho, of the seventh century BC. One of the fragments of Sappho's poetry that has come down to our time is translated by T. F. Higham in the original meter:

> The Moon
>
> Bright stars, around the fair Selênê peering,
> No more their beauty to the night discover
> When she, at full, her silver light ensphering
> Floods the world over.[1]

One can read all fourteen stanzas of Heermann's hymn in German (1630) along with an English translation of the whole by Catherine Winkworth (1863) in Erik Routley's *A Panorama of Christian Hymnody.*[2] The usual version in contemporary hymnals, however, is the five-stanza paraphrase by Robert Bridges, which appeared in his *Yattendon Hymnal,* 1899.

Bridges (1844–1930) was a poet of such distinction that he was made Poet Laureate of England in 1913 and received the Order of Merit in 1929.

His version follows the restrictions that the Latin poet Horace placed on sapphic meter: the long lines of eleven syllables must divide after the fifth or sixth syllable, and the fourth syllable should be stressed. Here in Bridges, each line of eleven falls into five plus six. The rhyme scheme is Heermann's—a a b b—as is also the double rhyme with the stress on the penultimate syllable: (of)-*fend*-ed and (de)-*scend*-ed; *pay* thee and *pray* thee; (un)-*swerv*-ing; and (de)-*serv*-ing, for example.

---

[1] T. F. Higham and C. M. Bowra, eds., *The Oxford Book of Greek Verse in Translation* (Oxford: Clarendon Press, 1938), 206.
[2] Erik Routley, *A Panorama of Christian Hymnody* (Chicago: G.I.A. Publications, 1979), 87.

Ah, holy Jesus, how hast thou offended
that man to judge thee hath in hate pretended?
By foes derided, by thine own rejected,
   O most afflicted!

Who was the guilty? who brought this upon thee?
Alas, my treason, Jesus, hath undone thee;
'twas I, Lord Jesus, I it was denied thee:
   I crucified thee.

Lo, the good Shepherd for the sheep is offered,
the slave hath sinned, and the Son hath suffered;
for man's atonement, while he nothing heedeth,
   God intercedeth.

For me, kind Jesus, was thine incarnation,
thy mortal sorrow and thy life's oblation;
thy death of anguish and thy bitter passion
   for my salvation.

Therefore, kind Jesus, since I cannot pay thee,
I do adore thee, and will ever pray thee,
think on thy pity and thy love unswerving,
   not my deserving.

Text: Johann Heermann, 1630; tr. Robert Bridges, 1899

The music of Johann Crüger (1598–1662) supports the text wonderfully. The two half notes that end each phrase slow the motion and encourage reflection. One cannot hurry. The deliberate, thoughtful character is reinforced by two half notes that close the first five notes in each case. All long phrases have the same pattern of half and quarter notes. Although the beginning of the six-syllable section suggests a gain in momentum, the phrase is soon halted.

The melodic shape is beautifully crafted as well. The first five notes pull downward in natural minor; the remainder of the phrase points upward. The second phrase moves toward brightness in the relative major key and the calmness of an arch shape, but the downward pull returns twice in phrase three, as it reflects the scale of the very beginning. The final phrase sounds like a desperate cry as it leaps upward an octave before it falls to the keynote.

The success of the Bridges-Crüger combination—its power to induce profound reflection—may be due in part to Bridges's deep respect for the music of a hymn. The words, he said, must be true to the mood and character of the tune.[3] In any case, the unity of this paraphrase and tune captures admirably the ethos of the Heermann-Crüger period.

---

[3] Robert Seymour Bridges, *Collected Essays, Papers &c. of Robert Bridges: [XXI–XXVI]* (London: Oxford University Press, 1935), 70–71.

Chapter 23

"VENI, SANCTE SPIRITUS"

Mary K. Oyer

One of the finest of the Gregorian chants that have made their way into hymnals is the medieval sequence "Veni, Sancte Spiritus," for use at Pentecost. Sequences came from adding texts to the elaborate vocalizations that developed on the final a of the Alleluia of the Mass. Eventually they were composed as pieces independent of the Alleluia, with unique characteristics.

"Veni, Sancte Spiritus" appears often in pairs of similar thoughts, recalling parallelism of Hebrew poetry, and its seven-syllable lines are organized into pairs of rhyming units and musical phrases. Here is the Latin of stanza 1:

	Rhyme		Music
Veni, sancte Spiritus,	a	⎫	
Et emitte caelitus	a	⎬	A
Lucis tuae radium:	b	⎭	
Veni, pater pauperum;	c	⎫	
Veni, dator munerum;	c	⎬	A
Veni, lumen cordium.	b	⎭	

All lines participate in double rhyme: lines one and two as well as four and five are paired. Lines three and six rhyme, thus dividing the stanzas into symmetrically balanced halves. Each half uses the same plainsong melody. The sequence is not strophic; rather, each succeeding stanza has new music, but always paired in the pattern of stanza one.

Reprinted, by permission of the publisher, from *The Hymn* 44, no. 2 (April 1993), 41. For background on this piece, see the introduction to chapter 22 of the present volume. The Taizé "Veni Sancte Spiritus" is #298 in *Hymnal: A Worship Book* (Elgin, IL: Brethren Press; Newton, KS: Faith and Life Press; Scottdale, PA: Mennonite Publishing House, 1992).

Probably the most familiar translation is the one by Caswall and the editors of *Hymns Ancient and Modern*. It is faithful to the meter and rhyme scheme of the original Latin, though it has single rather than double rhyme.

> Come, thou Holy Spirit, come!
> And from thy celestial home
> shed a ray of light divine.
> Come, thou Father of the poor!
> Come, thou source of all our store!
> Come, within our bosoms shine!
>
> Thou of comforters the best;
> thou, the soul's most welcome guest;
> sweet refreshment here below;
> in our labor, rest most sweet;
> grateful coolness in the heat;
> solace in the midst of woe.
>
> O most blessed light divine,
> shine within these hearts of thine,
> and our inmost being fill!
> Where thou art not, man is naught,
> nothing good in deed or thought,
> nothing free from taint of ill.
>
> Heal our wounds, our strength renew;
> on our dryness pour thy dew;
> wash the stains of guilt away:
> bend the stubborn heart and will;
> melt the frozen, warm the chill;
> guide the steps that go astray.
>
> On the faithful, who adore
> and confess thee, evermore
> in thy seven-fold gifts descend;
> give them virtue's sure reward;
> give them thy salvation, Lord;
> give them joys that never end!"[1]

---

[1] Thirteen century; translation based on Edward Caswall, 1849; altered in *Hymns Ancient and Modern*, 1861 and 1875. *Historical Companion to Hymns Ancient and Modern*, ed. Maurice Frost (London: William Clowes and Sons, 1962), 228.

Another remarkable version of the "Veni, Sancte Spiritus" emerged fifteen years ago at the Taizé Community in France—a community whose work is worship. It is a prose "paraphrase": memorable phrases from Caswall's translation appear, as these stanzas illustrate:

> Come, Holy Spirit,
> from heaven shine forth with your glorious light.
> > Veni Sancte Spiritus.
> Father of the poor
> Come to our poverty.
> Shower upon us the seven gifts of your grace.
> Be the light of our lives. O come.
> > Veni Sancte Spiritus.

In the absence of the regularity of meter and rhyme of the Latin and the English translation, the composer, Jacques Berthier (b. 1923), created unity with a congregational ostinato continuously repeating "Veni Sancte Spiritus."[2]

Example 1. Veni Sancte Spiritus

Over this a soloist or small group sings the stanzas, each of which ends with a return to the ostinato. The effect is spellbinding.

The peculiar needs of the Taizé Community produce a new kind of congregational musical experience. The people who come to worship there represent such diverse backgrounds and languages that simple, repetitive music is needed for full participation.

---

[2] *Music from Taizé*, vol. 1, conceived and edited by Brother Robert and composed by Jacques Berthier (Chicago: G.I.A. Publications, 1979), 36.

Latin, which is now no one's religious language, serves to unify the congregation. At times several languages are used simultaneously.

Why does such a piece function so well in worship? Surely the ancient phrases of the text, which remind the worshiper of earlier witnesses to the Spirit's work, have a role. The music brings something, too: the continuous repetition of a brief circular ostinato—somewhat like a mantra—frees the worshiper from wordiness and opens the possibility of another level of worship. Individuals are swept into an intense and unifying relationship with the congregation—an experience that can help them center in God. The duality of the repetitive ostinato and the more linear solo part is always present; those who sing the secure ostinato can anticipate the newness of the always-changing line.

Perhaps the ultimate value of this and similar works from Taizé is to offer, in Fred Pratt Green's words, "a new dimension in the world of sound" that leads us to "a more profound Alleluia!" (from "When in Our Music God Is Glorified").

Chapter 24

"THE STRIFE IS O'ER"

Mary K. Oyer

The Oxford Movement in England, beginning around 1830, brought with it an interest in ancient texts in Latin and Greek and Reformation hymns in German. By the 1860s fine translators such as John Mason Neale and Catherine Winkworth were publishing volumes of hymns in translation.

In 1861 a remarkable hymnal appeared, one that spoke to this ideal of the Oxford Movement: *Hymns Ancient and Modern*. It included many hymns in translation. Unlike most of the collections of the time, this book combined texts with musical settings. Some of these combinations remain prominent in present-day hymnals—"Holy, Holy, Holy" with NICAEA, "Abide with Me" with EVENTIDE, and "Eternal Father, Strong to Save" with MELITA, for example.

"The Strife Is O'er" first appeared with VICTORY in *Hymns Ancient and Modern, 1861.* The Latin text came from *Symphonia Sirenum,* Cologne, 1695. Its first stanza, 8 8. 8 with Alleluias, reads:

> *Alleluia, Alleluia, Alleluia.*
> *Finita jam sunt praelia,*
> *est parta jam victoria:*
> *gaudeamus et canamus,*
> *Alleluia.*[1]

Its first two lines rhyme, and the last line breaks into two rhyming sections of four syllables each.

Reprinted, by permission of the publisher, from *The Hymn* 44, no. 3 (July 1993), 39. For background on this piece, see the introduction to chapter 22 of the present volume. "The Strife Is O'er" is #263 in *Hymnal: A Worship Book* (Elgin, IL: Brethren Press; Newton, KS: Faith and Life Press; Scottdale, PA: Mennonite Publishing House, 1992).

[1] *Hymns Ancient and Modern: Historical Edition* (London: Clowes & Sons, 1909), 211.

222

Francis Pott (1832–1909) published a translation in five stanzas in *Hymns Fitted to the Order of Common Prayer* in 1861 but allowed its inclusion with alterations in *Hymns Ancient and Modern*. The translation has undergone many alterations since that time, so that hymnals now rarely agree on the form of text they present. All versions keep Pott's a-a-a rhyme scheme, however.

> Alleluia! Alleluia! Alleluia!
> The strife is o'er, the battle done;
> The triumph of the Lord is won;
> O let the song of praise be sung.
> Alleluia!

> The powers of death have done their worst,
> And Jesus hath his foes dispersed;
> Let shouts of praise and joy outburst.
> Alleluia!

> On that third morn he rose again
> In glorious majesty to reign;
> O let us swell the joyful strain.
> Alleluia!

> He closed the yawning gates of hell;
> The bars of heaven's high portals fell;
> Let songs of joy his triumphs tell.
> Alleluia!

> Lord, by the stripes which wounded thee,
> From death's dread sting thy servants free,
> That we may live, and sing to thee.
> Alleluia![2]

William Henry Monk (1823–89), the music editor *of Hymns Ancient and Modern* (in fact, he was the one who suggested the name for the book), adapted a chordal Gloria from a Palestrina Magnificat *(Magnificat in the Third Mode,* 1591)[3] to fit Pott's text. So both text and music came from earlier sources.

Monk wrote the music for three introductory alleluias and set the concluding alleluia in a climactic gesture. The combina-

---

[2] *Hymns Ancient and Modern* (London: Novello, 1861), no. 114.
[3] *Le Opere complete di Giovanni Pierluigi da Palestrina,* vol. 15 (Rome: Edizione Fratelli Scalera, 1943), 18.

tion well suits a festive and triumphant Easter spirit. The musical shape is upward, ending on the highest note of the soprano line. The triple meter contributes to the lively character.

A comparison of this setting with a musical version of the text from Malawi points up differences in ideals across cultures and offers to Western congregations an African expression that is quite manageable:[4] This version sounds "African": the solo part falls from high to low in the characteristic fashion not only of many African melodies but of ancient songs of other cultures—Native American, for example. The alleluia refrain moves downward also toward a kind of magnetic pull at the bottom. The entire hymn seems repetitive because it consists of only these two alternating musical phrases. The solo part makes its way through the text using the first phrase, always answered by the alleluia refrain sung by the group. The strophic effect of the Palestrina-Monk setting is not present except in the grouping of every three lines which the rhyme creates. The contrapuntal part of the refrain stresses the interval of a fourth rather than a third.

Example 1. The Strife Is O'er

The Malawi version was collected by Tom Colvin, a missionary of the Church of Scotland since 1954, and published in *Free to*

---

[4] Taken from the cassette tape: *African Praise from Iona Abbey,* vol. 1 (Iona: Iona Community, 1985).

Serve: Hymns from Africa. In the preface to another of his hymn collections, *Leap My Soul,* he writes;

> These are not simply a new body of hymns: they imply a new style of singing and even a different approach to worship. The sharing of a hymn between leader and worshippers ... introduces an element of drama and a greater excitement into the church's praise. The repetitive character of the melodies and the habit these hymns have of expanding to a climax can elicit a more spontaneous response and a fuller participation among the worshippers.[5]

Colvin's experiments with singing African hymns in the Iona Community are encouraging to Western music leaders who would like to experience the musical crossing of cultures.

---

[5] Tom Colvin, "Preface," in *Leap My Soul* (Glasgow: Iona Community, 1976), 5.

Chapter 25

"YE SERVANTS OF GOD"

Mary K. Oyer

The context of a hymn frequently offers insights into its meaning and enriches its use. "Ye Servants of God" emerged at a difficult time for Methodists, who were being falsely accused of rebelling against the King of England in favor of James II, who had abdicated in 1688, and his descendents.

As is often the case, the persecutions stimulated the writing of hymns. In 1744 a collection of thirty-three texts, entitled *Hymns for Times of Trouble and Persecution* appeared. Charles Wesley's "Ye Servants of God" was one of a group of four subtitled "To be Sung in a Tumult."

> Ye Servants of God, your Master proclaim,
> And publish abroad his wonderful name;
> The name all-victorious of Jesus extoll;
> His kingdom is glorious, and rules over all.
>
> The waves of the sea have lift up their voice,
> Sore troubled that we in Jesus rejoice;
> The floods they are roaring, but Jesus is here,
> While we are adoring, he always is near.
>
> Men, devils engage, the billows arise,
> And horribly rage, and threaten the skies:
> Their fury shall never our steadfastness shock,
> The weakest believer is built on a rock.

Reprinted, by permission of the publisher, from *The Hymn* 44. no. 4 (October 1993), 45. For background on this piece, see the introduction to chapter 22 of the present volume. "Ye Servants of God" is #100 in *The Mennonite Hymnal* (Scottdale, PA: Herald Press; Newton, KS: Faith and Life Press, 1969).

God ruleth on high, almighty to save;
And still he is nigh, his presence we have;
The great congregation his triumph shall sing,
Ascribing salvation to Jesus our King.

"Salvation to God who sits on the throne,"
Let all cry aloud, and honour the Son;
Our Jesus's praises the angels proclaim,
Fall down on their faces, and worship the Lamb.

Then let us adore, and give him his right,
All glory and power, and wisdom, and might,
All honour and blessing, with angels above,
And thanks never-ceasing, and infinite love.

The complete poem of six stanzas is needed for the full picture. Stanzas two and three, which tend to be omitted from our hymnals today, introduce the atmosphere of tumult. Elements of nature are personified: the waves lift the voice, the floods roar, the billows rage in fury. Yet God rules over all. God, rather than an earthly king, reigns and supports the believer. The language in this case is that of the book of Revelation—the Lamb on the throne, with angels and a great congregation falling on their faces as they bring adoration, honor, praise, and thanks to the true ruler of the world—the believer's King.

The remarkable craft of Charles Wesley shines out in this hymn, even with the omission of the two tumultuous stanzas. The grace and felicity of his lines are explained in part by Bernard L. Manning in his classic book, *Hymns of Wesley and Watts*: "More than most writers, Wesley makes the end of his lines correspond with the natural pauses in his thought. The sound and sense coincide. This it is that makes his verse specially suitable for singing."[1]

And from Frank Baker, on the craft of Wesley: "He wanted a stanza in which a theme could be announced, developed, and satisfactorily concluded—with a foreshadowing of the theme for the following stanza.... Within the stanzas themselves we find an orderly synchronization of thought and verse. In general, every line contains a complete idea, is in fact a clause or sentence. Similarly

---

[1] Bernard L. Manning. *The Hymns of Wesley and Watts* (London: Epworth Press, 1942), 59.

every stanza is a paragraph, and the whole poem a logically con-structed essay in verse."[2]

The meter of 10 10. 11 11. rhymes in an a a b b pattern. How-ever, the long lines break quite naturally in the middle, and even the inner pauses come at logical groupings of words—5 5. 5 5. 6 5. 6 5.—and form inner rhymes: a b a b c d c d.

The foreshadowing Baker mentions appears in the ending of stanza one, "And rules over all," connecting with the beginning of stanza four (or two, in most books) in "God ruleth on high." Stanza four's "Ascribing salvation to Jesus our King," foreshadows stanza five's "Salvation to God, who sits on the throne."

Wesley chose an anapaestic (light, light, strong) accent, which, though common in ballads, was unusual for hymns in his day. It lends the poetry a kind of energy and forward thrust—a lilt that matches well the triple meter of the musical settings.

HANOVER (LYONS and PADERBORN are used as well today) was first published in the sixth edition of the *Supplement to the New Version* of Tate and Brady, 1708, and set to the Sixty-seventh Psalm. William Croft may have been the composer, though we do not know for sure. The shape of the melody supports the natural pauses in the text. Through modulations it builds tension to the third of four phrases and then recedes on the fourth, resulting in the kind of arch shapes the Western world likes in its hymn tunes. The first and last lines of the melody end with an up-and-down motion which creates a duple, zigzag effect against the triple time.

"Ye Servants of God" was not a part of the *Collection of Hymns for the Use of the People Called Methodists,* 1780. It was included in the Supplement to the 1831 edition of the *Collection,* omitting the third stanza and adding a sixth from Wesley's *Funeral Hymns,* 1746:

> Come, Lord, and display thy sign in the sky,
> And bear us away to mansions on high;
> The kingdom be given, the purchase divine,
> And crown us in heaven eternally thine.

The four-stanza form (stanzas 1, 4, 5, and 6 of the original), however, has prevailed to the present day. It appears, usually unal-

---

[2] Frank Baker, *Representative Verse of Charles Wesley* (London: Epworth Press, 1962), xxxvi.

tered, in most of the hymnals of the last ten years. Perhaps it still has life today because it was vital and relevant when it was written in 1744.

Chapter 26

NURTURING SPIRIT
THROUGH SONG

Mary K. Oyer, with Rebecca Slough

This piece is based on an interview in which Mary Oyer explores an experience of lecturing and singing with teachers participating in the Lilly Fellows Program in Humanities and the Arts, Valparaiso University, Valparaiso, Indiana, 14–16 October 1994. The original intent of the interviewer, Rebecca Slough, was to create a prose article based on the interview. However, Mary's experience at Valparaiso was so alive for her, even three years later, that this free verse structure best honored the experience of the interview. In many presentations, Mary has talked about the power of singing. In an article appearing in The Mennonite[1] *she described the experience of singing as "a moment transformed." This time with the Lilly Fellows was one of those vividly transformed moments.*

The interviewer sought from Mary Oyer her reflections on helping people create works of art through her musical leadership. Here is what she said, in a form that fits the telling.

On October 15, 1994, I led a lecture-hymnsing for the Lilly Fellows Program for Humanities and the Arts at Valparaiso University. This was a group of a hundred administrators and teachers from fifty Christian colleges. The subject they gave me to explore was

---

Reprinted, by permission of the publisher, from *Mennonot: For Mennos on the Margins,* no. 10 (Fall 1997), 17–18.
[1] Mary K. Oyer, "Singing Celebrations: Hymns, Her and All of Them," *The Mennonite,* 12 May 1998, 5.

how music ministers to or nurtures the souls of Christians. I used the title "The Nurturing Spirit." They asked me to sing with the group, so I took *Hymnal: A Worship Book* and used illustrations from it. It was for me a fascinating topic, one I hadn't considered much before.

The planners called me while I was in Kenya
    at a time when I was playing chamber music with friends.
We all experienced how when we played together—
    as a group of persons
    with whom we had developed rapport—
    how much better each of us played
    than we could have alone,
    sometimes even better than we thought we could.

There was something nurturing about the experience
    of contributing something to playing together.
And it seems to me that that is what congregational singing is—
    though it isn't really chamber music,
    because the group is a whole lot bigger.
But what happens is the experience of being surprised—
    of being a part of something
    that you didn't know you could do,
    that is much bigger than yourself.

I was very conscious as I was working
and planning the presentation—
    having been given such an exciting subject—
    I was very conscious of the Holy Spirit hovering over the earth
    the way that Gerard Manley Hopkins talks
    about how "the Holy Ghost over the bent
        World broods with warm breast and ah! bright wings,"
    creating, enabling, enlightening.
I was very conscious of these feelings ...
    so that the whole experience of planning
    was almost as valuable as the experience
    of doing the presentation.
    (Though the experience of doing it was a great release, too.)

The experience of planning it kept being sort of an epiphany

or revelation of something emerging.
(I don't know why I never thought about it,
    but music does nurture the souls of Christians.)
That kind of experience I would like
    in the process of playing cello,
    but I don't get it there.
I get it sometimes in choir;
    but I got it very very strongly in this situation
    with the Lilly fellows.
Such openness—
    I was astonished.
These people were from Christian colleges,
    but usually in connection with education
    you don't talk about this kind of thing—
    music nurturing the soul.

As I think back to it,
    it was a very vivid experience
    when it actually was happening.
I knew right away as I began to talk that it was going to go.
I have an idea that,
    in part,
    it was because people don't expect to be able to sing.
I think they were surprised.
There was a kind of electricity in the air.
I knew something was vivid
    and something was happening to them.
There was a kind of vitality there
    and a freeing in them.

And I notice this in leading singing, if it goes well—
    that people are freed when they sing.
That something happens to the physical person in singing,
    a releasing.
And it is very wholesome.
Something comes to life
    that is beyond the ordinariness of many moments.

You asked whether the experience means anything now…
It doesn't really.

It was a disposable thing.
The presentation was planned for this particular group,
 at that particular time
 on a subject that excited me in that situation.
I remember telling some friends about the experience,
 since it had been such a landmark for me,
 a kind of watershed in understanding—
 this idea of the nurturing spirit.
So they invited me to a retreat of their small group.
It turned out to be a most disappointing thing for me.
I couldn't repeat anything from the original experience
 because the whole business had not been planned
 for that small group.
I should have started all over
 with something that was pertinent for them.
I couldn't do the presentation again,
 and haven't done it again.

There is something "one time" about works of this sort.
The moment,
 in that sense,
 cannot be revived.
It keeps moving on,
 and it's different every time.
The fundamentals are still there,
 but not the context in which to make it go.

You asked about the presence of evil.
I didn't experience it during the presentation itself.
Occasionally the texts we sang described how evil was overcome.
The music itself left us with the sense of overwhelming the evil.
There are forces that occur,
 that are present in a place,
 that keep a work from gelling—
 that keep a group from being able to be released—
 I think of singing as one of those releasing forces.
Something happens—
 and I think the Holy Spirit is at work
 enabling people to get outside of themselves,

to gain moments of recognition of something
way beyond themselves.

I suppose that evil comes in the forces that imprison the spirit
and keep it bound within a people.
Singing is the most releasing spiritual experience that I have.
Singing with other people is the most releasing experience I have.

Chapter 27

TWO CENTURIES OF AMERICAN MENNONITE HYMN SINGING

Mary K. Oyer

> *During her year in Scotland with Erik Routley, Mary Oyer became fascinated with hymnbooks. She found joy in tracing particular hymn texts and tunes back to their original sources and also cultivated a love for exploring whole collections of hymns. As a result of this newfound interest, she helped secure the J. D. Hartzler collection of hymnals for the Goshen College library in the 1960s. Such collections help scholars track changes in the theology of a denomination.*
>
> *Eileen Saner, librarian at Associated Mennonite Biblical Seminary, invited Mary to talk about Mennonite hymnody and singing at the 2006 annual meeting of the American Theological Library Association. This presentation outlines a brief history of Mennonite hymnal developments in North America. Those attending the lecture sang many of the musical examples.*

It is a pleasure and a privilege to speak to librarians. You are such a valuable link in any research effort. I knew this during my graduate work, but it was more obvious to me when I began working with hymnody. I had always sung hymns, but I had no idea of the richness of the field until I worked in Edinburgh, Scotland, in 1963 and 1964. In the Scottish National Library anything published in Great Britain was available, and the librarians could find it with the

This paper was presented at the American Theological Library Association 2006 Annual Conference in Chicago, IL, 22 June 2006.

slightest hint. Every morning they brought me my stack of books, reserved from day to day. I worked also in New College Library of the university. There the librarian lamented that the hymnals were not fully catalogued, so he gave me a dust cloth and sent me to the stacks to explore. And in this country there are wonderful treasures. I mention only the Newberry Library here in Chicago, with its fine collection of American hymnody, and the Mennonite Historical Library at Goshen College, where Librarian Joseph Springer even anticipates what I might need.

I have organized this presentation around Mennonite hymnbooks, which are listed in chronological order (see table 27.1). I plan to spend more time with the early books because of their distinctive characteristics. Recent Mennonite hymnals resemble more closely the contents of mainline Protestant books, without the service music of the liturgical churches.

Mennonites originated in the 1520s in three areas of Anabaptist reform movements: Switzerland and South Germany, Holland, and Eastern Europe—Austria and Moravia. They left the Roman Catholic Church because they believed in baptizing adults, not children. When they chose to be baptized again, they were called Anabaptists. Their interest in the Sermon on the Mount led them to seek peace rather than war, and to speak the truth, without taking oaths. They rejected the authority of the Pope, the power of the sacraments, and the sale of indulgences. Their radical views led to disputations with both Catholic and the new Protestant leaders. Many of them were persecuted, imprisoned, and even killed.

The Anabaptists believed, along with Luther and Calvin, in the active participation of the congregation in worship. They chose the vernacular language over Latin and created a congregational hymnody. Beginning in the late 1520s, the Swiss Brethren began to write verses about their martyrs and to sing them to tunes they knew. For example, "Who Now Would Follow Christ," 535 in *Hymnal: A Worship Book* (HWB; see example 1),[1] is an anonymous hymn of twenty-seven stanzas about Jörg Wagner, whom both Lutherans and Anabaptists claimed. He was imprisoned, tortured, and burned in 1527. The translator created three stanzas out of the

---

[1] *Hymnal: A Worship Book* (Elgin, IL: Brethren Press; Newton, KS: Faith and Life Press; Scottdale, PA: Mennonite Publishing House, 1992).

Table 27.1. Two Centuries of American Mennonite Hymnals

Background: European Anabaptists (Mennonites and Amish)
1564 *Ausbund, Das ist etliche schöne christenliche Lieder ...*
      2nd ed., 1583

Mennonite Church (Old)	**General Conference Mennonites**
1803 *Harfe der Kinder Zions*	
1804 *Ein Unpartheyisches Gesangbuch*	
1832 *Genuine Church Music (Harmonia Sacra, 1847)*	
1847 *A Selection of Psalms, Hymns, and Spiritual Songs*	
1890 *Hymns and Tunes*	1890 *Gesangbuch mit Noten*
	1894 *Mennonite Hymns: A Blending of Many Voices*
1902 *Church and Sunday School Hymnal*	
1911 *Supplement*	
1915 *Life Songs [Number 1]*	
1927 *Church Hymnal*	1927 *Mennonite Hymn Book*
1938 *Life Songs Number 2*	
	1940 *Mennonite Hymnary*

Cooperative
1969 *The Mennonite Hymnal*
1992 *Hymnal: A Worship Book*
2005 *Sing the Journey*

first five, paraphrasing the hymn to represent martyrdom in general rather than to include the specific details of Wagner's death.

Not all hymns were about martyrs. Praise songs were prominent. Other hymns articulated Anabaptist beliefs or encouraged new believers. "We Are People of God's Peace" (HWB 407; see example 2) comes from the prose writings of the Dutch leader Menno Simons (whose name the group adopted). It is a versification of his "Reply to False Accusations," 1552.

The Dutch Mennonites were the first to produce hymnbooks, but the most significant Anabaptist hymnal was the *Ausbund*, published in 1564 by the Swiss Brethren. Its importance lies in its con-

Example 1. Who Now Would Follow Christ (WARUM BETRÜBST DU DICH, MEIN HERZ)

1 Who   now would fol-low Christ in life   must scorn the world's
2 Christ's ser-vants fol-low him to death   and give their bod -
3 Re - noun-cing all, they choose the cross, and claim-ing   it,

in - sult   and strife,   and bear the cross each day. For this
y,   life,   and breath   on cross and rack and pyre. As gold
count all   as loss,   e'en hus-band, child, and wife. For-sak-

a - lone leads to the throne; Christ is   the on - ly way.
is   tried and pu - ri - fied   they stand the test of fire.
ing gain, for - get-ting pain, they en - ter in - to life.

Text: "Wer Christo jetzt will folgen nach," *Ausbund*, 1564; tr. David Augsburger, 1962, *The Mennonite Hymnal*, 1969, revised 1983. Translation copyright © 1969, 1983 David Augsburger. Used by permission.
Music: Bartholomeus Monoetius, 1565; harmonized by J. Harold Moyer, 1965. Harmonization copyright © 1968 Faith and Life Press/Mennonite Publishing House, Scottdale, PA 15683. Used by permission.

tinuous use, virtually unchanged since its second edition in 1583. It is the hymnbook for most Amish congregations today.

The core of the book consists of fifty-three hymns composed by Anabaptist prisoners in the dungeons at Passau on the Danube from 1537 to 1540. In the second edition (1583) eighty hymns from the entire Anabaptist output were included. By the early seventeenth century a few more additions brought the total number to 140, its present state. Only German texts were printed, but at the head of each hymn was a tune name, usually a folk song or German Lutheran chorale tune, with an occasional Catholic chant.

Example 2. We Are People of God's Peace (AVE VIRGO VIRGINUM)

1 We are peo-ple of God's peace   as   a   new cre-a-tion.
2 We are chil-dren of God's peace   in   this new cre-a-tion,
3 We are ser-vants of God's peace,   of   the   new cre-a-tion.

Love u-nites and strengthens us,   at   this   ce-le-bra-tion.
spreading joy and hap-pi-ness, through God's great sal-va-tion.
Choosing peace, we faith-ful-ly   serve with heart's de-vo-tion.

Sons and daugh-ters of   the Lord, serv-ing one an-oth-er,
Hope we bring in spir-it meek, in   our dai-ly liv-ing.
Je - sus Christ, the Prince of peace, con-fi-dence will give us.

a   new cov-en-ant of peace binds us   all to-geth-er.
Peace with ev-ry-one we seek, good for   e-vil giv-ing.
Christ the Lord is our de-fense; Christ will nev-er leave us.

Text: Menno Simons, 1552; tr. Esther Bergen, *Mennonite World Conference Songbook*, 1990
Translation copyright © 1990 Mennonite World Conference. Used by permission.
Music: Johann Horn, *Ein Gesangbuch der Brüder im Behemen und Merherrn*, 1544; revised in *Catholicum Hymnologium Germanicum*, 1584

Their choice of tunes tells us how freely they borrowed from their surroundings, even from the repertoire of their persecutors. The *Ausbund* was published in Europe in eleven editions after 1600.

In 1683 the first Mennonites migrated to Pennsylvania, taking advantage of William Penn's offer of land to Germans. Ten years later a group of Swiss-German Anabaptists under Jakob Ammann's leadership broke away from the Mennonites, on issues of strict church discipline, to form what became the Amish church. They, too, migrated gradually to America. There the *Ausbund* was reprinted many times between 1742 and the present. The forty-seventh printing, 2005, is the most recent.

The Amish and Mennonites in America illustrate differing approaches to tradition and to assimilation with the culture around them. Their hymnody offers one good way to examine the differences. The Amish used (still use) the *Ausbund* exclusively for their worship. Mennonites, although they talked about "separation from the world," gradually expanded their worship practices to embrace new ideas. To illustrate the Amish approach, see the Amish *Loblied,* or praise hymn, always the second hymn in their worship (HWB 33, translated at HWB 32; see example 3).

The text retains High German. The music is always a single melody, sung without an instrument and introduced by a male leader. The congregation joins after the first syllable of each phrase. The entire hymn will take close to twenty minutes, five for each stanza.

The tune name, AUS TIEFER NOT, comes from Luther's metrical setting of Psalm 130. He also wrote a fine tune in the Phrygian mode; but an anonymous tune from Strassburg, 1525, was the one they must have known because, hidden within the ornamentation on each syllable, it can be found (see example 4).

The ethnomusicologist George Pullen Jackson has explained that when a group sings very slowly, it is unable to maintain the pitch without wavering. Over centuries of slow singing, the waverings have become a part of an ornamented version of the original.[2]

---

[2] George Pullen Jackson, "The Strange Music of the Old Order Amish," *Music Quarterly* 31 (July 1945), 75–88.

Example 3. O Gott Vater (AUS TIEFER NOT)

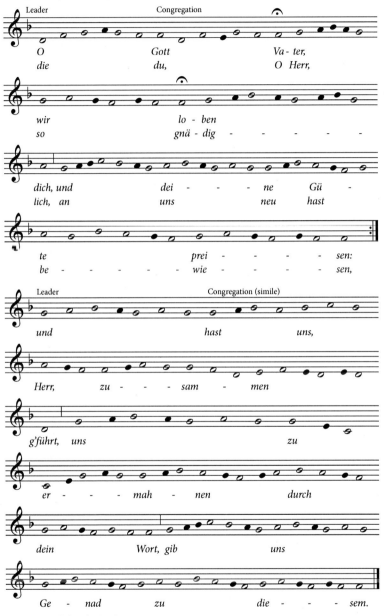

Text: Leenaerdt Clock, *Ausbund*, 17th c.

Music: based on the notation of J. W. Yoder in *Amische Lieder*, 1940, and Olen F. Yoder in *Ausbund Songs with Notes*, 1984
Adapted to current singing east of Goshen, IN, by Mary K. Oyer.

Example 4. Aus tiefer not in O Gott Vater

The Mennonites, in contrast, published hymnals in the early nineteenth century that fully accepted the hymns of Lutheran and Reformed churches. *Die kleine Geistliche Harfe der Kinder Zions (Zions Harfe),* published in 1803 in the Franconia area of eastern Pennsylvania, included thirty psalms from Calvin's Genevan Psalter, translated into German by Ambrosium Lobwasser. The bulk of the book of 475 hymns consisted of German chorales, with only two *Ausbund* hymns. In 1804 the nearby Lancaster Conference of Mennonites published *Ein Unparthyeisches Gesangbuch* with sixty-one Calvinist psalms and many German chorales. But the inclusion of sixty-three of the *Ausbund* hymns (16 percent of the 390 total) retained some continuity with the Mennonite German heritage.

See "As the Hart with Eager Yearning" (HWB 500) for Genevan Psalm 42, and "Blessed Jesus, at Your Word" (HWB 13; "Liebster Jesu, wir sind hier") for a Lutheran chorale, used in both books, but as the first chorale in *Zions Harfe.*

The shift to English in America presented a dramatic change in Mennonite singing. It appeared in written form first in *Genuine Church Music,* 1832—a shape-note book in an oblong format. Joseph Funk, from the Shenandoah Valley in Virginia, compiled this book for singing schools, in the manner of predecessors *Wyeth's Repository of Sacred Music* and *Kentucky Harmony;* the more familiar *Sacred Harp* came in the decade following.

Significant changes in Mennonite hymn singing came in both text and music:

1. The poetic meter (that is, the number of syllables per line and the number of lines per stanza) was much more regular and far less varied than in the French or German psalms and hymns. The earliest English psalms, written in the mid-sixteenth century, followed ballad meter—8.6.8.6. or 8.6.8.6.D (doubled). This came to be called common meter, abbreviated CM in our hymnals. Common meter could expand to long meter (LM), 8.8.8.8., or contract to short meter (SM), 6.6.8.6., either of which could be doubled. Only three or four other meters appeared occasionally. Rhyme schemes were limited basically to two. Calvinist psalms, in contrast, used "no fewer than 110 varieties of stanza structure ... and 33 different rhyme schemes."[3] German hymns, like the French, offered much variety in stanza structure and rhyme. Our languages shape the poetic form of our hymns.

2. English texts and music often appear in pairs of phrases creating question-answer relationships. German hymns often used the Meistersinger rule for writing a song: A A B (as in "A Mighty Fortress Is Our God," for example). French psalms were sometimes organized in A A B, but frequently fell into seven or eight unique phrases.

3. Texts were often anonymous and dealt with the brevity of life and the inevitability of death. Isaac Watts was by far the favorite author in America. Twenty-two percent of the hymns in the twenty-fifth edition of *Genuine Church Music (Harmonia Sacra)*, 1993, were by Watts. The next favored author, Charles Wesley, had only one-third of Watts's total number.

4. American folk tunes predominated. They were probably tunes from Great Britain that were kept alive in the Appalachian Mountains and chosen for the shape-note books. Lowell Mason, the New England composer, teacher, and hymnal compiler, was represented prominently. Examples of folk tunes include FOUNDATION (HWB 567), TENDER THOUGHT (HWB 556). Examples of Lowell Mason tunes include HAMBURG (HWB 259) and NASHVILLE (HWB 166).

---

[3] Emily Brink, in *Psalter Hymnal Handbook,* ed. Emily Brink and Bert Polman (Grand Rapids, MI: CRC Publications, 1998), 32.

5. The singing schools taught part singing in three voices: soprano, tenor, and bass. The tenor carried the melody in the style of Renaissance and pre-Renaissance music. By the middle of the century a fourth part was added, and the music of Lowell Mason shifted the melody to the soprano part. The style was a cappella. No instruments were permitted. The emphasis on reading music and the mode of singing influenced Mennonite congregations through much of the twentieth century.

The Mennonites compiled their first English hymnal in 1847: A *Selection of Psalms, Hymns, and Spiritual Songs.* It consisted of texts only. The singers were directed to use the tunes of *Genuine Church Music.* Specific tunes were indicated at the head of each hymn. Texts were often those of *Genuine Church Music* (now called *Harmonia Sacra).* Seventy-two percent of them were in the traditional English psalm meters. There were thirty other meters, but these were often represented by only one hymn.

It was more than forty years before Mennonites created another hymnal. For the first time *Hymns and Tunes,* 1890, combined texts with tunes. Only the first stanza was placed between the staves; the others were set out in poetic form, as was the custom with nineteenth-century hymnals such as Beecher's *Plymouth Collection,* 1855, and the famous *Hymns Ancient and Modern,* 1861, in England. The usual format for the double page of *Hymns and Tunes* was one tune with two or three texts of the same poetic meter.

Hymns and Tunes was the first hymnal since the *Ausbund* to include original Mennonite texts, perhaps thirty. Seventeen tunes were attributed to "The Committee." One, "I Owe the Lord a Morning Song" (HWB 651; see example 5), managed to survive to the present. It conveys something of the Mennonite character of the times: "I owe" suggests the sense of duty rather than pleasure, and the serious, straightforward language offers no poetic imagery; yet it has worn well.

The compilers perpetuated the tradition of singing American folk tunes by borrowing from *Harmonia Sacra,* and they were beginning to sing hymns from the middle of the nineteenth century. William Bradbury, for example, wrote music for singing schools, following in Lowell Mason's direction. *Hymns and Tunes* used these hymns of his that are still sung today:

Example 5. I Owe the Lord a Morning Song (GRATITUDE)

1 I owe the Lord a morn - ing song, of
2 He kept me safe an - oth - er night; I
3 Keep me from dan - ger and from sin, help
4 Keep me till thou wilt call me hence, where

grat - i - tude and praise, for the kind mer - cy
see an - oth - er day. Now may his Spir - it,
me thy will to do, so that my heart be
me by cr night can be, and save me, Lord, for

he has shown in length - 'ning out my days.
as the light, di - rect me in his way.
pure with - in, and I thy good - ness know.
Je sus' sake; he shed his blood for me.

Text: Amos Herr, *Hymns and Tunes*, 1890
Music: Amos Herr, *Hymns and Tunes*, 1890
   Text and music copyright © 1927 Mennonite Publishing House, Scottdale, PA 15683. Used by permission.

"Sweet Hour of Prayer" (HWB 11)
"Savior, Like a Shepherd Lead Us" (HWB 355)
"Just as I Am, without One Plea" (HWB 516)
"My Hope Is Built on Nothing Less" (HWB 343)

But Bradbury also wrote for the growing Sunday school movement. Sabbath school songbooks appeared by the hundreds, at first in the format of the hymnals of the times with texts only. The new style of the 1860s enlarged the dimensions and included the music.

Its ornate covers presented flowers, angels, and decorative letters. Fanciful names, such as *The Golden Casket, Gems for the Sunday School, Bright Jewels,* and *The Shining Strand,* replaced the simple title, *Hymnal.* Mennonites of 1890 liked these songs, too. For example, they included:

"Jesus Loves Me" (Bradbury) (HWB 341)
"He Leadeth Me" (Bradbury) (HWB 599)
"I Love to Tell the Story" (Fischer) (HWB 398)
"Shall We Gather at the River" (Lowry) (HWB 615)

Another group of Mennonites immigrated to the North American Midwest in the 1870s. Their ancestors were Dutch Mennonites who had helped build dikes in Prussia in the seventeenth century and from there moved to the Ukraine to farm, at the invitation of Catherine the Great in 1783. They joined those Mennonites who, as a part of the spiritual awakening movement around 1860, had formed a new branch called the General Conference Mennonite Church. Together they published a German hymnal parallel in name and date to *Hymns and Tunes: Gesangbuch mit Noten,* 1890. It consisted of German chorales and eighteenth- and nineteenth-century hymns, with simplified harmonies, and German and American folk songs. There were occasional American composed tunes of Lowell Mason.

One Sunday school song, "Oh, have you not heard of that beautiful stream" (HWB 606; see example 6), had an unusual history. Written by Torrey and Hull and published in 1864 in *Sabbath School Gems,* it was taken by Baptist missionaries to Germany and translated into German. It became a favorite of German-speaking Mennonites in Ukraine, who brought it with them when they immigrated to America. Here at various times they have translated it back from German into English.

Although these two books were alike in a number of ways, their poetic meters contrasted. Three-fourths of the texts in *Hymns and Tunes* were in English psalm meters, with only eleven other meters listed in the metrical index. *Gesangbuch mit Noten*'s 109 meters for its 600 hymns reveal its Germanic base.

But General Conference Mennonites also wanted an English hymnal. They chose the best they could find on the market: *A Blending of Many Voices,* published by A. S. Barnes. They made a few changes and gave it a new title: *Mennonite Hymns: A Blending of Many Voices.* The contents represented a wide range of "classics" in hymnody, with only a few representatives of their German heritage.

The *Church and Sunday School Hymnal,* 1902, replaced *Hymns and Tunes,* 1890, as the official hymnal for the (Old) Mennonites (those who had come to America and used English). To link it with the Sunday school movement was a progressive move; there were Mennonites who feared and resisted the changes Sunday schools might bring. Progressive also was the inclusion of gospel hymns. Although their publication began with *Gospel Hymns* (1874), *Hymns and Tunes* barely touched them in 1890. But now more than a third of the book came from the Moody-Sankey revival movement, with its musical roots in Chicago popular music. Prominent names were Fanny Crosby, William Doane, Robert Lowry, and P. P. Bliss. Gospel hymns rarely used English psalm meters. They added to the iambic and trochaic accents the livelier, rollicking rhythms of dactylic and anapestic organization. For example, "When Peace, like a River" (HWB 336) flows along with more syllables per line. The repetitions of the refrain give opportunity for the singer to reflect on the stanza.

Only nine years later a supplement of 119 hymns enlarged the *Church and Sunday School Hymnal.* Now more than half of the contents were gospel hymns. Momentum for a change of style grew to the making of a separate supplement, *Gospel Hymns* (1915), which consisted largely of this new type.

A hymnal reflects the character, theology, and piety of the church it represents. This was a period of the rise of Fundamentalism and an opposing emphasis on social concerns—the Social Gospel. It was a divisive time in Mennonite life. Both Mennonite groups published hymnals in 1927. English Victorian hymns appeared in both; otherwise they were quite different. The (Old) Mennonite *Church Hymnal* included the gospel songs Fundamentalists demanded (it seems that church leaders linked gospel songs with Fundamentalism), as well as nineteenth-century American hymns.

The General Conference Mennonites in *Mennonite Hymn Book* chose to focus on hymns from liturgical traditions, emphasizing

Example 6. Oh, Have You Not Heard (THE BEAUTIFUL RIVER)

flow-ing for thee, O seek that beau-ti-ful stream.

1 Ich weiss einen Strom, dessen herrliche Flut
fliesst wunderbar stille durchs Land,
doch strahlet und glänzt er wie feurige Glut,
wem ist dieses Wasser bekannt?

2 Wohin dieser Strom sich nur immer ergiesst,
da jubelt und jauchzet das Herz,
das nunmehr den köstlichsten Segen geniesst,
erlöset von Sorgen und Schmerz.

3 Der Strom ist gar tief und sein Wasser ist klar,
es schmecket so lieblich und fein;
es heilet die Kranken und stärkt wunderbar,
ja machet die Unreinsten rein.

4 Wen dürstet, der komme und trinke sich satt,
so rufet der Geist und die Braut,
nur wer in dem Strome gewaschen sich hat,
das Angesicht Gottes einst schaut.

Refrain: O Seele, ich bitte dich: Komm!
und such diesen herrlichen Strom!
Sein Wasser fliesst frei und mächtiglich,
O glaub's, es fliesset für dich!

Text: R. Torry, Jr., *Sabbath School Gems*, 1864 (English); German tr. Ernst H. Gebhardt, *Frohe Botschaft*, 1875
Music: Asa Hull, *Sabbath School Gems*, 1864

the church year. That book did not last long, but the *Mennonite Hymnary* of 1940 replaced it brilliantly. The editor grouped the hymns into books—a book of psalms, a book of children's songs, one of gospel songs, another of chorales, and so on. The denomination was well satisfied.

These two Mennonite groups decided to build a hymnal together in the 1960s—the *Mennonite Hymnal*. The (Old) Mennonites brought the folk tradition of early America and the General Conference Mennonites the German chorale. Together they looked for the hymns that sustain and nourish the ecumenical church. Both continued the practice of four-part congregational singing—the (Old) Mennonites singing a cappella and the General Conference using keyboard, for the most part.

Other influences of the 1960s helped shape that book. New translations of the Bible in the 1950s had brought insights but also revealed growing difficulty in understanding King James Version language. The Second Vatican Council asked Catholics around the world to use their vernacular languages, rather than Latin, and their own musical styles. These songs began to enter Western hymnbooks, including the Mennonite ones. The human rights

movement raised justice issues and alternate ways of perceiving
the Christian life. The Mennonites joined the mainline churches
in fully researching the texts and tunes they chose and carefully
documenting sources for each hymn.

In the 1970s and 1980s Mennonites produced supplementary
books in the new styles of the 1960s. Many of these needed instrumental accompaniment. Songs sung by Mennonites on five continents were collected for a Mennonite World Conference in 1978,
and choirs from Africa and Asia brought their songs and dances to
the occasion. By the end of the century the majority of Mennonites
lived in the southern hemisphere and outside of Western culture,
and cross-cultural songs enriched Mennonite hymn singing. For
example, the Cheyenne hymn *Jesus A, Nahetotaetanome* (HWB 9;
see example 7) brings a new kind of spirituality in the words and
music. The Cheyenne retained their own traditional melody, and
John Heap of Birds wrote Christian words to fit. The Plains Indian
tune typically moves too high and too low for many voices and calls

Example 7. Jesus A, Nahetotaetanome

Text: John Heap of Birds, *Jesus A, Nahetotaetanome*; tr. David Graber and others, *Tsese-Ma'heone-Nemeotòtse*, 1982
  Copyright © 1982 Mennonite Indian Leaders' Council. Used by permission.
Music: Plains Indian melody

for reaching the whole range of one's voice. The melody begins high and falls downward, as is the pattern in many ancient songs.

"Asithi, Amen" (HWB 64; see example 8), is a South African hymn with a Zulu text. A limited number of words, often repeated, is the usual pattern for cultures that use oral rather than written means for learning songs. The solo-response pattern creates high energy. Drums and shakers, which are needed, supply a network of lines of rhythm. Africans help Westerners accept the dancing body as part of worship; the whole person, mind and body, is involved.

Example 8. Asithi: Amen

Text: South African hymn
Music: S. C. Molefe

"Ah, What Shame I Have to Bear" (HWB 531; see example 9) is a Japanese response to the parable of the prodigal son, set to an

Example 9. Ah, What Shame I Have to Bear (ɪᴍᴀʏō)

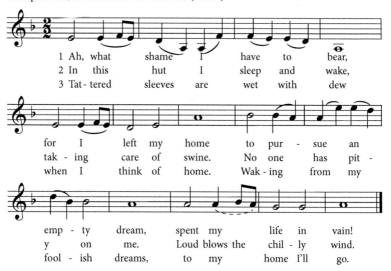

```
1 Ah, what      shame    I     have    to     bear,
2 In   this     hut      I     sleep   and    wake,
3 Tat- tered    sleeves  are   wet     with   dew

for   I      left   my   home   to   pur - sue   an
tak - ing    care   of   swine. No   one  has   pit -
when  I      think  of   home.  Wak- ing from  my

emp - ty    dream,   spent my       life in    vain!
y      on   me.      Loud blows the chil - ly  wind.
fool - ish  dreams,  to   my        home I'll  go.
```

Text: Sogo Mōtsumoto, 1895; tr. Esther Hibbard, 1962
Music: Traditional Japanese Air, 12th c.
Copyright © The Hymnal Committee UCC in Japan. Used by permission.

ancient Japanese tune. Japanese Christians have often tried to sing Western English hymns translated into Japanese, but they say that ballad meter (8.6.8.6.) does not fit their language easily. Hymns written by Japanese are often in 7s and 5s (haiku can be 5.7.5.), as in this hymn. The melody covers a wide range and often has two or three notes for a syllable of text.

In 1992 Mennonites and the Church of the Brethren—both historical peace churches with Anabaptist connections—produced *Hymnal: A Worship Book*. With this worship book Mennonites have moved very close to the hymnals of the mainline churches. Gender equality in language was a strong component in the compilation. The expansion of musical styles of the previous decades revealed a much greater variety of styles than ever before.

And with the publication of this hymnal German chorales and gospel songs are no longer opposing styles but belong in the same camp, as traditional Mennonite singing faces contemporary Christian music projected on a screen and led by a band of instrumentalists and singers. The new style presents several challenges:

1. It involves moving from a distinct church style to one that borrows heavily from popular culture (perhaps a bit like the approach the Reformers in the sixteenth century used for their new hymns).

2. It means communicating music by ear rather than eye—by oral means rather than by the written page. Historically Mennonites valued the ability to read music.

3. It is not just a method of catching the music and bringing it to sound; it also entails accepting a musical style with far more repetition and improvisation than we find in our traditional hymnals.

4. It represents a shift in emphasis from harmony to rhythm. The tensions and resolutions at the heart of four-part harmony are replaced by the tensions of rhythm. Rhythm rather than harmony becomes the heartbeat of the hymn; it gives energy and emotional power to the singing.

A 2005 supplement, *Sing the Journey,* points strongly toward this new approach to congregational singing. Once again, as in the 1920s, piety and musical style threaten to divide members within a congregation as well as congregations from one another. In the climate of polarization present in North America today, there is an urgent need for mediating conversations and models for developing understanding. Thomas Troeger and Carol Doran present such a model in their *Trouble at the Table,*[4] in which they discuss approaches to change in worship. They see hymns, for example, falling into three categories, represented by three concentric circles around a vertical axis. In the center, the structural circle, we collect all those hymns that are basic to our congregation's life—those that continue to nourish us over the years. The outer circle, ephemeral, brings in all the new possibilities. We test these hymns as they move toward the center through the intermediate conjunctural circle. If the church is alive, there will be constant motion in and out through this evaluating process.

---

[4] Carol Doran and Thomas H. Troeger, *Trouble at the Table: Gathering the Tribes for Worship* (Nashville: Abingdon Press, 1992).

A JOYFUL SONG I'LL RAISE
Bibliography of Works by and about Mary K. Oyer

When All Thy Mercies, O My God

When all thy mercies, O my God,
  My rising soul surveys,
Transported with the view, I'm lost
  In wonder, love and praise.

Ten thousand thousand precious gifts
  My daily thanks employ;
Nor is the least a cheerful heart,
  That tastes those gifts with joy.

Through every period of my life
  Thy goodness I'll pursue;
And after death, in distant worlds,
  The glorious theme renew.

Through all eternity, to Thee
  A joyful song I'll raise;
But O eternity's too short
  To utter all Thy praise!

Joseph Addison, 1712

WORKS BY MARY K. OYER

compiled by Mary Swartley
with annotations by Rebecca Slough

> *"When one reads these essays, ... if one has had the stimu-*
> *lating experience of hearing a Mennonite congregation sing*
> *in four strong parts without an instrument, one realizes*
> *that in this denomination, its congregations and its leaders,*
> *is probably a flowering of hymns unmatched by any other*
> *group—and Mary Oyer [is] its present dean."—Ellen Jane*
> *Porter*[1]

1949

"Selecting Songs for Children, Part 1." *Gospel Herald* 42, no. 49 (December 6), 1192.

1950

"Selecting Songs for Children, Part 2." *Gospel Herald* 43, no. 1 (January 3), 10.

1955

"A Philosophy of the Use of Music in Mennonite Meetings." Address, First Mennonite Musicians' Meeting, Chicago, 4–5 March.

> Printed as chapter 14 of the present volume.

1957

"A Philosophy of Mennonite Church Music: As Related to Beauty." Address, Second Mennonite Musicians' Meeting, Iowa City, IA, 22–23 March.

"A Christian View of the Fine Arts." In *Proceedings of the Eleventh Conference on Mennonite Educational and Cultural Problems,* Bethel College, North Newton, KS, 6–7 June 1957. [N.P.]: Council of Mennonite and Affiliated Colleges.

> Reprinted as chapter 15 of the present volume.

---

[1] Ellen Jane Porter, Review of *Exploring the Mennonite Hymnal: Essays,* by Mary Oyer, *The Hymn* 33 (October 1982), 264.

"Christianity and the Fine Arts: Basic Problems Which Confront Mennonites Participating in the Fine Arts." Paper, Goshen College Faculty Discussion Meeting, 21 November.

1959

"Questions Which Arise with the Consideration of Instruments for Mennonite Worship." Presentation, Laurelville Mennonite Church Center, Mt. Pleasant, PA, September.

> Printed as chapter 17 in the present volume.

"The Church's Responsibility for Artistic Discrimination." Paper, Mennonite Graduate Fellowship, Columbus, OH, 2 January.

> Printed as chapter 16 in the present volume.

1962

"The Use of Music in Mennonite Worship." Presentation, Ontario Mennonite Conference on Music, 10–11 November.

> Copy in Mennonite Historical Library, Goshen College, Goshen, IN.

1964

"Walter Yoder: A Tribute." *Gospel Herald* 57, no. 47 (December 8), 1040.

(ca. 1964)

"Possible Uses for Organ in the Goshen College Mennonite Church."

1965

"The Life and Method of Music." *Mennonite Life*, January, 30–31.

> Reprinted as chapter 18 in the present volume.

1967

"Cultural Problems in the Production of a Mennonite Hymnal." In *Proceedings of the Sixteenth Conference on Mennonite Educational and Cultural Problems,* Hesston College, Hesston, KS, 8–9 June 1967. [N.P.]: Council of Mennonite and Affiliated Colleges.

> Reprinted as chapter 19 of the present volume.

"Hymnal Revision." Paper, meeting of Indiana-Michigan Mennonite Ministers, 25 April.

1969

"Introduction." In *The Mennonite Hymnal,* edited by Lester Hostetler and Walter E. Yoder. Newton, KS: Faith and Life Press; Scottdale, PA: Mennonite Publishing House.

> This hymnal was published jointly by the (Old) Mennonite Church and the General Conference Mennonite Church. Mary served as executive secretary of the joint hymnal committee. Drawing from *The Church Hymnal* (1927) and *The Mennonite Hymnary* (1940), the committee also added hymns from other sources. With 619 hymns, thirty-three musical worship resources, and ninety-eight worship resources for congregational use, this hymnal was intended to "increase and deepen an appreciation among the

church for the rich hymnody of the Christian church" (from the preface). This hymnal included six hymns from Asia as an experiment. Number 606, "Praise God from Whom All Blessings Flow," placed in the choral hymn section of the collection, soon became a beloved Mennonite anthem.

1972

with Philip Clemens, Eleanor Kreider, Orlando Schmidt, and Marilyn Houser. *Festival of the Holy Spirit Song Book.* Goshen, IN: Goshen College.

This songbook signaled a new approach to Mennonite congregational song. The committee now assumed the use of instruments—guitars and pianos, if not organs—in worship. Many of the songs in the collection appear in unison or in two-part arrangements; some would be sung with improvised harmonies. The previous generation of church leaders would have considered these "lighter songs" more appropriate to the campsite than the congregation's worship. But because it was not an authorized book of the Mennonite Church, Mary could take risks. Her classical training, her experience with the 1969 hymnal, and her emerging awareness of African music expanded the musical sensibilities she applied to the task of selecting 125 songs: scripture songs, post–Vatican II Catholic folk songs (including then-popular Medical Mission Sisters compositions), African-American spirituals, Black gospel songs, Latin American songs, songs in a folk idiom by Mennonite writers, songs in a jazz idiom, songs by Sydney Carter, and international songs from Israel and the West Indies.

1975

"Hymn Singing among Mennonites." *Festival Quarterly* 3, no. 2 (May, June, July), 32.

1976

"Reflections of a Church Musician." *Mennonite Reporter* 6, no. 6 (22 March), 5; *Gospel Herald* 69, no. 13 (March 30), 256–57.

1976–77

"Cheers for the Book Collectors among Us!" *Festival Quarterly* 3, no. 3 (November, December, January), 21.

1977–78

"The Tape Recorder." *Festival Quarterly* 4, no. 4 (November, December, January), 19.

1978

"A Folksong from *The Mennonite Hymnal.*" *Festival Quarterly* 5, no. 3 (August, September, October), 28.

Review of *Lead Us, Lord; A Collection of African Hymns,* compiled by Howard S. Olson. *The Hymn* 29 (July), 194.

1979

"606, *Mennonite Hymnal.*" *Festival Quarterly* 6, no. 1 (February, March, April), 29.

1980

Exploring the Mennonite Hymnal: Essays. Newton, KS: Faith and Life Press; Scottdale, PA: Mennonite Publishing House.

> Thirty-four essays explore musical, poetic, and historical dimensions of hymns found in *The Mennonite Hymnal.* Each essay starts with one text and tune combination, but as Mary guides the reader into a text or tune, she connects one quality of the song with the same quality found in another song. This approach adds depth and texture to the study of each hymn by setting it in a larger context. This series of essays displays in prose style the center-and-spokes diagram method that Mary used extensively in her later teaching.

1983

"The Cold, White Peaks of Art, the Foothills of Warm Humanity." *Goshen College Bulletin,* November, 3–5.

> Mary tells of her "conversion" from the cold peaks of a disembodied and unfeeling artistic aesthetic to an understanding of art that includes the mind but also the warmth of the heart and body. It was her study of hymns and her opportunities to lead hymns in congregations that made her question the validity of aesthetic experience separated from human contexts. Hymns, in particular, serve functions and do not exist for their own sake. She explains why learning African music also helped refine her view of art as a profoundly human expression best understood within the context of a human community.

ed., with Orlando Schmidt, Harry Loewen, and Leonard Gross. *Assembly Songs: A Hymnal Supplement—Hymns Both New and Old.* Newton, KS: Faith and Life Press; Scottdale, PA: Mennonite Publishing House.

> This songbook was published for the joint Mennonite Church–General Conference Mennonite Church assembly at Bethlehem, PA, in 1983. The first ninety-nine hymns were drawn from earlier Mennonite collections (*The Mennonite Hymnal* and *Sing and Rejoice,* for example). Sixty songs were new texts and/or tunes drawn from historical, international, or contemporary ecumenical English-language sources. This collection was an early Mennonite experiment in making inclusive language changes and an important precursor to *Hymnal: A Worship Book* (1992).

with Alice Loewen and Harold Moyer. *Exploring the Mennonite Hymnal: Handbook.* Newton, KS: Faith and Life Press; Scottdale, PA: Mennonite Publishing House.

> This resource provides basic hymnological information on the sources, texts, and tunes of each hymn in *The Mennonite Hymnal,* usually with additional narrative material. Because of the book's format, it is difficult to discern which entries Mary wrote. This handbook was not published until fourteen years after the release of *The Mennonite Hymnal.*

1983–84

"Should Our Hymnody Be More Specific?" *Festival Quarterly* 10, no. 3 (November, December, January), 28–29.

1984

"Crossing Musical Cultures." *Festival Quarterly* 11, no. 1 (Spring), 42.

1985

"Extending Our Experience of Mennonite Hymnody." *Festival Quarterly* 12, no. 1 (Spring), 34.

Review of *Fill Us with Your Love, and Other Hymns from Africa*, by Tom Colvin. *The Hymn* 36, no. 2 (April), 31–32.

1986

"Amish and Mennonite Music." In *The New Grove Dictionary of American Music*, 1: 42–43. London: Macmillan Press Limited.

> Mary describes the beginning of the Anabaptist movement; the hymns written by Anabaptist prisoners at Passau, which became the core of the *Ausbund* (1583); the origins of the Amish and their use of the *Ausbund*; Amish singing; two Mennonite hymns published in America at the beginning of the nineteenth century; the shape-note tune books of Joseph Funk (*Genuine Church Music*; later *Harmonia Sacra*); the origins of part singing among North American Mennonites; first American Mennonite hymnals in English (*A Selection of Psalms, Hymns, and Spiritual Songs* [texts only], 1847; *Hymns and Tunes for Public and Private Worship, and Sunday School Songs Compiled by a Committee*, 1890); the origins of the General Conference Mennonite Church; the Dutch/Russian hymn heritage; and *The Mennonite Hymnal* (1969). She also mentions the Mennonite Brethren and the Mennonite Indian Leaders' Council.

"Music and Worship: New Styles, New Life." *Festival Quarterly* 13, no. 1 (Spring), 25.

1987

"Is It Possible to Keep a Tradition?" *Festival Quarterly* 14, no. 1 (Spring), 24.

1988

"Hymnody in the Context of World Mission." *Internationale Arbeitsgemeinschaft für Hymnologie Bulletin* (Rijksuniversiteit te Groningen Instituut voor Liturgiewetenschap) 16 (June): 53–74; German translation: 75–95.

> This essay is based on a presentation Mary gave at an international conference on hymnody in Lund, Sweden, in August 1987. Using examples from Africa, she outlines ways people can use study of hymnody to help bridge gaps to another culture: (1) participate in music-making activities; (2) discuss the character and function of hymns with the music leader of a local congregation; (3) read literature written by natives of the countries of interest; and (4) read the work of anthropologists, ethnomusicologists, linguists, and theologians who have studied the culture. She explores the cultural

meanings of sound, instruments, melody, harmony, rhythm, circularity, and embodied music. Western missionaries routinely misunderstood how these aspects of music worked within specific cultural contexts including worship in the church. Reprinted in *Hymnology Annual* 1, edited by Vernon Wicker. Berrien Springs, MI: Vande Vere Pub., 1991.

1989

"Hymn Leading among Mennonites." Part of a larger article, "Hymn Leading Practices in American Churches," by David W. Music. *The Hymn* 40, no. 1 (January), 21.

Mary sketches the hymn-leading practices of Mennonites who came to North America in the seventeenth century and those who came in the nineteenth century by way of Russia. Leadership in the latter group of immigrants used keyboard accompaniment for their four-part singing. The leadership style of the seventeenth-century immigrants was shaped by the singing school movement and by a distinctive Amish singing style. She explores briefly Joseph Funk's singing school movement and the style of Amish singing led by the *Vorsänger*. Women as well as men were likely to lead Mennonite congregational singing by the 1960s. She concludes by saying that Mennonite congregations in the 1980s could sing in four-part unaccompanied styles led by a song leader in one part of a worship service and by organ or guitar later in the same service.

ed. *Hymnal Sampler*. Findlay, OH: Church of God General Conference; Elgin, IL: Brethren Press; Newton, KS: Faith and Life Press; Scottdale, PA: Mennonite Publishing House.

The sampler was created for the joint assembly of the Mennonite Church and the General Conference Mennonite Church held in Normal, IL, in August 1989. It was also used at the Church of the Brethren Annual Conference that year and at the Churches of God General Conference. The collection of 117 songs and twenty worship resources was designed as a preview of the 1992 hymnal. The collection included chorale and psalm tunes, gospel songs, Black gospel numbers, contemporary hymns, contemporary worship songs, songs from the Taizé Community, and international songs.

1990

"A 'Singing School' for the '90s." *Festival Quarterly* 17, no. 2 (Fall), 18–19.

"Dedication anthem: 606." *The Builder,* January, 10–15.

"East African Church Music: Three Decades of Change." Lecture, joint meeting of the American Musicological Society, the Society for Ethnomusicology, and the Society for Music Theory, Oakland, CA, September.

Mary describes how hymnody has developed in East Africa, especially Tanzania, since the arrival of white missionaries, whose musical patterns overtook the indigenous African patterns. She notes four types of hymns found in East Africa in the late 1980s: (1) Western hymns that were translated into the local language with Western-style music, usually paired unsuccessfully because of differences in language structure and accent patterns; (2) hymns in Kiswahili, the national language of Tanzania, also used in Kenya; (3) vernacular hymns and music, which are closest to the spirit of the worshipers; and (4) original work in an indigenous style.

"Evolving African Hymnody." *Mission Focus* 18, no. 4 (December): 52–56.

> Reprinted as chapter 20 in the present volume.

Review of *Tumshangilie Mungu* [Let Us Praise God]. *The Hymn* 41, no. 2 (April), 40–41.

1991

Review of *Sing and Rejoice: Help for Hymn Singing with Alice Parker,* videotape. *The Hymn* 42, no. 4 (October), 44–45.

Review of *The Anabaptist Hymnal. Festival Quarterly* 18, no. 1 (Spring), 26.

Theological Lectureship on Church Music: An Ethnomusicological Perspective. Associated Mennonite Biblical Seminary, Elkhart, IN, 14–15 February.

> Mary's five presentations were: "Hymnody: A Key to Culture," "Crossing Cultures—Africa and the West," "My Pilgrimage with Music and the Church," "Artistic Dimensions of a Hymn," "The Future of Hymnody among Mennonites." Cassette recordings stored at AMBS library, Elkhart, IN.

1991 (1998, 2003)

"African Music." Elder Hostel course, Eastern Mennonite University, Harrisonburg, VA, 19–25 May 1991; Amigo Centre, Sturgis, MI, 4–9 October 1998; Amigo Centre, Sturgis, MI, 18–23 May 2003.

1992

"Hymns in the Life of the Church." In *On Being the Church: Essays in Honour of John W. Snyder,* edited by Peter C. Erb, 67–87. Waterloo, ON: Conrad Press.

> The essays in this collection were contributed for the retirement celebration of John W. Snyder, pastor of Rockway Mennonite Church for thirty years. Mary explores the cultural contexts that shaped the use of the Amish Lobg'sang "O Gott Vater"; "O Have You Not Heard of that Beautiful Stream," loved by Russian Mennonites; and "Amazing Grace," which has become a favorite song among North Americans, Christian or not. From this base of traditional songs, she looks at new styles of texts and tunes entering North American Mennonite churches in the early 1990s: new Roman Catholic songs in the wake of Vatican II; Native American hymns; contemporary worship songs; contemporary ecumenical hymns; favorite hymns and songs from other Christian traditions (for example, "My Life Flows On," a favorite among the Quakers); and music from the Taizé Community. The resources currently available to Mennonites would enrich their musical palette and reflect the time in which the songs were written and something about the people who sing them.

"Learning to Sing Another's Hymns." *Festival Quarterly* 19, no. 2 (Summer), 33.

"On the Table of Contents of a Hymnal," *Festival Quarterly* 18, no. 4 (Winter), 36.

> An article in a column Mary wrote for *Festival Quarterly* during 1992. Reprinted as chapter 21 of the present volume.

1993

"'Ah, Holy Jesus' & HERZLIEBSTER, JESU." Hymn Interpretation column. *The Hymn* 44, no. 1 (January), 37.

"'The Strife Is O'er.'" Hymn Interpretation column. *The Hymn* 44, no. 4 (October), 37.

"'Veni, Sancte Spiritus.'" Hymn Interpretation column. *The Hymn* 44, no. 2 (April), 41.

"'Ye Servants of God.'" Hymn Interpretation column. *The Hymn* 44, no. 3 (July), 45.

> The four hymn interpretations listed above appeared in the quarterly publication of the Hymn Society of the United States and Canada. They are reprinted as chapters 22–25 of the present volume.

"Introduction." In *The Harmonia Sacra: A Compilation of Genuine Church Music,* 25th ed. Intercourse, PA: Good Books.

> Mary's introduction reviews the editorial changes in the various editions of *Genuine Church Music,* first published in 1832 by Joseph Funk and Sons; renamed *Harmonia Sacra* in 1851.

1994

"Ethnic Hymns in *Hymnal: A Worship Book.*" *Builder,* August, 10–13.

"The Nurturing Spirit: How Music Teaches by Forming the Souls of Christians." Address, Fourth Annual National Conference of the Lilly Fellows Program in Humanities and the Arts, Valparaiso University, Valparaiso, IN, 14–16 October.

"Singing across Cultures: The African Gospel," and "Hymn Festival in *a cappella* Style: The Congregation as Choir and Organ." Workshop and presentation, Choristers' Guild Regional Meeting, Dallas, TX, 13–14 January.

1995

"African Hymnody." Paper, meeting of the Japanese Hymnal Committee, United Church–Kyodan, 1 September.

1996

"African Hymnody." *Kyodan Journal,* January 1996.

> This article is in Japanese translation.

1997

"Hymnody." Three lectures, Westminster Choir College, Princeton, NJ, 23–26 April.

"Nurturing Spirit through Song." *Mennonot: For Mennos on the Margins,* no. 10 (Fall 1997), 17–18.

> Reprinted as chapter 26 of the present volume.

with John S. Oyer. "Anabaptist Hymns Described and Sung." Presentation, meeting of Michiana Anabaptist Historians, Waterford Mennonite Church, Goshen, IN, 22 March 1997.

> This is a transcription of the program on hymns drawn from the *Ausbund* (1564) and *Die Lieder der Hutterischen Brüder.* Print copy and cassette re-

cording are housed in Mennonite Historical Library, Goshen College, Goshen, IN. John and Mary chose traditional martyr hymns and hymns still sung by the Amish. Their comments explain aspects of songs sung by a small group. The songs included in the program were:

"Aus tiefer Not schrei ich zu Dir" (*Ausbund* 61); "Out of the depths I cry to thee"

"Ein grosse Freud ist ingemein" (*Ausbund* 18)

"Herr Gott Vater von Himmel" (Hutterite hymnal)

"Trauren will ich stehen lassen" (*Ausbund* 17)

"Come, thou Holy Spirit, come" (translation of a Latin sequence hymn)

"Herr, ich bitt dich mit grosser Gier" (Hutterite hymnal)

"Wir kommen, Herr, zu dire" (Hutterite hymnal)

"O Gott Vater, wir loben Dich" (*Ausbund* 131); "Our Father God, thy name we praise" in an English translation

"Als Christus mit sein'r wahren Lehr" (*Ausbund* 7)

"Es sind zween Weg in dieser Zeit" (*Ausbund* 125)

1998

"Global Music for the Churches." In *Music in Worship: A Mennonite Perspective*, edited by Bernie Wiebe, 67–82. Newton, KS: Faith and Life Press; Scottdale, PA: Herald Press.

> *Music in Worship* contains fourteen essays by authors exploring issues related to music in Mennonite worship. Mary's essay describes several ways attention to various cultural influences has had an impact on Mennonite worship. She traces the emergence of new musical expressions for worship arising from Vatican II and the cultural unrest of the 1960s. New sources for international hymns have expanded Mennonite singing. She also discusses three levels of historical memory –borrowed from Thomas Troeger and Carol Doran (who had borrowed the concept from Edward Schillebeeckx)—as a way of evaluating how memory is expanded and challenged. The essay concludes by exploring what music reveals about the culture that gave it voice.

1999

"Amish and Mennonite Hymnody of the Reformation." Part of a series on hymnody at Yale University, New Haven, CT, 21 January.

"Congregational Song." Six sessions at Westminster Choir College, Princeton, NJ, 21–23 June.

"The Holy Ghost over the Bent World Broods." In *She Has Done a Good Thing: Mennonite Women Leaders Tell Their Stories,* edited by Mary Swartley and Rhoda Keener, 137–44. Scottdale, PA: Herald Press.

> This essay is an adaptation of a commencement address Mary gave at Eastern Mennonite College (Harrisonburg, VA) in 1994. It first appeared in *Christian Living* (June 1998). The title is taken from Gerard Manley Hopkins's poem, "God's Grandeur"; Mary retraces transformations in her heart and mind, attributing surprising shifts to opportunities presented by the Spirit's presence and activity in her life.

2000

Hymn Singing Sessions, ELCA Jubilee 2000, Navy Pier, Chicago, IL, 9–14 July.

2001

The Erik Routley Lectures, on the theme Common Ground—Celebrating the Worldwide Church. Albuquerque Presbyterian Association of Musicians, Conference on Music and Worship, Albuquerque, NM, 15–19 July.

> Mary's lectures were titled "African Hymns," "Asian Hymns," "Hymns in History," and "'Common Ground' Revisited."

2002

"History of Mennonite Music" and "Where Are We with Music in Mennonite Churches." Addresses, Mennonite Society of Musical Heritage, First Mennonite Church, Denver, CO, 19–21 July.

"Hymns in History" and "Celebration of Christian Song through the Ages." Class presentation, lecture and hymnsing, Regent College, University of Vancouver, Canada, 5 July.

"The History of Mennonite Singing" and "*Songs of the Church:* The Legacy of Walter E. Yoder." Presentations, conference on Our Musical Roots, Illinois Mennonite Historical and Genealogical Society, Metamora, IL, 5 May.

2004

"Hymnody" and "African Music." Lectures, Anderson Seminary, Anderson, IN, 17–18 March.

"Issues in Ethnic Music." Lecture, discussion, hymnsing, Faculty Seminar: Teaching Theology through Music, sponsored by The Wabash Center for Teaching and Learning in Theology and Religion, and The Department of Theology and Institute for Church Life at the University of Notre Dame, Oakwood Retreat and Conference Center, Syracuse, IN, 23 May–4 June.

"Music in My Life—A Retrospect," Afternoon Sabbatical series, Goshen College, Goshen, IN, 16 March.

> Mary narrates her life by decades, focusing on turning points.

"The Poetry and Music of Hymns." Presentations, Amagi Sanso Retreat Center, Izu Peninsula, Japan, 23–25 January.

> The titles of Mary's presentations were: "When in Our Music God Is Glorified," "Historical Hymns: Our Heritage," "Hymns as Support for Scripture," and "Cross Cultural Hymns."

2005

"A Brief History of the Organ Program at Goshen College." http://www.gcmusiccenter.org/php/facility/special.features/organ.php

> Program notes on the occasion of the dedication of a pipe organ, Opus 41, in Reith Recital Hall, Goshen College, Goshen, IN, in May 2005. In this brief introduction, Mary outlines reasons why prior to the 1960s acquiring

an organ at Goshen College was fraught with difficulties. She tells how an organ was secured for the arts building in 1960. Myron Casner began teaching on the instrument at a time when the (Old) Mennonite Church was considering whether organ music could be used in worship without threatening congregational singing. Through the donation of a Goshen alumna, Fannie (Rupp) Severson, an organ was placed in the church chapel in 1968. Through the creative research of Bradley Lehman and the craftsmanship of John Boody and George Tayler, the Opus 41 organ installed in the Reith Recital Hall—a space not specifically identified for worship—opens new possibilities for teaching and performing a variety of organ works.

"Crossing Cultures in Hymnody," and "Reformations in Hymnody." Lectures, University of Iowa, Institute for Sacred Music, 27–29 January. Hymn festival at First Mennonite Church, Iowa City, Iowa.

Introduction for *In Thee is Gladness*. CD produced by Martin Hodel, trumpet; and Bradley Lehman, organ.

"The Sound in the Land." In *Sound in the Land, Essays on Mennonites and Music*, edited by Maureen Epp and Carol Ann Weaver, 21–33. Kitchener, ON: Pandora Press.

> Mary created this essay from a lecture she gave as the keynote speaker at the Sound in the Land conference (Conrad Grebel College, Waterloo, ON, 28–30 May 2004). She explores several hymnals significant in the history of Mennonite Church and General Conference Mennonite Church and seeks to reveal something of their character. In a brief overview of the *Ausbund* (1564); *Zions Harfe* (1803); *A Selection of Psalms, Hymns, and Spiritual Songs* (1847); *Hymns and Tunes* (1890); *Gesangbuch mit Noten* (1890); *The Church and Sunday School Hymnal* (1902); *Church Hymnal* (1927); *Mennonite Hymn Book* (1927); *Mennonite Hymnary* (1940); *The Mennonite Hymnal* (1969); and *Hymnal: A Worship Book* (1992), Mary highlights the collections' unique characteristics and ways each contributed to Mennonite singing practices. She points out two contemporary trends that she believes will influence future Mennonite singing: (1) songs for congregational singing from countries in the southern hemisphere—from Africa, Latin America, and south Asia; and (2) Western music that builds on music styles that have more in common with oral cultures than written ones. Mary concludes by posing questions that could guide discussions of music in congregational settings, and by describing a model for cultural change developed by Thomas Troeger and Carol Doran in *Trouble at the Table* (1992).

"Using Music from Other Cultures in Worship: A Conversation with Mary K. Oyer." In *Music in Christian Worship: At the Service of the Liturgy*, edited by Charlotte Kroeker, 156–90. Collegeville, MN: Liturgical Press.

> Charlotte Kroeker interviewed Mary on a wide range of topics related to music in worship. The printed version of this exchange deals with the differences between music in North American culture and other cultures. Reading the written interview is much like following one of Mary's circle-and-spokes diagrams. Each section of the interview addresses the primary focus through what Mary has learned during different eras of her life: learning musicological analysis, teaching fine arts, finding *Dunblane Praises* in Scotland, coming to terms with gospel songs, crossing cultures, playing African

instruments, and learning how oral cultures work with music. Quality is determined by the context in which music is made, the function of the music within the context, and whether the music sits in the collective memory of the group sharing the music or whether it is out on an experimental edge. The interview demonstrates the variety of ways Mary has crossed cultures in her life, beyond her time in Africa and Asia.

2006

"African Music." Presentation, Lifelong Learning Institute, Goshen College–Greencroft Series, 1–10 May.

"Two Centuries of American Mennonite Hymn Singing." Lecture, American Theological Library Association, 2006 Annual Conference, Chicago, IL, 22 June.

Reprinted as chapter 27 of the present volume.

WORKS ABOUT MARY K. OYER

compiled by Mary Swartley
with annotations by Rebecca Slough

"A Quiz: Music-Making among the Mennonites." *Festival Quarterly* 5, no. 4 (November, December 1978; January 1979), 24, 29–30.

Biographical sketch and photograph. *The Hymn* 28 (July 1977), 138.

Burkhardt, Ferne. "Important to Go to Zimbabwe." Mennonite World Conference news release, 18 April 2003.

Erb, Paul. "Gathered with a Purpose." *Gospel Herald* 57, no. 36 (16 September 1969), 804.

Geiser, Linea Reimer. "Worship." In *College Mennonite Church, 1903–2003*, ed. Ervin Beck. Goshen, IN: College Mennonite Church, 2003.

"Goshen College Professor Received Honorary Doctorate." *Goshen News*, 25 June 1994.

Growing in Faith: Practices That Shape the Changing Lives of Christians, DVD. Produced and directed by Christopher Salvadore. Notre Dame, IN: Institute for Church Life, University of Notre Dame.

> The University of Notre Dame's Institute of Church Life produced this video based on Dorothy Bass's book *Practicing Our Faith: A Way of Life for a Searching People*. It explores ways that five people of faith across the generational spectrum seek and find God through practices of daily life. A young adult couple with three young children discuss the practices of saying yes and saying no, discernment, and honoring the body. A Latina young adult energetically talks about shaping communities through her ministry of peace and justice with young people in New York City. An African-American man, a respected community leader in North Carolina, remembers the painful discrimination of his youth and describes how he chooses to practice hospitality and forgiveness across barriers that would divide races. The segment on Mary explores the practices of singing our lives to God and honoring the body. She represents the adult nearing the end of life. Film footage was taken as she was preparing to go to Taiwan in 1999. The film crew later followed up with her after she was settled there. The film makes clear that Mary has lived her life well. It leaves the poignant hope that she will also die well.

Hawn, Michael C. "Can Songs Bring Reconciliation? A Conversation with I-to Loh, Patrick Matsikenyiri, Mary Oyer, and Pablo Sosa, with C. Michael Hawn, Moderator." *Reformed Worship* 68 (June 2003): 26–28.

This article is available online at http://www.reformedworship.org/magazine/article.cfm?article_id=1227.

———. "The Church Musician as an Enlivener." In *Gather into One: Praying and Singing Globally*. Grand Rapids, MI: Eerdmans, 2003.

Publication of this book was celebrated at The Calvin Symposium on Worship and the Arts, 10–11 January 2003, Calvin College, Grand Rapids, MI. Three composers included in Hawn's book—Pablo Sosa (Argentina), I-to Loh (Taiwan); Patrick Matsikenyiri (Zimbabwe)—were, along with Mary Oyer, "the enlivener"—the panelists for four sessions: (1) Introduction of panel members; (2) Sing the World Round; (3) Worship and Justice! and (4) Can Songs Help Bring Reconciliation? *Siyahamba!* Connecting with African Worship Songs (see preceding bibliographic entry).

Hawn's essay is the first scholarly attempt to understand Mary's leadership of international—particularly African—music in congregational settings. The first half of the essay discusses the cross-cultural dynamic of leading songs from one culture in another cultural environment. The song leader (*enlivener* is the term Hawn borrows and adapts from Michael Warren and Joseph Gelineau) has responsibility for interpreting and communicating the song in its new cultural context. He describes the attitudes and skills required for the "office" of enlivener. Mary is his primary example, and he examines her personal history and her scholarly approach to the songs she leads. The essay is a significant contribution to the growing literature on appreciating music cross-culturally. Hawn also gives theoretical depth and texture to Mary's approach to leading music in the congregation.

"Hymnody as an Expression of Culture." *The Hymn* 40, no. 2 (April 1990), 36.

Announcement that Mary is to be one of the panelists to make a presentation at the joint meeting of the American Musicological Society, the Society for Ethnomusicology, and the Society for Music Theory, in Oakland, CA, September 1990.

Indiana Women's History Association. "Mary K. Oyer." http://www.iwh.iupui.edu/bios.html

This web site includes a brief biographical sketch of Mary in a listing of notable women in Indiana history.

Kauffman, Kathy. "Eight Women of the Academy." Oral History Project 1993–94, Hist. Mss. 6–295, Box 2, Folder 1, Mennonite Church USA Archives–Goshen [IN].

Kathy Kauffman interviewed eight women, including Mary, who began teaching at Goshen College in the 1940s and 1950s.

Listing as a Fellow of The Hymn Society of the United States and Canada. *The Hymn* 48, no. 4 (October 1997), 66.

The Hymn Society is an elite society of musician scholars. Mary had been named a Fellow in 1989; at that time, the group consisted of fifty-one scholars, nine of whom were women.

Music, David. "An Interview with Mary Oyer." *The Hymn* 45, no. 1 (January 1994), 14–17.

In this interview conducted by David Music, 8 July 1992, Mary narrates her early history, work on the 1969 Mennonite hymnal, contributions to the Hymn Society, her dismay surrounding language issues in the project to produce *Hymnal: A Worship Book* (1992), Mennonite congregational singing, and her time in Africa.

Photograph of Mary Oyer leading a workshop on African hymnody, a special interest session of the National Convocation of the Hymn Society of United States and Canada, 22–24 April 1979 at Dallas/Fort Worth, TX. *The Hymn* 30 (July 1979), 192.

Porter, Ellen Jane. Review of *Exploring the Mennonite Hymnal: Essays,* by Mary Oyer. *The Hymn* 33, no. 4 (October 1982), 263–64.

Porter's review praises the rich variety of illustrations and connections Mary makes within and between hymns. She refers to Mary as the musical dean of congregational singing among Mennonites.

"Quilts from the Attic." *Mennonite Weekly Review,* 6 March 2006, 1, 10.

This news item announces an exhibit of quilts found in the attic of Mary's home; Goshen College Library Gallery, 12 March–7 July 2006.

"Research Committee Chairmanship Changes." *The Hymn* 28 (October 1977), 185.

This piece announces that Mary Oyer will be chair of The Hymn Society's Research Committee.

Routley, Erik. "Three American Hymn Books of 1969." *Bulletin of the Hymn Society of Great Britain and Ireland* 119, no. 7 (Summer 1970), 96.

Sherer, Michael. "Mary Oyer and Music: 'There Are Some I Don't Like, but I'm Working at It.'" *Gospel Herald* 84, no. 4 (22 January 1991), 6–7.

Smith, Cynthia Neufeld. "Singing Our Way to Heaven." Sermon, Topeka, KS, 26 June 2005.

Stoltzfus, Duane. "Still Turning to 606." *The Mennonite,* 18 November 2003, 8–11.

Swartley, Mary. "Mary K. Oyer, Classicist, Scholar, Minister of Music: The Influence of Mary K. Oyer on Hymnology in the Mennonite Church." Paper for hymnology class taught by Mary Oyer at Associated Mennonite Biblical Seminary, May 1996.

This paper is the first extended treatment of Mary's life and influence on Mennonite singing, based on interviews with Mary and others involved with hymnology and congregational singing in the Mennonite Church. The project drew together the first bibliography of Mary Oyer's written work.

Thornton, Denise. "For Mennonite Teacher, Music Opened Doors around the World." *South Bend Tribune,* 31 March 1991.

Tschetter, Kimberly. "The Truth about Other Cultures." *The Falcon Online,* 3 March 1999.

Report about a chapel address by Mary K. Oyer at Seattle Pacific University.

Yoder, Jessica. "Former Faculty Profiles." *Goshen College Bulletin,* September 2002.

Mary K. Oyer is one of the former faculty profiled in this article.

NURTURING SPIRIT THROUGH SONG

The Legacy of Mary K. Oyer

The legacy of Mary Oyer, as a scholar, educator, hymnologist, and church musician, is brought to life in this DVD teaching resource. Watching Mary lead hymns, teach classes, and describe her life and passion for church music provides a small glimpse of her world and dynamic personality.

Hear also from former students and colleagues, each with their own distinguished careers: Alice Parker, Ken Nafziger, Marlene Kropf, C. Michael Hawn, Vance George, Debra Brubaker, Jean Kidula, and J. D. Martin.

Designed for church musicians, congregational song leaders, students interested in learning the art of leading congregational singing, and music teachers in college, university, and seminary settings, the DVD contains eight sections (study guide included), making it a useful resource in a variety of settings:

DVD Menu

Leading Hymns

Visual Arts

Music in Worship

(1969)
The Mennonite Hymnal

In Her Own Words

African and Asian Music

Doxology (606)

Circles of Influence

Produced by Mennonite Media Productions
To order online go to mennomedia.org/resources
Or call 800-999-3534 / U.S.
800-565-1810 / Canada